Slings and
Arrows

Slings and Arrows

Narcissistic Injury and
Its Treatment

Jerome David Levin, Ph.D.

JASON ARONSON INC.
Northvale, New Jersey
London

Production Editor: Judith D. Cohen

This book was set in 11 pt. Baskerville by Lind Graphics of Upper Saddle River, New Jersey, and printed and bound by Haddon Craftsmen of Scranton, Pennsylvania.

Library of Congress Cataloging-in-Publication Data

Levin, Jerome D. (Jerome David)
    Slings and arrows : narcissistic injury and its treatment / by
Jerome D. Levin.
        p.   cm.
    Includes bibliographical references and index.
    ISBN 0-87668-550-5 (hardcover)
    1. Narcissistic injuries.   2. Psychotherapy.   I. Title.
    [DNLM: 1. Narcissism.   2. Self Concept.   3. Mental Disorders—
therapy.   WM 460.5.E3   L665s   1993]
RC455.4.N3L48   1993
    616.85'85—dc20
    DNLM/DLC
    for Library of Congress   93-13285

Manufactured in the United States of America. Jason Aronson Inc. offers books and cassettes. For information and catalog write to Jason Aronson Inc., 230 Livingston Street, Northvale, New Jersey 07647.

In Memory of My Mother

Edith Levin

To be, or not to be: that is the question:
Whether 'tis nobler in the mind to suffer
The slings and arrows of outrageous
    fortune,
Or to take arms against a sea of
    troubles,
And by opposing end them? . . .
For who would bear the whips and
    scorns of time,
The oppressors's wrong, the proud man's
    contumely,
The pangs of dispriz'd love, the law's
    delay,
The insolence of office and the spurns
That patient merit of the unworthy
    takes,
When he himself might his quietus
    make
With a bare bodkin? who would fardels
    bear,
To grunt and sweat under a weary life,
But that the dread of something after
    death,
The undiscover'd country from whose
    bourn
No traveller returns, puzzles the will
And makes us rather bear those ills we
    have
Than fly to others that we know not of?
Thus conscience does make cowards of
    us all;
And thus the native hue of resolution
Is sicklied o'er with the pale cast of
    thought,
And enterprises of great pith and moment
With this regard their currents turn
    awry,
And lose the name of action.

Hamlet act 3, scene 1

Contents

ix

It didn't take psychoanalysis to establish that life is suffused with pain. Injury, loss, rejection, and death are ineluctable concomitants of our earthly journey. Humanity has always known this. Nor does psychoanalysis primarily seek to nor claim to ameliorate that pain. On the contrary, Freud wrote that the aim of psychoanalytic psychotherapy is to "convert neurotic misery into ordinary human unhappiness," not an especially inspiring statement perhaps, yet it does have the virtue of not promising too much. I trust the acerbic Freud far more than I do the ubiquitous panacea hucksters of whatever nostrums who pervade the contemporary mental health scene.

This is a book on narcissistic injury and its treatment. It too doesn't promise too much. In some cases, as Jewish folk wisdom would have it, *Gar nicht helfen*—nothing helps. Nevertheless, patients do come to us for some sort of balm for the "slings and arrows of outrageous fortune," for some sort of help in healing life's inevitable injuries. What can we honestly offer them? Insight? Companionship while they mourn? Hope for restitution of some sort? The answer to these questions is neither obvious nor easy. As therapists we feel the pressure that patients, one after another of whom tells us "Nobody knows the troubles I've seen," bring to bear on us to relieve their pain. Sometimes we can; more often we cannot. What we have to offer isn't what the patient wants. Our countertransferences range from sorrow to helplessness to compassion to rage at demands we cannot meet.

All human pain isn't narcissistic injury or its consequence. The pain of childbirth is intense, but it isn't usually experienced as a narcissistic wound. Narcissistic wounds are special kinds of hurts—those that cut to the quick, that assail us where we live, that threaten our identity or our self-image, or our ego-ideal or our self-esteem. They are the hurts that go to the core. The emotional response to narcissistic injury is hurt, shame, and rage.

In this book, I will look at the narcissistic injuries of life from our unceremonious ejection from the womb to our usually involuntary exit from this mortal coil. In addition to examining these ineluctable narcissistic wounds, I will discuss a special kind of narcissistic injury—that of being a psychotherapeutic patient. This book examines what therapists can do to assist patients in integrating, mourning, sealing over, healing, or otherwise ameliorating the characteristic injuries of different life stages. Unfortunately, the treatment of narcissistic injury is itself a narcissistic injury, certainly for the patient, and not all that infrequently for the therapist. I will try to elucidate the nature of the injuries to each party and consider ways to minimize them. The therapist cannot but help injuring his or her patients: hurt is built into the very role of being a patient. Additionally, the therapist's unavoidably imperfect attunement, the therapist's countertransferential hate, the therapist's own narcissism and grandiosity, and the therapist's messianic strivings and misguided passion to heal all contribute to the narcissistic injury of patienthood.

Therapists get mangled too. They are the recipients of the patient's possessive love, desire to control, hatred, devaluation, primitive idealization, and contempt. Besides, as we so often hear, we aren't helping. How can a therapist help but feel injury from 8 or 10 hours a day of this kind of barrage? Narcissistic injury inflicted in the transference–countertransference nexus is alive, immediate, ready at hand for our interventions. It is an opportunity, yet it must be minimized. After all, patients do not come to us to be hurt. Our goal must be to simultaneously get the most therapeutic mileage out of the inevitable injuries of patient-hood and to minimize those injuries.

The impetus for this book came from my publisher, Jason Aronson, who "cooked up" the project with me during a phone conversation. His support and encouragement continued during years of interruptions during which I wrote two other books. I am grateful to him for his vision and gentle nudging.

Extraordinary appreciation is due to and extended to Virginia Wray for her seemingly effortless conversion of cassette dictation into errorless manuscript. Judith Cohen proved to be a flawless production editor. I thank her.

I am deeply grateful to my patients and supervisees, from whom I learned so much, and to my students at the New School for Social Research and the Post-Graduate Center for Mental Health, who gave me a much-needed opportunity to bounce my developing thoughts off a perceptive audience. Their feedback has been invaluable.

I am deeply appreciative of the support and intellectual stimulation my wife and best friend Ginny extended throughout the writing of *Slings and Arrows*.

Some readers may prefer to begin with Chapter 2, returning to the theoretical after reading the clinical chapters. Although I don't particularly recommend this, it is a feasible way of approaching some difficult material. I have made the clinical material self-sustaining for those readers who wish to proceed in this manner. I have also deliberately built in some degree of redundancy by discussing such difficult concepts as projective identification, ontological anxiety, and Kohutian metapsychology in several places. Hopefully, the theoretical and the clinical integrate giving you, the reader, a binocular "fix" on the treatment of narcissistic injury.

1

Narcissistic Injury, Narcissism, and the Self

As we say in Vienna, all roads lead to the *Zentralhoff* (main cemetery)," wrote the still young Sigmund Freud in a characteristic mood of acerbic realism to his friend Wilhelm Fliess. Freud, a poor Jew and a medical heretic and thus no stranger to narcissistic injury, was, of course, highlighting the one narcissistic injury none of us escapes. Narcissistic injuries come in all shapes and sizes, from minor rebuffs to crushing awareness of the shortness of our days. It is this, our awareness of our mortality, that inflicts the ultimate and deepest narcissistic injury. It brings to mind our powerlessness, the universe's indifference to us, and the impotence of our parents to protect us from being snuffed out, from ceasing to be.

Narcissistic injury is a concomitant of, or at least a constant possibility in, every life stage from birth to death. Of course it is well known that life is not a bowl of cherries, and it did not take psychoanalysis to discover that it isn't. Psychoanalysis does, however, have much to say about narcissism and about the self—their metapsychology, epigenesis, vicissitudes, and vulnerability

3

to injury. Not all psychological pain is narcissistically injurious, nor is all somatic pain. What characterizes narcissistic injury is its depth and centrality; it inextricably lowers self-esteem and disrupts our sense of self—our unconscious, preconscious, and conscious notions of who and what we are. Narcissistic wounds hurt where it counts, where we live.

A wound to ourselves and to our narcissism. What does that mean? The nature of self is a vexed question; its status, ontological and epistemological, has been much debated. Thinkers like David Hume and the logical positivists have cast doubt upon the very reality of the self. Look all you will, says Hume, and you can't find the self—what you actually experience is a succession of sensations, perceptions, and affects; but not a senser, a perceiver, or a feeler. The succession of impressions is all there is. The reality of the psychosomatic self as we usually experience it has been challenged from another direction, that of the various mystical traditions. For an Eightfold Buddhist or a Zen master, the self is an illusion concealing the ultimate reality in which we are embedded. Separateness is illusionary. Be this as it may, each of us has a conviction that we exist, that we endure in time, that we are such and such and not this or that; that is, that we have relatively enduring personalities, values, and character traits. Experientially the self exists. We feel that we are we and have some concept of that we-ness which each of us can activate at any time. The empirical psychological notion of a "self-concept" operationalized in such instruments as the adjective checklist in which the self is defined through self-description—by checking which adjectives do or do not apply to and define us—reflects this universal subjective experience of having a self with definitive and distinctive qualities. However, the empirical psychological self is not a psychoanalytic notion, because it is limited to the realm of the conscious. Psychoanalytic notions of the self have evolved and changed, but all of them take cognizance of the fact that self is not entirely, or even primarily, conscious.

The self as experience certainly has some reality even if it is in some sense illusionary. People at least think they know what they are talking about when they refer to "I myself. . . ." The self has degrees of centrality and of peripheralness, of coreness and of adjunctiveness. A narcissistic wound is a wound to the core, to that which is vital for us. Psychoanalytic understanding of the self started with the self as person, as body and mind, and evolved into the notions of self-representations; self-representations with affective coloring; self-representations merged with object representations, and differentiating from them; to self as an organization that is primary both experientially and theoretically in the psychic economy of human beings. I shall have more to say about the philosophical, psychological, and psychoanalytic understanding of the self shortly.

Narcissism, love of self, is also a vexed term interpreted in a multitude of ways. However, regardless of how the word narcissism is used or understood, it always refers to self-love. So a narcissistic wound or injury always entails some diminution of our love of ourselves, some disruption of our amour propre. A narcissistic wound always lowers self-esteem and engenders the affective states of shame, humiliation, and rage. To be narcissistically wounded is to join the ranks of the "insulted and injured." The lowered self-regard, shame, humiliation, and rage are frequently deflected, isolated, split off, projected, acted out, or repressed. These defenses are themselves narcissistically injurious and compound the injury. The treatment of narcissistic injury must address each of the components of the wound. Is the injury so deep and lacerating because of antecedent excessive narcissistic vulnerability? In that case, some repair of the vulnerable self structure is in order, some of what traditional psychoanalysis denoted strengthening the ego. That, of course, is long-term stuff and not distinct from the aims of modern psychoanalytic practice in general. Reducing narcissistic vulnerability is a highly desired outcome of treatment, but it reduces vulnerability to new injury rather than assuaging present and past injuries. The key to facilitating the healing of narcissistic injury is raising the patient's self-esteem. Anything that raises self-regard is curative. But raising self-esteem is not enough. The affects engendered by the injury must be made conscious, owned rather than projected or acted out, and worked through. This is particularly true of shame and rage. Narcissistic rage is frequently turned against the self, resulting in intense depression, which may be of suicidal proportions. So narcissistic injury is a wound to our core selves that lowers self-esteem and elicits powerful feelings of shame, humiliation, and rage—which may or may not be experienced as such.

Let me give you some examples of nonnarcissistic injury and contrast them with narcissistic injury. Perhaps all pain carries with it some degree of damage to self and self-love, but that need not be the salient feature of that pain. In narcissistic injury, *per contra*, it is the most salient feature of that pain.

I remember moving to upstate New York from Philadelphia at the age of 11 and finding an unbridled, unsaddled horse in a field and trying to ride it with another youngster. Naturally we were thrown, and I broke my wrist. The pain was excruciating and the fracture couldn't be set immediately. I certainly didn't like the pain, and I liked the restrictions imposed by the cast (which I mostly ignored or circumvented) even less, but this was not a narcissistic wound. Being a horseback rider was not part of my ego-ideal; I felt daring for even having tried to ride the beast. I suffered no loss of self-esteem; on the contrary, I was something of a hero to the other kids, and my parents were caring and supportive. A few years later, I was walking to the movies with one of my closest friends; we started arguing and he punched me in the nose. I went down. It bled and hurt some, but the pain was in no way comparable to the pain of the broken wrist; yet this was a narcissistic injury, albeit not a particularly serious one. I did care about winning fights, so losing one after a single punch lowered my self-esteem. I felt diminished. Further, my friend's turning on me so savagely deeply upset me. I felt shame, I felt humiliated, and I felt rage—the three affective correlatives of narcissistic injury.

I experienced a far more serious narcissistic wound at the end of my first term in college. I had always considered myself talented in science. Then I encountered college physics, finding it surprisingly difficult; nevertheless, I thought that I was doing pretty well. I was wrong. I blew the final and received a C+ for the course. I was crushed. I remember riding home in the train feeling so heavy I thought that I would literally sink through the floor. Once home I felt tormented, especially when trying to fall asleep. I would spend hours tossing and turning, trying to throw off my disappointment and self-hatred. Although I wasn't conscious of it, I was deeply ashamed. I didn't feel my rage either, but it was surely there, albeit turned against myself. What I did feel was depressed.

Narcissistic wounds are also concomitants of the humiliation of revered self-objects, idealized loved ones experienced as extensions of self, especially parents. Sigmund Freud's father told him a story about being called a dirty Jew and being pushed into the street by a gentile. Freud asked his father what he did. "Nothing," said Father. "I just picked up my hat and continued walking." On hearing of his father's unheroic behavior, Freud was overcome with shame. It was a traumatic disillusionment. To think of his tall, strong father behaving in a cringing way caused the boy to cringe. It was a narcissistic wound from which Freud never completely recovered. He retold his father's story and his reaction to it, revealing his disillusionment, in his associations to a dream in *The Interpretation of Dreams* (1900). The little boy's pain still comes through in the mature man's masterpiece. So deep was this narcissistic wound that the whole theory of the Oedipus complex and of the primal father, both of which require strong, powerful fathers, can be seen as a reaction formation to the boy's abhorrence of his father's powerlessness and humiliation. Several years ago I briefly treated a concentration camp survivor who became symptomatic when her husband became ill. His illness, which meant that her husband could no longer serve as a powerful protector, recapitulated her parents' powerlessness in the face of the Nazi onslaught. Of all the horrors she had experienced, it was the failure of her parents to be able to protect her that had inflicted the deepest narcissistic wound. When I suggested this to her, she dismissed it as nonsense — what could they do? They didn't have an army, or any safe refuge, but as she thought about it, my interpretation resonated and opened up mourning possibilities that helped alleviate her depression. It was not only the powerlessness of her parents, but also their humiliation without the possibility of retaliation that was so painful for her. On a less tragic plane, another patient recalled once seeing his father walk home down the street leading to their apartment looking downcast and defeated. The patient was then about age 5 and didn't understand what was happening. His father was out of work and looking for a job without success. Years later, his mother characterized his father as coming home "looking like a whipped dog" during that period of unemployment. Her so describing him caused my patient searing pain — deep narcissistic injury. He didn't want to think of his beloved Daddy as a whipped dog. He was furious at his mother for thinking of his father in that way and even more for telling him that she thought of him in that way. Speaking of the incident 40 years later in therapy, my patient became extremely disturbed. The humiliation of the beloved parent was a deep narcissistic wound.

I have defined narcissistic injury as a wound to the core self accompanied by feelings of humiliation, shame, and rage and have extended that definition to include shame at the humiliation of those we love and with whom we identify. Well and good. But what is the self or core self that is injured? The concept of self is one of the most vexed in philosophy, psychology, and psychoanalysis; the confusion surrounding the term *narcissism* is almost as great. So let us start by trying to define these key terms. Both have a history and it will be of some use to have a look at those histories. Once we have decided on a workable understanding of self and of narcissism, it will be useful to return to the notion of narcissistic injury and redefine it in the light of our researches and conclusions.

THE SELF

The self is the ego, the subject, the I, the me, as opposed to the object, or totality of objects — the not-me. *Self* means "the same" in Anglo-Saxon (Old English). So hence self carries with it the notion of identity, of meaning the selfsame. It is also the I, the personal pronoun *ipse* in Old Gothic. Thus, etymologically, self comes from both the personal pronoun *I* — I exist, I do this and that — and from the etymological root meaning "the same"; it is the same I who does this, who did that. All this sounds unproblematic, but that is far from the case.

The self is elusive. Now you see it, now you don't. What is this self that is so elusive? Is it a psychosomatic existence? Is it a verbal representation? Is it an organizing principle around which experience accrues? Is it substantial — indeed, the most substantive thing there is? Is it a kaleidoscope, a mere stream of thought and feeling? Does it evolve? Is it static? Is it something that unfolds? Is it something that is paradoxically emergent only in relationship with others? Is it an illusion? Is it a cybernetic program? What is the ontological status of the self, and what is its phenomenal reality? Over the course of human history, these questions have been pondered and answered in myriad ways.

Whatever the ontological status of the self, we do have a sense of self. How do we develop this sense? Depersonalization is no longer so much a psychiatric diagnosis as it is a normative experience and a theoretical stance. For the ancient Hindus, the *Atman* was the *Brahma*; that is, the Self Imminent was the Self Transcendent. For modern man, the very existence of the self has become problematic. This, in itself, constitutes a narcissistic wound. From the seventeenth century on, there has been a powerful conflict between those who thought that the self was either an illusion or a grammatical fiction, and those who thought that the self was our one indubitable datum, our only certainty.

As we have seen, the root meaning of the word *self* is "same." So in some sense, the self is what remains constant throughout the vicissitudes of life. This is not to suggest that there is no development, but rather that what develops is enduring and continuous. On the other hand, experiences of discontinuity are certainly real, so a theory of self must account for both the ongoingness and the disjunctiveness of the self-experience. Self, which has been understood in so many ways—as an aspect of being that transcends the body; as a grammatical fiction; as an illusion; as an organizing principle; as something experienced; as a synthesis; as something substantive; as something that unfolds; and as something that develops only in relationship with others— is sometimes there and sometimes not there.

PREANALYTIC THEORIES OF THE SELF

When the ancient Hindus said the *Atman* was the *Brahma*, the Self Imminent was the Self Transcendent, they were adumbrating a notion of self as the ground of reality, which is the part of us beyond the reach of time. It is a notion found in many cultures. The Self in this sense is something like what is usually denoted as the soul. For the Hindu sages, the task of man is clearing the delirium of desire and aversion so that this Self in its pure essence can be experienced. This Self is equated with a void, with *Nirvana*, that is, with what is eternal and transcendent in the universe; it is the Divine within, not in a personal sense but in a transpersonal one. Taoism and Buddhism have similar beliefs. The biblical concept of self is rather more personal. For the writer of Exodus, God is He who He is ("I am that I am"), a concept that reflects and is a projection of an individuality and sense of selfhood that it embodies both as autonomy and as mystery— incomprehension of the nature of that self.

For Plato, the self is tripartite. In a famous metaphor, which anticipates Freud, Plato compares the self to a chariot driver trying to rein in two spirited steeds, representing appetite and ambition, respectively. Plato's (1961a) concept of self as developed in *The Phaedrus* is dynamic—forces contend with each other and may or may not achieve integration and harmony. The Socrates of Plato's dialogues emphasizes the depth of the self, and our ignorance of those depths. Socrates' self is an unknown to be discovered through introspection and dialectic (dialogue aimed at the discovery of truth). The most salient feature of Plato's presentation of self is its exemplification of the profundity of and difficulty of the Delphic oracle's injunction, "Know Thyself."

The Stoics (Epictetus, Marcus Aurelius, and Seneca) emphasized the freedom of the self; its potential liberation and detachment from the slings and arrows of outrageous fortune. If the self is identified with the *Logos*, the rationality behind the apparent irrationality of existence, then nothing can touch that self. For the Stoics, the ultimate freedom of the self lies in the capacity for suicide, to refuse participation in the morally evil, the painful, and the transitory.

St. Augustine (354–430 C.E.) approached self in a way that was new in the Western tradition, through psychological autobiography. He was the first to trace the development of self from infancy through adulthood, doing so through both introspection and memory, and infant observation. In his *Confessions* (1961), his spiritual autobiography, Augustine emphasizes the incompleteness of the self and its longings for union with that which completes it—in Augustine's case, God. Augustine, like Plato, anticipates Freud in describing the drives or at least their derivatives, emphasizing the innateness of aggression.

The modern debate on the nature of the self starts with the seventeenth-century philosopher René Descartes. Although primarily interested in providing a philosophical basis for science, Descartes's (1637, 1642) philosophizing has important implications for a theory of self. He begins by questioning both received wisdom and common sense in his search for certainty. In his famous, or perhaps I should say infamous, method of radical doubt, he proceeds to cast into question all that can be questioned. After successively discarding the senses, book learning, and traditional wisdom as sources of certain knowledge, he comes to doubt the external world and his own body as objects the existence of which he can know with certainty. Continuing to doubt, Descartes arrives at an indubitable truth, namely, that he is thinking. Since doubting is itself a form of thought, he seemed to be on safe ground, and he concluded, "*Cogito, ergo sum*" ("I think, therefore I am"). According to his own account, he arrived at this insight while resting from the wars alone in a huge Dutch oven. Thus modern thought starts out with a strange notion of self arrived at in isolation. Descartes's self is disembodied, detached from an external world that may not even exist, minimally affective, and asocial. It is a purely mentalistic (thinking, perceiving, judging, doubting), solipsistic self devoid of object relations and connectedness. Twentieth-century philosophers have pointed out that on his own premises Descartes can only maintain that "thinking is occurring now," not even that there is a thinker. From thinking to thinker is an inference not supportable given his strict criteria of certainty. Descartes has traded certainty for vacuity. His is a self that can do mathematical physics and not much else. As many have pointed out, its extreme intellectualism is pathognomic of the isolation of modern life.

Descartes's critics were of two sorts; those who, like Blaise Pascal (1966), saw too much head and not enough heart in the Cartesian self; and those like John Locke, who thought his concepts of self and of world were arrived at by *a priori* reasoning rather than by examination of the date. Pascal has no quarrel with Descartes's way of philosophizing nor with the centrality of self in his system. What he objects to is the intellectualization. He sees the infinitely large and infinitely small spaces revealed by the new scientific instruments of the seventeenth century and cries out, "These infinite spaces terrify me." His self is a feeling, anxious, insecure one filled with fear before the emptiness and enormity of the universe. He deals with his fear by espousing a form of religious mysticism. When asked how he can believe this, he replies, "The heart has its reasons, which the reason knows not." Pascal's contribution to the theory of the self was to demonstrate the primacy of affectivity in the self-experience.

Locke, on the other hand, was primarily an epistemologist examining how we know what we know and the limits of that knowledge. The founder of philosophical empiricism, he maintained, in contradistinction to Descartes who believed in "innate ideas," that all knowledge came from experience. "Nothing is in the mind that was not first in the senses."

In his *Essay on Human Understanding* (1690), Locke has a long section on "Personal Identity." Here, for the first time, is a full appreciation of the problematic nature of identity and of the self. Locke is aware of the unconscious, of multiple personalities, and of discontinuities in the experience of self. After an examination of the meaning of identity, as a result of which he concludes that there is logical identity (A is A); material identity (this stone is the same stone I saw a minute ago); organizational identity (this man is the same man as the child that was, because their respective relations of parts is invariant); and finally, personal identity. He asked, How is the sense of personal identity, of being the same person across time and across experiences, possible? Locke is acutely aware of the discontinuities, during sleep for example, of our experience of self; after struggling with a number of possibilities, including a multiplicity of selves, he concludes that *consciousness* and *memory* are what confirm the ongoingness of the self and give us a sense of personal identity. The memory of self-consciousness across time is the basis of our sense of personal identity. Consciousness of self is an invariant accompaniment of every moment of consciousness, and by remembering those moments, I, so to speak, create a personal identity.

Locke (1690) explicitly rejects any role for the unconscious in his psychology and theory of personal identity. He does so because he fears that the unconscious brings with it a means of readmitting innate ideas. Since we don't have access to the unconscious through experience, its contents may very well be inscribed from the beginning—a phylogenetic inherence. Locke wishes to exclude innate ideas for political and ethical as well as epistemological reasons. In his view, they have too often served as the alleged justification for fanatical belief and religious persecution. Locke is prescient here. Freud and Jung do indeed include in their notions of the unconscious innate ideas in the form of phylogenetic inherences.

Philosophers like Locke, who emphasize experience, or who confer exclusivity on experience as the source of knowledge, are known as empiricists, while philosophers like Descartes, who emphasize the importance of reason in the acquisition of knowledge, are called rationalists. In general, the empiricists have been far more wary of the existence of self than have the rationalists, who tend to put self at the center of their systems. Locke's heir, David Hume (1738), maintained that the self is illusionary. His argument is essentially empirical. He says, introspect and try to find the awareness of self that Locke alleges accompanies every mental event—thoughts, feelings, and judgments. According to Hume, you never find it. The only mental events you will find are sensations such as pain, pleasure, hot, cold, red, blue, noise, quiet, and so forth; but never a self. Hume is here concerned to abolish the notion of self as enduring mental substance, an underlying substrate, to which experience happens, or in which mental events—thoughts and feelings—adhere. Hume does not doubt that we have a sense of personal identity and he too attributes it to the synthesizing power of memory. What he does doubt is that we have any evidence whatsoever of the existence of a substantive enduring self. If his view of self be correct, experience is atomistic and so are we.

Immanuel Kant attempted to answer Hume. Kant's philosophizing is obtuse and complex, but his contribution to the theory of self is relatively clear. Kant's (1781) reply to Hume was essentially that we contribute the connectedness to world and self. He reasoned that it would not be possible to experience any degree of coherence or continuity if the experiencer was not himself coherent and continuous. He calls this a logically necessary condition of a world that makes any sense at all, and the world does, or science would not be possible. Yet science exists and is able to formulate verifiable predictions, which implies some sort of coherence and continuity. For that to be possible, there must be coherence and continuity within me. Kant calls the source of that coherence and continuity the "transcendental unity of the apperception." By this Kant means that, Hume notwithstanding, there must be a self that endures, that manifests itself as the self-consciousness that accompanies every perception, and that is in some sense consistent and continuous. This unity is "transcendental" because it precedes; in other words it is logically, but not necessarily temporally, prior to any experience that is not chaotic. The ground for believing this is logical necessity, and it is not necessary to introspect to find it. So much for Hume.

Kant's further contribution to the theory of self was to envision two selves, the *phenomenal self* and the *noumenal self*. The phenomenal self is part of the causal sequence of nature and is the subject of a science, psychology. This self exists in time and is in principle knowable. Since for Kant, the mind is very active in the act of knowing, the empirical or phenomenal self that we know is known only through the "categories of the understanding." It is the self screened through our sensibilities and the apparatuses of our minds; not the self-in-itself, not the self as it exists apart from our knowing it.

The self-in-itself, the noumenal self, is not knowable, at least not by the science of psychology. For Kant, the noumenal self is known, if at all, "practically," not theoretically. For him, that means in moral life, in making ethical decisions. In this strange formulation, the two selves are quite different: one is strictly determined and scientifically knowable, the other is free and unknowable.

G. W. F. Hegel was the most prominent of Kant's successors. Extremely difficult to understand, he both builds on and rejects Kant. His early work, *The Phenomenology of Spirit* (1807) has some interesting things to say about self. It is a history of consciousness as embedded in the products of that consciousness: religions, philosophies, works of art, systems of government. Its implications for a theory of self are that the self can only be known through its objectifications, the things that it creates; and further, that the self objectified is an alienated self that must be (re)introjected before it can be integrated. Another way of saying this is that we only know ourselves through our acts, which have objective consequences, but then they are no longer subjective, no longer within us, and we must in some sense re-own them — make them our own again — before they can become part of ourselves. This is an early philosophical version of the psychoanalytic notion of projective identification, in which self is at least in part built up through reintrojection of that which has been disavowed and projected.

Hegel has other important things to say about the self, including the notions that the self is developmental, that it isn't given but becomes, and that that development is conflictual. Hegel maintains that "life is strife," and that growth occurs only through conflict. His theory of development is both dynamic and dialectical: each stage of human development is incomplete and every viewpoint is one-sided; this incompleteness and one-sidedness give rise to a corrective antithesis, which in turn is incorporated into a higher synthesis. This is an epigenetic theory of development. Later stages both incorporate (transform and preserve) and destroy (annihilate) earlier stages. This gives us a clue to understanding the continuity of self. That which went before is simultaneously preserved in an altered form and destroyed by being transcended and left behind, and this is one sense in which the self is both continuous and discontinuous.

The self, for Hegel, is dynamic, realized only through conflict with itself and with other selves; is known only by its acts and their objective consequences, which must then be re-owned by the self; and is a continuous process of development, which both embodies and discards earlier developmental stages.

Søren Kierkegaard was the founder of existentialism. Much of his thinking is a reaction to Hegel, whom he found far too "rational." The late Hegel had frozen his developmental schema into a System. Kierkegaard (1843, 1849) wrote that the System is magnificent; it is like a grand castle; the only trouble is that I don't live in the castle but in the outhouse. Kierkegaard's self is the self in the privy. He is interested in the self scared shitless.

His categories are dread and despair. For him, the self is the act of deciding in "fear and trembling." In Kierkegaard's eyes, truth is subjectivity—passionate commitment—and the more passion, the more self. Like his atheistic existential heir (Kierkegaard himself was a passionately believing Christian), Jean-Paul Sartre, Kierkegaard believes that man is "condemned to freedom" in the sense that there is no ultimate reason, no intellectual or logical justification for the decisions that matter. The self is that which decides. It is volitional in its very essence. Unconscious emotionally plays an important role in Kierkegaard's theory of self. For him, both dread and despair, anxiety and depression are ontological, that is, built into the very nature of being human. They may be conscious or they may be unconscious; either way, they are always with us.

The more consciousness, the more self, says Kierkegaard. So the self is not a given; it is an achievement, something that is accreted in the hard-won struggle to not repress the anxiety ineluctably attendant upon being a finite and mortal being. The self is that which is known, indeed comes into being, through contact with finitude, limitation, mortality, and the realization that one's decisions have no ultimate justification. It is the emotions attendant upon that contact. Kierkegaard's theory of the self is more normative than descriptive. In many ways it is a restatement of the oracle's injunction "Know Thyself," but with a more highly developed notion of the unconscious.

William James (1890) has a fascinating, highly complex theory of self that he developed in his *Principles of Psychology*. Somewhat parallel to Kant, James conceives of an *Empirical Self* and a *Pure Ego*. The Empirical Self is constituted by three sub-selves: the material self, the social self, and the spiritual self. The material self includes not only my body, but all that I have an emotional investment in—my home, my career, my children—all that I can call mine. This is reminiscent of Freud's theory of cathexis through libidinal energy going forth to invest and capture objects in the world. James's notion is new in our review of theorizing about self, in that here, self is not bounded by the boundaries of the body but, on the contrary, encompasses everything that I identify as mine. James points out that loss of that which is loved diminishes self; I shrink and become less when I suffer the loss of a loved one.

The social self is the self constituted by the reflected appraisals of others. I have as many social selves as I do "significant others" (an original Jamesian phrase). In addition, I construct an "ideal other" and fantasize the evaluation of me that that ideal other would make. This is somewhat like the ego-ideal aspect of Freud's superego reprojected and then constituting the most powerful of my social selves. The social psychologist George Herbert Meade (1934) developed James's social self into a theory of self as "generalized other." Historically, James's notion is important, being the first, albeit primitive, object relational theory of self.

The spiritual self is our inner or subjective being, our psychic facilities and dispositions. It is the most enduring and intimate part of the self—that which we seem to be. The central part of the self is *felt*; it is not merely rational or a sum of memories, nor is it the sound of the word "I." James thinks that what is felt as the spiritual self is actually a bodily sensation that is concomitant with acts of attending, asserting, negating, and so forth. The spiritual self seems "to reside" in the interneurons between the afferent and the efferent nerves. It is the place where decisions are made and the moral life lived.

The "Pure Ego" is the source of our sense of personal identity. It is the judgment that I am the same self today as I was yesterday. That which is mine comes with a characteristic brand; it is identified as mine and as part of me; it has a particular warmth that the nonself lacks. The Pure Ego is both James's version of Kant's transcendental unity of the apperception (or as James puts it, "only a connected world can be known to be disconnected" and that connected world can only be known by a connected self) and a consequence of James's description of the "stream of consciousness" in which each segment of the stream flows out of, and in some sense still contains, its immediate preceding segment, which in turn connects it, segment by segment, to its source. The image of the river that you can never step in twice but which is still the same river everywhere is powerful. It provides a visualization of the self that never is, yet always is, the same. For James (1890) "this unbrokenness in the stream of selves, like the unbrokenness in an exhibition of 'dissolving views' in no wise implies any further unity nor contradicts any amount of plurality in other respects" (p. 318). How much unity is an empirical question. James's is a rich and evocative theory of the self.

So far the self has been seen as thinker, as terrified cosmic insignificant, as memory, as nonexistent, as the logically necessary condition of experience, as simultaneously determined and free, as realized in action and in conflict, as alienated, as conscious and unconscious dread and despair, as the totality of what I care about, as the collated opinions of significant others, as the sensation arising from bodily concomitants of thought, and as a stream.

PSYCHOANALYTIC THEORIES OF THE SELF

Freud doesn't use the word self; instead he talks about the ego. Ego means "I." His use of the word *ego* is inconsistent. In his earlier writings and sometimes in his later writings, ego means self, self here being used in the same way it is used in ordinary language. Here it means the bodily and the mental self. In 1923, Freud developed the "structural model" of the mind in which the mind is constituted by three agencies defined by their function: the id (it), the ego (I), and the superego (over-I). Here ego is not self as usually understood, but rather that part of the mind whose functions are memory, judgment, motility, perception, and psychological defense. The ego as mental organ is partly conscious and partly unconscious, but consciousness is intrinsic to it in the sense that perception and consciousness are among its functions. The defenses in particular tend to be unconscious. The id consists of the biological drives, while the superego is the internalized parent resident as both ego-ideal and conscience. In Freud's writings after 1923, one must be careful to distinguish the two meanings of ego and to decide from the context whether the self or an agency of the mind is being denoted.

Freud: Self as Developmental Achievement

Freud (1915a, 1923) had several interesting and not always consistent things to say about the self. He wrote, "The ego (self) is the precipitate of abandoned object cathexis." The underlying notion is that we can only give up that which we love by making it a part of ourselves. So the self is built up through internalizations of libidinal attachments. This is an extraordinarily interesting notion. It implies that love of others is antecedent to a sense of self. It is both an object relational notion and an affective one. It is the process of investing libidinal energy in objects and their subsequent incorporation into self. In the same vein, Freud wrote, "The shadow of the object fell on the ego." Here he is talking about object loss and the way in which fury at the object who abandons us, now introjected, becomes fury at ourselves. Freud also spoke of the ego being "first and foremost a bodily ego." Here he emphasizes the importance of somatic sensations in the awareness of selfhood. So for Freud, self seems to be a construct the components of which are identifications with those we love and bodily sensations. Self is not here primordial, but rather an integration of many sensations and experiences. It is ongoing and developmental. Freud (1914a) said that "a unity as complex as the ego (self) cannot exist in the individual from the start" (p. 77).

Edward Glover (1956) developed this notion into his theory of ego nuclei—many islands of self-experience—which coalesce into a unified ego (self). At the end of his life, Freud wrote a paper, "Splitting on the Ego for Purposes of Defense" (1940), in which ego again means self and in which a very important concept, splits in the self, emerged. For Freud, self is not necessarily unitary. On the contrary, many sorts of splits are induced by the defenses of repression, disavowal, projection, and denial. Integration of self is an achievement, not a given; and one purpose of analytic therapy is to bring about that integration. Freud (1933) wrote that "where id (it) was, ego (I) shall be," but there can be no I until the disavowed and split-off portions of that I are reclaimed.

The notion that the task of psychoanalytic therapy is the conversion of it to I, of the biologically given into the personal, of owning the facticities of my life, is a recurrent one. Winnicott, describing it as a developmental rather than a therapeutic task, calls it *personalization*. During personalization, biological urges — hunger, thirst, and pain — come to be experienced as mine rather than as coming from the environment. The conversion of it to I is implied in Spinoza's statement that "freedom is the acceptance of necessity"; in the existentialists' injunction to face one's "contingency, thrownness, and facticity"; and in Erikson's statement that one must finally agree that the life one has lived is the one and only life possible. In its various forms, this is a notion implying differing mixtures of acceptance and mastery. It is the project of overcoming the "id's living us" (Groddeck 1930). In the present climate of biological psychiatry's insistence that the etiology of psychopathology is the inherence of neurochemical (the modern id) abnormalities, Freud's notion of personalizing the biologically given through insight and control, thereby creating a self, provides a rationale for psychotherapy. Therapists, who often feel a sense of futility in the face of the biological revolution in psychiatry, need not. There is plenty of legitimate reason for them not to do so. This is one narcissistic injury that can be ameliorated. Neither id nor neurotransmitters are a self, and the consolidation of the self is of the essence of therapy.

Jung: Self as Life's Goal

Self is not a primary category for Freud, and it was left for his disciples to develop a more explicit theory of self. Carl Jung, his erstwhile successor and later bitter rival, developed a decidedly non-Freudian theory of self. For Jung (1945, 1961), the self is life's goal. It is the search for wholeness, sometimes although not necessarily, through religious experience. Before the self can emerge, various components of the personality must be fully developed and individuated. The archetype (pattern) of the self doesn't emerge until middle life, which for Jung is a time of serious effort to change the center of the personality from the conscious ego to a midpoint between the conscious and the unconscious. Selfhood is balance and integration of opposites. Neither introverted nor extroverted, centered neither in consciousness nor in unconsciousness, neither feminine nor masculine, but encompassing both. Self is the progressive unfolding and differentiation of a primal potentiality, and in the second half of life, reintegration of that which had been differentiated. In selfhood, that which had not been expressed, the "Shadow" part of personality, is also represented. Self is an ideal that nobody realizes but that each strives to approximate as fully as possible. Jung's notion of self(hood) is partly normative and partly descriptive. He clearly believes that striving for selfhood, in his sense of achieving equidistance between his sets of paired opposites, is desirable and the goal of his therapy, but he equally believes that he is describing a structural component of personality that emerges at midlife.

Adler (1927) came up with a notion of self strikingly similar to Jung's, in his theory of the "creative self." Adler originated the concept of self-actualization. The creative self is an integration; it expresses all components of self, resulting in self-fulfillment.

Hartmann: Self-Representations

Heinz Hartmann (1958, 1964) developed the notion of self nascent in Freud and clarified some of the confusion caused by lack of consistent terminology. Hartmann did this by distinguishing between self, self-representation, and ego. For Hartmann, self is one's — yours or mine — bodily and mental existence. It is what I see in the mirror and my stream of consciousness insofar as I identify it as mine; I recognize you as a self because I see your body and dialogue with your mind. The self is something that exists in the world and is public, or at least potentially so. Not so my self-representation. It is neither my body nor my mind, rather it is my mental representation of them. My self-representation is a construct around which I organize experience. It is related to but not identical with the empirical psychological notion of a self-concept, which is operationalized as various forms of self-description; adjective checklists, Q-sorts, and the like. The self-concept is conscious or preconscious while Hartmann's self-representation can be (dynamically) unconscious; that is, unavailable to consciousness because of psychological defense. For example, one's goodness or one's badness may be unavailable to consciousness because awareness of them would be too threatening. So Hartmann's self-representations may be conscious, preconscious, or unconscious. There may be more than one self-representation and these competing self-representations are not necessarily consistent. Hartmann's ego is Freud's system ego: the ego as agency of the mind. Hartmann's clarification was much needed, and subsequent psychoanalytic literature is indebted to him. His notion of the self-representation has borne fruit.

Jacobson: Affective Coloring of Self-Representations

Edith Jacobson (1964) built affectivity into Hartmann's theory of the self-representation. She slightly modified and made more precise Hartmann's formulations defining *self* as the whole person of the individual — including body, psychic organization, and their respective parts — while defining self-representations as the unconscious, preconscious, and conscious endopsychic representations of the physical and mental self in the system ego. They are never purely cognitive but always have an affective quality. Her distinction between the preconscious and unconscious reflects Freud's formulation of the *descriptive unconscious*, which includes all mental contents that are out of awareness, and the *dynamic unconscious*, which encompasses that part of that which is out of awareness that cannot be called to consciousness by an act of will because it is walled off by psychological defenses. (The preconscious is that part of the descriptive unconscious that can be voluntarily assessed and retrieved.)

According to Jacobson, in the initial stage of human development there is a *primal psychophysiological self*, the undifferentiated psychosomatic matrix from which self-representations and object representations as well as the libidinal and aggressive drives differentiate. Prior to this differentiation, there are no self-representations (or object representations) and the basic drives are fused. Jacobson is a dual-drive theorist, holding that libido and aggression are innately programmed manifestations of biological energy. Once the self- representations arise, they are always cathected by one of the two basic drives. The term *cathexis* is James Strachey's translation of Freud's *Besetzung*, which literally means occupation, as in a military occupation. In Freud's model, psychic energy flows out from the self and grasps hold of objects in the environment. They are emotionally invested, and this investment has a certain amount of aggression inherent in it. Freud's metaphor is that of an amoeba putting forth pseudopodia to engulf food particles. Jacobson reformulated Freud's picture of cathectic action. In her version, it isn't objects, but rather self-representations and object representations that are cathected. This cathexis may be by libido or by aggression, so that the self-representations are *always*, to some degree or another, loved or hated. The self as experienced has now become the self-representations. These representations are multiple and are contents of the system ego, may be conscious or unconscious, and are affectively colored; that is, loved or hated. The multiplicity of self-representations opens up potential for conflict between self-representations, particularly between conscious (or preconscious) representations and unconscious representations. This sheds new light on, or is at least a different way of conceptualizing, Freud's splitting of the ego (self) for the purposes of defense.

Kernberg: Object Relations Development

Otto Kernberg (1975) used Jacobson's concept of self- and object representations to delineate four stages in the development of object relations. He, too, starts with the undifferentiated matrix. In his second stage, self and object are not differentiated, but there are endopsychic structures, self-objects, that are affectively colored. Memory traces of gratification result in positive (libidinally cathected) self-object representations, while memory traces of frustrating experiences result in negative (aggressively cathected) self-object representations (self-objects), which do not differentiate between the I and the not-I, between self and world. In normal development, gratifying experiences predominate in early infancy.

Fixation at either of the first two stages results in psychosis. In the third stage, the self- and object representations are differentiated, resulting in four endopsychic structures: a positive (libidinally cathected) self-representation, a negative (aggressively cathected) self-representation, a positive (libidinally cathected) object representation, and a negative (aggressively cathected) object representation. Self and object are now differentiated, but self- and object representations reflecting gratifying and frustrating experiences are not yet integrated. Thus, the object (usually mother) who both gratifies and frustrates is experienced as two separate objects, the "good mother" and the "bad mother." Similarly, there is a "good self" and a "bad self," which are not experienced as the same self. Fixation at this stage, or regression to it, results in borderline pathology. Borderline personalities have severe difficulties in interpersonal relationships, chaotic emotional lives, poor impulse control, and are prone to acting out.

Kernberg's fourth stage involves the integration of self- and object representations. Successful completion of this process results in a stable self-representation and in *object constancy*. Frustrations are tolerable because there are stable representations (internal objects) of loving, albeit humanly flawed caretakers. The attainment of object constancy indicates that there is a cathexis (libidinal) of the constant mental representation of the object regardless of the state of need. Similarly, there is a predominantly libidinal cathexis of a self-representation resulting in a firm sense of identity.

In normal development, psychic structuralization resulting in the establishment of the ego and the id as separate psychic systems emerging from the undifferentiated matrix of earliest infancy proceeds concomitantly with the establishment of differentiated, affectively complex self- and object representations. Stable self- and object representations (internal objects) are normal components of the system ego. In emotional health, these images integrate the gratifying and frustrating aspects of experience and are differentiated from each other.

Kernberg also envisions the process of self-development (i.e., the development of normal self-representations) going sour. When development goes awry, there is either fixation to the predifferentiated stages, or the development of a pathological self-structure (representation) which he calls the *grandiose self*. This grandiose self is a pathological condensation (fusion) of ideal-self, real-self, and ideal-object representations. This introduces a new aspect of self-representation — the ideal self, a mental representation of what we would like to be. William James had the same concept in nascent form, but here it is fully developed. This opens yet another potential for intrapsychic conflict, here between real- and ideal-self representations.

Kernberg draws not only upon Jacobson (1964), but also, importantly, on Margaret Mahler's (1975) now familiar discussion of separation-individuation. Although Mahler didn't use the language of object relations, her developmental sequence of autism, symbiosis, and separation-individuation is another way of describing the establishment of a sense of autonomous identity, of selfhood. In Mahler's view, the infant starts life without a sense of self or of objects; there is just need and its gratification. The world of the neonate is, in William James's words, a "buzzing, blooming confusion." Out of this primordial state of sensation without a sensor, of archaic perception without a perceiver, comes a nascent sense of being and a dim sense of others who attend that being. This dawning sense of separateness is but momentary; ineluctably frustration and overwhelming feelings of helplessness lead to hallucinatory union with the mother, and the stage of symbiosis is reached. Mahler's autistic stage is parallel to Kernberg's stage of undifferentiation, while Mahler's stage of symbiosis is an ego psychological postulation of Kernberg's object relational self-object representation. According to Mahler, the child acquires a sense of selfhood — of enduring identity as a person apart from Mother — by going through a complex developmental process, which she calls separation-individuation characterized by four substages: differentiation, practicing, rapprochement, and finally separation-individuation proper. Her stages are behavioral but the changing behavior is reflected endopsychically. Thus, the development of locomotion and speech enhances the process of separation leading to differentiation. "I am different from Mother." This differentiation is tested and affirmed during practicing; rapprochement is the developmentally vital opportunity to regress in the face of pain and frustration and to reunite with Mother both interpersonally and intrapsychically. Sufficiently gratifying rapprochement experiences build ego strength so that the child can finally "hatch" and become a separate person with a sense of identity, including gender identity. In the process, I not only become separate from Mother, I become me; that is, individuate. Mahler doesn't have much to say about the nature of the self that emerges.

Kohut: The Bipolar Self

Heinz Kohut, founder of the psychoanalytic school called "self psychology," was not primarily a theorist; he was a clinician. His theory of the self arose from his work with a group of patients he called "narcissistic personality disorders" (see section on Narcissism below). His theory of self is an inference from clinical data, particularly that derived from transference phenomena, gathered in working with adults.

Kohut (1971, 1977) defines the self as a unit both cohesive in space and enduring in time, which is a center of initiative and a recipient of impressions. It can be regarded either as a mental structure superordinant to the agencies of the mind (id, ego, and superego) or as a content of those agencies. Although Kohut believed that these conceptualizations were complementary rather than mutually exclusive, he emphasizes the self as a central or superordinant principle in his later writings. The self is, so to speak, the organized and organizing center of human experience, which is itself experienced as cohesive and enduring. How does this sense of an I (self) that coheres in space and endures in time develop? According to Kohut, the infant develops a primitive (fragmented) sense of self very early. That is, each body part, each sensation, each mental content is experienced as belonging to a self, to a me, as mine; however, there is no synthesis of these experiences as yet. There are selves, but no unitary self. Nor are there clear boundaries between self and world. Kohut designates this stage the stage of the *fragmented self*; it is the developmental stage at which psychotic persons are fixated or to which they regress. Although there are important differences, Kohut's stage of the fragmented self corresponds to Freud's stage of auto-eroticism (see Freud and Narcissism below); it is another way of understanding the stage of human development that precedes the integration of the infant's experienced world.

At the next stage of development, an *archaic nuclear self* arises from the infant's experience of being related to as a self rather than as a collection of parts and sensations. This self is cohesive and enduring, but it is not yet securely established. Hence, it is prone to regressive fragmentation. It is nuclear in the sense of having a center, or nucleus, and it is archaic in the sense of being a primitive (that is, grandiose and undifferentiated) precursor of the mature self. The archaic nuclear self is bipolar in that it contains two structures, the *grandiose self* and the *idealized parental imago*. That is, in this stage there is a differentiated self, which is experienced as omnipotent, but there are no truly differentiated objects. Objects are still experienced as extensions of the self, as self-objects. At this stage, the child's grandiose self attempts to exercise omnipotent control over his objects. In healthy maturity, all loved objects have a self-object aspect.

The internalization of what Kohut calls *psychic structure*, which is perhaps better understood as functional capacity, is codeterminous with the formation of the nuclear self. As Kohut (1977) puts it, "the rudiments of the nuclear self are laid down by simultaneously or consecutively occurring processes of selective inclusion and exclusion of psychic structure" (p. 183). Failure to adequately internalize functions originally performed for the child by self-objects (i.e., caretakers experienced as self-objects) results in deficits in the self. Of crucial importance are the internalization of tension regulation, self-soothing, and self-esteem regulation, as well as the self-object's function as stimulus barrier.

Kohut conceives of the mature self as continuing to be bipolar. In maturity, the grandiose self becomes one's realistic ambitions while the idealized parental imago becomes one's ideals and values. Maturation of self is a process of depersonalization in the sense that attributes and functional capacities that were acquired from others take on an autonomy and become integrated into us in such a way that they are no longer identified with those from whom they were acquired. This is important to a healthy sense of selfhood. I need to feel that I can soothe myself, maintain my self-esteem, and modulate my anxiety. The fact that others once did these things for me until I internalized these abilities as "psychic structure" is now irrelevant.

Kohut's theory is intriguing. Implicit in it is the notion that the self arises both from the inside and the outside. The grandiose self seems to be preprogrammed to emerge organically from fragments of self-experience, while the idealized parental imago is an identification with and internalization of idealized parents. Both the grandiosity and the idealization are related to and reactive from the sense of infantile helplessness. The delusional, but phase-appropriate and normal, beliefs that I am omnipotent and those who love me are omnipotent provide the security for emotional growth to proceed. In addition to providing a developmental sequence the success of which significantly depends on the (human) environment, as that self paradoxically arises from experiences with others, Kohut's theory introduces a new dimension to the understanding of the self: cohesion and its opposite, fragmentation. The self can be more or less cohesive and more or less subject to regressive fragmentation. The cohesive self feels bounded, ongoing, centered, and active. It has a sense of agency. Although Kohut recognizes self as self-representation in the id, ego, and superego, his emphasis is on the sense of selfhood, the lived experience of wholeness, the process of human interactions leading to that experience, and the vicissitudes that result in malformation of the self.

Erikson: Identity

Erik Erikson is another psychoanalytic theorist whose work is relevant to the understanding of the self. He speaks of identity and the sense of identity rather than the self. Self seems to encompass or be defined by the answer to two questions: What am I? and Who am I? Identity seems to be primarily concerned with the answer to the later. Erikson's (1950, 1968) central notion is that identity comes from identification. We are, or better we become, so to speak, an integrated composite of our identifications with people—parents, siblings, peers, public personages, historical and fictional figures; and with causes, movements, and ideals. So for Erikson there is an almost infinite number of possibilities for identification, a plenitude of material out of which to build an identity. Obviously some sort of selection occurs. The possibilities are narrowed in several ways: one's historical, economic, and cultural situations are limited. As much as I might admire, idealize, and seek to emulate a Comanche warrior, an identity as an Indian brave is not possible for me.

Here it becomes clear that for Erikson, identity is both an intrapsychic construct and a social-political-economic-cultural role, or set of roles. Further, my possibilities for identification are limited by my genetic endowment, my early object relations, and my family constellation. I can only become what my culture allows; even if I am an extraordinary individual who creates a new identity, I am still limited by my historical situation. Erikson is interested in creative individuals who forge new identities and thereby create new possibilities for identification. He has written studies of Luther, Gandhi, Freud, James, Hitler, and Maxim Gorky illustrative of the process of identity formation, in cases in which hitherto unavailable identities come into being. Erikson emphasizes the dialectical interplay of personality and culture in the formation of an identity. Once an innovator creates a new identity, it becomes available for identification by the next and succeeding generations. A new identity can be constructive (e.g., psychoanalyst), or demonic (e.g., concentration camp guard).

Erikson has an epigenetic developmental scheme in which each stage is folded into the succeeding stage. No developmental battles are won once and for all; on the contrary, the process of identity formation is lifelong and provides creative opportunities as well as potential for disastrous regression over the life span. Although adolescence is, par excellence, the stage for identity formation — a period of detachment from family and search for idealizable models, heroes, to serve as raw material in the creation of self through selective identification — the process of identity formation is inherent in every stage. Erikson's stages are discrete periods of challenge during which the self changes for better or for worse. Consolidation occurs during the intervals between crises. In this formulation, self becomes self only through realization in the world, and that which is realized is the outcome of interaction of culture and personality. Identity may be integrated or diffused. Identity diffusion, sometimes called identity confusion, is a form of self pathology in which there is no centeredness, nor any superordinate identity that unifies the identity fragments formed through identification. In its more severe form, identity confusion is pathognomic of borderline personality disorder.

Erikson's epigenetic stages are dichotomous; the first of each pair of developmental possibilities is dominant in the healthy self, but the secondary possibility is to some degree inevitably realized and expressed. This lends a richness and complexity to the evolving self. Erikson's stages are basic trust versus basic mistrust, autonomy versus shame, initiative versus guilt, industry versus inferiority, identity versus identity confusion, intimacy versus isolation, generativity versus stagnation, and ego integrity versus despair. They characterize oral-sensory, muscular-anal, locomotive-genital, latency, puberty and adolescence, young adulthood, adulthood, and late maturity stages, respectively.

Self is more than identity, more intrapsychic than sociological, yet Erikson's conception of identity evolving over a series of life stages with their unique potentialities for maturation, identification, and objective realization, eventuating in affirmation of the "one and only life that has been possible"; that is, in affirmation of one's self in the final stage of ego integrity, gives us a new and significant way of understanding self. Erikson the refugee, the wanderer, and the polycareerist has much in common with William James, who also saw self as complex and evolving. Although Erikson's view is uniquely his, it clearly owes something both to Freud — the ego is the precipitate of the abandoned object cathexis — and to the American social psychologists George Herbert Meade (1934) and Charles Cooley (1902) — "the self is the generalized other." What Erikson's theory doesn't adequately address is the nature and origins of self, which must exist antecedently to the choosing; which chooses, consciously and unconsciously, objects with which to identify.

Winnicott: True and False Selves

Donald Winnicott is not a systematic thinker. In some ways more of a poet than a scientist, his insights into self are diffused throughout his deceptively simple papers. Winnicott's thinking about self encompasses a developmental schema, a notion of self pathology, and an object relational notion of self. Developmentally, Winnicott (1965) postulates three stages of ego development: integration, personalization, and object relating. Though he explicitly disavows that he is using ego to mean a self and says he is using it in its structural sense, it is clear that Winnicott's ego stages are self precursors. To steal a phrase from the title of one of Winnicott's books, ego development comes about through the interaction of "maturational processes and the facilitating environment." Winnicott's (1965) notions of ego and self are object relational; they come into being only in the presence of and through interaction with others. As he says, "There is no such thing as a baby," meaning that there are no babies unrelated to mothers. Thus self is defined in relation to others from the outset, or to be more precise, before the inception of self. That is, the precursors of self are already related to others. The first stage of ego development is *integration*. Integration is the process by which the paradoxically undifferentiated *and* unintegrated infant begins to differentiate from the experience of merger, which Mahler calls symbiosis and Kohut calls the archaic self, into separateness. It is the beginning of the separation of me from not-me. This me is fragmented, as isolated me experiences, which following differentiation begin to cohere or integrate into an "I." During integration, and indeed during all of Winnicott's developmental stages, the experience of continuity and "going-on-being" is vital to the establishment of a healthy self. Going-on-being is threatened by "impingement," traumatic disruptions that fragment experience. Impingement is the precursor and prototype of narcissistic injury. Adequate ("good enough") maternal care minimizes impingement and establishes going-on-being. Self cohesion comes from continuity of care. Personalization is the achievement of psychosomatic collusion, of living in the body rather than in fantasy. It is the "holding environment," initially literal holding, later symbolic holding, provided by maternal handling that enables the infant to feel whole and not merely a collection of parts. Winnicott's account is strikingly similar to Kohut's notion that the move from the stage of the fragmented self to the stage of the archaic nuclear self is dependent on the experience of being treated as an integral self, cohesive in space and continuous in time, by loving caretakers (self-objects). I gain the sense of being one self who continues to be that self, and who can initiate action, by being treated as a unit that endures and acts rather than as a collection of distress signals. The establishment of psychosomatic collusion, the sense of being one with my body, is vital for mental health; failure to succeed to do so leaves one prone to experiences of depersonalization. In this stage, the body comes to be experienced as a "limiting membrane," as a boundary, further establishing the distinction between me and not-me. The move from integration to personalization is a move from "I" to "I am," to some sort of affirmation, or preverbal recognition, of personal existence.

In the third stage of ego development, *object relating*, complex processes, starting with the experience of omnipotence and progressing through destruction of the fantasy object (mother) and her replacement with a real mother, leads the infant to the depressive position, a developmental stage in which separateness is consolidated and ambivalence accepted. The child's experience is now "I am alone," but "there are others I can relate to and make part of me" (as internal objects) so that being alone is tolerable and even enjoyable. In the process of ego development, the id comes into being as the source of sensations come to be felt as arising from within rather than coming from the environment. Paradoxically, I cannot internalize Mother or other loving caretakers until I separate from her, experience omnipotence over her, destroy her as a fantasy object, reconstitute her as a real object, make restitution or reparation for my aggression to her, and experience her as one person who both gratifies and frustrates. In the process, I too become one person. So in the course of ego development, the infant and the toddler goes from the not-I (fragmentation and merger) to "I," to "I am," to "I am alone but related," and self comes into being. This self is the product of

the interaction of biological maturation and the human environment, facilitating or otherwise.

Winnicott now turns Descartes on his head, saying, "I see that
I am seen, therefore I know that I am." "When I look, I am seen,
so I exist." This is a thoroughly object relational notion of self.
Self is not a lonely cogitator; on the contrary, self is established by
refraction through another. Being held and being seen are the
basis for ontological security, the experience of selfhood and of
identity.

This brings us to a final Winnicottian concept, that of the true
self and the false self. The true self is the self with all of its
feelings, drives, and id-derived instincts striving for expression.
The true self is messy, egocentric, unsocialized, filled with hate
and envy and destructiveness. But it is also the repository of love,
gratitude, and creativity, as well as the repository of yearning and
of the desire to be loved. The true self is not id, but includes id
as owned, as personalized. It is "it" become "I," without being
deinstinctualized. If the true self is unduly threatened by a
nonfacilitating environment, it goes into hiding deep within the
recesses of being to be replaced (as far as social reality is
concerned) with a false self, which is a compliant, "people-
pleasing" self that looks for approval at all cost. False-self
organization often leads to outward success, especially in intellectual pursuits, but at the cost of vitality, feelings of aliveness
and genuineness. The experience is of hollowness and absence of
deep satisfaction. But the true self has not been destroyed; it is
merely in hiding. The true self contains within it, and protects, all
that is felt to be threatened by destruction. In fact, Winnicott
defines God as "the repository of the good aspects of self, which
we need to project outward to protect from our inner badness."
Successful psychotherapeutic intervention surfaces the true self,
establishing experiences of wholeness, aliveness, genuineness,
and worthwhileness.

In summary, Winnicott sees the self as coming into being
during the process of ego development through interaction with
loving caretakers who treat the child as a self and reflect back

their experience of the child's selfhood. In health, the true self is secure enough to express itself freely; in disease, the false self predominates, striving to keep the true self safely hidden.

Stern: The Four Selves

Daniel Stern importantly differs from other psychoanalytic developmental theorists in denying the existence of an autistic, fused, merged, symbiotic stage out of which separateness, autonomy, and self emerge. On the contrary, he maintains that the template for the organization of experience into self-experience and non-self-experience is innate, and that it is meaningful to talk about self-experiences occurring in the infant from the age of 2 months on. For Stern (1985), selfhood is an epigenetic development of four types of self-experience: emergent, core, subjective, and verbal. These are successive in time, distinct and discrete, yet coexistent from about the age of 4, when the verbal self is established, to the end of life. Thus, there are four selves: the *emergent self*, the *core self*, the *subjective self*, and the *verbal self*, each contributing its harmonies and disharmonies to the symphonic structure of the adult self, in which the components retain their uniqueness, yet blend into a unitary experience. Stern based his theory largely upon the infant observational and experimental research of the last two decades, taking note of psychoanalytic clinical notions, the validity of which he does not deny, yet insisting that they are adultomorphic retrospective projections onto the infant. What Stern does validate in the psychoanalytic notions of self is their emphasis on the reality, indeed the saliency, of inwardness, of subjective experience, in contradistinction to the outwardness, the behavioralistic bias, of most empirical psychological work. Stern believes in an unconscious, although he doesn't much deal with it.

For Stern, the self is experiential. Explicitly, he defines it as the *sense* of agency, the *sense* of physical cohesion, the *sense* of continuity, the *sense* of affectivity, the *sense* of a subjective self that can achieve intersubjectivity with another, the *sense* of creating organization, and the *sense* of transmitting meaning. Definitions are prescriptive as well as descriptive, and Stern opts for a self or series of selves that are sensate, consisting of vaguely inchoate or sharply experienced sensations and organizations of sensations. These selves are essentially preconscious most of the time, although for the most part they can emerge into consciousness without difficulty. It is not clear how or how much the Sternian selves are dynamically unconscious. Perhaps figure and ground is a better metaphor than conscious–unconscious: Stern's selves most commonly serve as ground, albeit an active and organizing ground, but they can and do become figure.

Let us look at Stern's selves in a bit more detail. They correspond to discontinuities, quantum leaps in development. In this way, they are reminiscent of Spitz's (1965) "organizers of the psyche." The sense of the emergent self comes into being during the first 2 months of life. It is a "sense of organization in the process of formation" (Stern 1985, p. 38). Stern emphasizes the experience of the process more than he does the product. This process is the ongoing organization of bodily concerns ("the ego is first and foremost a bodily ego,") resulting in experiential cohesion of the body, its actions, and inner feeling states. These will form the core self, which is now emergent. The emergent self is both the process and product of forming relations between isolated events. It is the giving of coherence. In adult life, the emergent self is the basis of creativity and potential for ongoing development.

In the next stage, that of the core self, there is a consolidation of that which has emerged from the emergent self. The core self is characterized by experiences of *self-agency* (can do things); *self-coherence* (I have boundaries and I am a physical whole); *self-affectivity* (I have patterned inner qualities of feeling that are the same across experiences); and *self-history* (I endure, go-on-being because there are regularities in the flow of my experiences, in my stream of consciousness). These four self-experiences of the core self are preconceptual. Stern (1985) says, "A crucial term here is 'sense of' as distinct from 'concept of' or 'knowledge of' or 'awareness of' a self or other" (p. 71). They are not reflexive or reflective. The core self is a self without self-consciousness. In normal development, it is consolidated at about 8 months.

The subjective self develops from 8 to 15 months. Essentially, it is the discovery that there are inner subjective experiences — thoughts and feelings — that are mine. Simultaneously, or slightly later, the infant "discovers" that others also have "minds"; that is, thoughts and feelings that are potentially the same as his. This opens up the possibility of intersubjectivity. I can share (or not share), connect (or not connect) with other creatures who are subjects like me, who have an inner world of sensations, feelings, and thoughts. For Stern (1985), self and objects are coemergent not from a symbiosis but from genetically and temporally prior, less organized, inwardly experienced experiences of self and others. There is a prior primitiveness of self and others — primitive in the sense of less organized, less self-aware — but no prior confusion or merger. In the stage of the subjective self, the subjectivity of the other is also established and multitudinous possibilities for relatedness come into being. It is only now that merger or symbiosis becomes possible, but only as a union of that which was initially experienced as distinct. The distinctness of self and other, self and world, are preprogrammed as is the development of the four selves. However, development does not take place in a vacuum; it takes place in a social matrix, and there is a dialectical relationship between the emergent selves of the infant and response of the adult caretakers. As the child changes, the response he or she elicits changes, which in turn elicits further changes in the child. Here Stern's notion is similar to those of Winnicott and Kohut, but the balance is more on innateness and response to it than on environmental provision — being treated as a self — creating a self. The emphasis is different, but all these thinkers see both innate and environmental input as necessary for the formation of the self.

During the second year of life, the verbal self comes into being. Now the self can be represented as a narrative, the story one tells to oneself about who and what one is. The verbal self opens up new possibilities for interpersonal experience, but language also increases the possibilities for deception and concealment. The verbal self cannot adequately represent the emergent or the core selves. We are now in the world of conceptualization and abstraction, which carries with it the dangers of alienation from the vividness and vitality of the preverbal experience characteristic of the emergent, core, and subjective selves. Thus, the four selves are equally necessary, the temporally later does not supplant the temporally earlier; rather they provide different self-experiences. The four selves endure and mutually enrich each other across the life span. In the full flower of the Sternian self, it is simultaneously the experience of coming into being, the experience of being, the experience of interiority of self and others, and the experience of giving a history verbally — a narrative.

What can we conclude about self? Self is *developmental*; self is *emergent*, emergent from an innately programmed template and from experiences of merger; it comes out of a preselfhood; self is *affective*; self is *not body but neither is it disembodied*; self is *conflictual*, in conflict with various components of itself and with the environment, but not only conflictual; self is *object relational*, coming into being through interaction with others and always mediated by such interactions; and self is *constitutive*, a synthesizer and a synthesis.

Self is experienced as, and indeed is, an interaction between innate potential and environmental response. Feelings of aliveness, cohesion, agency, continuity (ongoingness), and self-worth come from both within and without. I agree with Winnicott's and Kohut's beliefs that the feelings of being coherent, enduring, and worthwhile, indeed of existing, come, at least in part, from the outside. I become a self by being treated as a self. I learn who and what I am by the ways in which I am treated. Self is both organizer and organization. It always has an affective quality; it is never purely conceptual; it encompasses verbal and preverbal levels; it is more or less consistent and coherent (the degree of which can only be empirically determined); it is unconscious as well as preconscious, and less frequently conscious; it is a construct and a synthesis; it is a fiction (narrative) and a reality (experience); it is a dialectic of conflict and reconciliation with others and with itself carried out by projection, identification, and introjection; it is partly dependent on memory; it evolves over a lifetime; and it is subject to injury. (For a more detailed discussion of the metapsychology of self, see Levin 1992.)

NARCISSISM

Narcissism, love of the self, is an old concept given a modern meaning by psychoanalysis. Our word *narcissism* comes from the Greek *narka*, to deaden. It is the same root that is used in narcotic and narcotize. Both narcotics and (excessive) narcissism deaden, attenuate sensation and feeling. That says something interesting about addiction and its relation to narcissism. The Greek root took on its meaning of deadening from the name of a protagonist of a legend, Narcissus. In the legend, Narcissus, a beautiful youth, becomes so entranced by his reflection in a pool of water that he remains frozen gazing upon his own face until he perishes. At his death, he was transformed into a flower, the narcissus. His infatuation with self gives narcissism its meaning of self-love. Both *narka* and the tale of Narcissus remind us that there is something dangerous about self-love, yet without it we would also perish. So there must be a healthy self-love that is life-enhancing, and a pathological self-love that deadens.

Freud (1914a) turned narcissism into a scientific concept in his prescient paper, "On Narcissism: An Introduction." In it, Freud distinguishes several meanings of narcissism: as a sexual perversion in which the self is taken as a primary sexual object; as a libidinal component of the instinct of self-preservation; and as the libidinal cathexis of self. He cites a number of phenomena as evidence for the existence of narcissism: the existence of the above-mentioned sexual perversion in which pleasure in looking at, admiring, and fondling the self provides complete sexual satisfaction; the normal and universal love of self; the megalo-mania of schizophrenia, in which all of the libido seems to be directed onto the self; the clinical evidence of the distinction between the object libido and ego libido as manifested in the transference neuroses in which a libidinal bond is formed with the analyst, and the narcissistic neuroses (i.e., psychosis) in which such a bonding does not take place; organic illness during which self-absorption is normal; hypochondria, in which libido is also directed onto the self or fragments thereof; the egoism of sleep; homosexual love between men in which object choice is choice of a replica (in some sense) of self; and parental love with its excesses and denial of reality, which Freud views as narcissistic love once removed.

Freud (1914a) described a normal developmental process in which there is a progression from autoeroticism (love of isolated body parts) to narcissism (love of self) to object love (love of others). The infant first derives pleasure from body parts, experienced as yet as isolates, not as parts of a self; these sensory experiences are later integrated into a self, or ego, which is experienced as tenuous and unclearly demarcated from the not-self (the world), and this ego is loved; and finally a portion of this primeval self-love or primary narcissism overflows and is projected out as object love. Thus, our instinctual energy is first invested in our own body parts, then invested in ourselves before the distinction between self and others has been established, and finally flows outward to emotionally invest (cathect) objects. Narcissistic libido becomes object libido.

According to Freud (1914a) disappointment in object love can lead to withdrawal of interest (libido) from the world and reinvestment of that libido in the self. Freud denoted this phenomenon *secondary narcissism* to distinguish it from *primary narcissism*. Freud postulated that normal self-esteem results from a reservoir of self-love that remains from the stage of primary narcissism and that continues to exist alongside object love. He thought that secondary narcissism was the basic mechanism of psychotic withdrawal from the world and that the psychotic delusion of the end of the world reflected the reality of the withdrawal of libido from the world of objects and its redirection onto a now impoverished and isolated self.

Jacobson (1964), who saw the initial stage of human development as an undifferentiated "psychosomatic" matrix in which neither self-representations and object representations nor the libidinal and aggressive drives are yet differentiated, does not believe that it makes sense to speak of narcissism in a stage preceding the differentiation of self and object representations. Therefore, she defines narcissism as the *libidinal cathexis of the self-representation*. Analogously, object love is seen as the libidinal cathexis of an object representation. She conceptualizes severe psychopathology in terms of regressive fusion of self- and object representations.

Kernberg (1975) conceptualizes normal narcissism as the libidinal investment of the self-representation. This self is a structure in the ego that integrates good and bad self-images. Normal self-love predisposes successful completion of Kernberg's fourth stage of object relations development. To review, in his first stage, there is an undifferentiated matrix; in his second, good and bad self-objects; in the third, good self-representations, bad self-representations, good object representations and bad object representations; in stage four, these good and bad representations are integrated, and separate self- and object representations established. That is, self- and object representations that incorporate the good and bad aspects of self and object come into being. In normal narcissism, the self, which is seen as a complex and integrated self-representation in the system ego, is libidinally cathected. Being suffused with libido, it is loved.

In Kernberg's (1975) view, those who suffer from pathological narcissism develop a pathological self-structure, the *grandiose self*. This grandiose self is a pathological condensation (fusion) of ideal-self, real-self, and ideal-object representations. It is not found in normal development. It is, however, a stable psychic structure, a characteristic that makes possible relatively smooth social functioning. Narcissistic personalities typically relate to others not as separate people but as extensions of themselves. They do not really experience others as others, but rather as projections of their grandiose selves. Hence, what appear to be object relations are really relations of self to self.

Characteristic defenses in narcissistic personalities include primitive idealization, projective identification, splitting, and devaluation. In one way or another, these defenses distort the object to meet the needs of the narcissist. These mechanisms are in the service of omnipotent control. True dependence on another human being, experienced as separate and autonomous, would entail the risk of intolerable emotions of rage and envy toward the person depended upon. Thus, what appears to be dependent relating in the narcissistic personality is, in reality, another aspect of the need for omnipotent control, in this case the control of the source of supply. Such a pseudodependency cannot possibly meet the real dependency needs that are part and parcel of the human condition, and a vicious cycle of need and failure to meet it is set up.

Kohut's (1971, 1977) view of narcissism differs from both Freud's (1914a) and Kernberg's (1975). In contradistinction to Freud's notion of narcissistic libido as the precursor of object libido, Kohut believes that narcissistic and object-libidinal strivings develop along independent lines. That is, narcissism is seen not as a stage in the development of object love, but rather as an aspect of human life that has its own developmental history in which the self and its libidinal investments evolve from a fragmentary stage into a cohesive, archaic form (the nuclear self) and finally into a mature form. The development of mature object love and mature self-love are parallel but independent processes.

Kohut (1971, 1977) differs from Kernberg (1975) in believing that the grandiose self is a normal, albeit archaic structure, rather than a pathological one. As we have seen, Kohut is particularly interested in two early self-structures: the grandiose self and the idealized self-object (or idealized parental imago). These structures constitute the nuclear self. Kohut's stage of the archaic self corresponds to Freud's stage of primary narcissism. However, it does not develop into object love, but rather into a mature narcissism characterized by realistic ambitions, enduring ideals, and secure self-esteem.

Pathological narcissism is the regression/fixation to the stage of the archaic self. It is characterized by the presence of a cohesive but insecure self, which is threatened by regressive fragmentation; grandiosity of less than psychotic proportions that manifests itself in the form of arrogance, isolation, and unrealistic goals; feelings of entitlement; the need for omnipotent control; poor differentiation of self and object; and deficits in the self-regulating capacities of the ego (self). Affect tolerance is limited. The tenuous cohesion of their selves makes narcissistically regressed individuals subject to massive anxiety which is, in reality, fear of annihilation (fear of fragmentation of the self). They are also subject to empty depression, reflecting the emptiness of the self — its paucity of psychic structure and good internal objects. These manifestations of the grandiose self and/or the idealized self-object may either be blatantly apparent or deeply repressed and/or denied, with a resulting facade of pseudo-sufficiency. In pathological narcissism, archaic self-structures are not integrated into the mature self, as is the case in healthy narcissism. The pathologically narcissistic are more vulnerable, more subject to narcissistic injury yet ill equipped to deal with it.

In Kohut's formulation, the overtly grandiose self is a result of merger with (or lack of differentiation from) a mother who uses the child to gratify her own narcissistic needs. It is a "false self." Kohut envisages this false self as insulated from the modifying influence of the reality ego by a vertical split in the self. The reality ego is in turn impoverished by repression of archaic, unfulfilled narcissistic needs by a horizontal split (repression barrier) in the self.

Kohut emphasizes the normality of our narcissistic needs and the deleterious consequences of repression or disavowal of those needs. For him, a healthy narcissism is a vital component of mental health and at least as important as the ability to achieve instinctual gratification. Kohut is highly critical of what he calls the "maturity morality" implicit in much of psychoanalysis, which he views as unaccepting of the narcissistic sphere of personality. He is equally critical of the Judeo-Christian religious tradition's denial of the centrality and legitimacy of our need for self-affirmation. He sees many factors working to deny or disapprove of the fulfillment of narcissistic needs and believes that as with any repression, it will fail, and the repressed will return. If narcissistic needs are not met in healthy ways, they will be met in unhealthy ways—the ravages of narcissistic rage with its unquenchable desire for revenge and the idealization of demonic leaders such as Hitler and the Reverend Jones.

Whatever their differences, these theorists—Freud, Jacobson, Kernberg, and Kohut—all see narcissism as having healthy and pathological forms, as being love of self, as occupying a co-central place in human life with object love (although they differ in their views of the relationship between these kinds of love). The introduction of the concept of narcissism changes our notion of narcissistic injury. Now narcissistic injury denotes not only injury to the self, but also injury to our capacity to love ourselves. This is a subtle yet meaningful distinction. Further, insofar as we are identified with others, their injury becomes our injury and the "shadow of the object falls on the ego."

NARCISSISTIC INJURY

Freud (1930) wrote that humankind had suffered three great narcissistic wounds. The first was inflicted by Copernicus when he moved the center of the universe from the earth to the sun. Instead of being at the center of a universe, humankind became inhabitants of an average planet of a minor star in one of an almost infinite number of galaxies. The persecutions suffered by those who upheld the Copernican theory confirms the narcissistic injury and the intensity of the defense against it. The second great narcissistic wound was inflicted by Darwin. Instead of the lord of creation, à la Genesis, man became merely an animal among animals, the end product of a natural evolution independent of mind or purpose, not the proudest creation of a divine Creator. Humankind became part of nature rather than apart from and above it. The demotion was not gladly accepted. The response to narcissistic injury is narcissistic rage—mindless, unquenchable questing for revenge as retaliation for humiliation and damage to the self. The response to Darwin was hardly less irrational than to Copernicus; witness the recent resurgence of Creationism. The third injury was inflicted by Freud himself when he demonstrated that man is not the master in his own house. On the contrary, we are, in George Groddeck's words, "lived by the id." Unconscious drives, instincts, and impulses determine our lives. Consciousness, civilization, and morality are but their veneers. As a neurologist once put it, the cortex, seat of consciousness and rationality, merely ratifies the decisions of the limbic system, seat of emotionality. Freud's infliction of yet another narcissistic injury was and is also met with denial, defense, mockery, repression, co-option and domestication, and at times persecution.

What we can conclude from this is that the essence of narcissistic injury is an affront to our grandiosity. In his essay "On Narcissism" (1914a), Freud spoke of "His Majesty the Baby." Infantile grandiosity never goes away; we simply learn to package it in more or less acceptable ways. That grandiosity cannot be confirmed by reality—His or Her Majesty, the Baby lives uncertainly and briefly in a universe whose grandeur is matched only by its indifference. Thus, narcissistic injury is intrinsic to human life. It is an inevitable and ineluctable part of living. The prototype of narcissistic injury is impingement—disruption of going-on-being. Anything that threatens our continuity, our boundaries, our centeredness, our feelings of agency, our self-object transferences, or that brings about regressive fragmentation is narcissistically injurious, as is the diminution of self through objectification—being turned into an object by another. Narcissistic injury is everywhere. The question is, How do we handle it? How do we absorb and transmute the slings and arrows of outrageous fortune? Can we relinquish at least a part of our grandiosity so that affronts to it sting less? How can we help our patients mourn their losses, treat their wounds, deal with the shame and rage that are ineluctable concomitants of narcissistic injury, and lessen their vulnerability? The rest of this book is an attempt to answer these questions.

Treatment should help ameliorate narcissistic injury, yet paradoxically, it often inflicts it. Assuming the role of patient is inherently narcissistically injurious. Yet so much of narcissistic injury in treatment is gratuitous, surplus injury—to steal and modify a term from Marx—over and above unavoidable injury. Patients aren't the only ones injured in treatment; therapists are as well. How can the therapist minimize the injury inherent in conducting therapy, as well as process and integrate that which can't be avoided? These questions too must be answered. Therefore, the case discussions that follow will deal not only with the injury sustained by the patient in life, but also with the injuries to each of the partners in the therapeutic relationship in the course of that relationship.

2

Roberta: Injured by Life; Injured by Therapy

A number of years ago, I spoke to an audience of mental health professionals. Among the therapists in the audience was an overly intense, youngish man who was apparently much taken with what I had said about narcissism. I forgot about him. Several months later, I started getting calls from patients who had been in therapy with Mr. Stone. He had decided to stop practicing therapy and was referring his patients to me. They were uniformly severely disturbed, often engaged in bizarre behaviors, and powerfully emotionally bonded to the retiring Mr. Stone. Their involvement with him was virtually a merger. None of these patients was able to transfer their allegiances to me, and our contacts were brief. I felt hurt. I'm not used to having a string of patients walk. It rankled. What did this Stone have that I didn't? Stone and all of his patients were members of a religious community, so I tried to tell myself that as an outsider, it was only natural that these patients didn't stay in therapy with me. It helped but was emotionally unsatisfying. It seemed clear that since they all belonged to the same, closely knit sect, they weren't about to trust a nonmember, but damn it, my forte is relating to all sorts of people from all sorts of cultures. My ability to do so is a source of pride and self-esteem. It is a salient part of my self-concept, and doubtlessly, my unconscious self-representation as well.

Several months went by with no more calls from Stone's patients. I occasionally thought of my string of therapeutic failures, feeling a bit of the shame and rage that are the ineluctable concomitants of narcissistic injury. I told myself "You're being unreasonable. You know members of tightly-knit religions don't engage in therapy with those who are not part of their subculture. You're being absurdly vain." It worked. Stone and his patients faded from my consciousness. Intense transference generally facilitates treatment, but there are certainly unhealthy, antitherapeutic transferences, and I had no doubt that Stone's patients had "antitherapeutic" transferences to him. My hunch proved to be correct, but I didn't know how true it was. I like patients to be passionately engaged in therapy with me. Their love and hate are what make the work possible. That much is objective truth, but there is another factor here; I like the attention, the concentration of feelings on me. Unfortunately, Stone elicited a remarkable loyalty from his patients. Damn it, what does Stone have that I don't? In analyzing my countertransference, I realized how much I need my patients. Needing to be loved (or hated) gets in the way of being an effective therapist, yet it is always there, however much denied. I tell my supervisees, "Don't take it personally," and I tried to take my own advice. For the most part, it's *unconscious* countertransference that disables the therapist, so I was ahead of the game in having realized that I want to be felt about and I'm hurt when I am not. When I say the countertransference of which we are aware generally does not harm the patient, this assumes that we do not act on our countertransference feelings. There certainly are cases (and as it turned out, Stone's was one of them) in which a conscious countertransference can damage the patient. But mostly, that is not the case.

Thinking about my own countertransference, I thought of Freud writing somewhere, I think in a letter to Lou Andreas-Salomé, "The patient doesn't transfer to me; I'm too old." Poor Freud, 80, fatally sick with cancer, yet still wanting to be loved. His hurt is palpable in that letter. The narcissistic wound of Stone's referrals rapidly dropping out was compounded by my anger at myself for caring. Well, if Freud had had similar problems, maybe I wasn't so bad after all. Feeling comforted, I decided to retire before I hit 80. Other patients came and stayed. Who wants those religious fanatics anyway? I forgot Stone. Then Roberta called.

In *Civilization and Its Discontents* (1930), Freud wrote:

> We are threatened with suffering from three directions: from our own body, which is doomed to decay and dissolution and which cannot even do without pain and anxiety as warning signals; from the external world, which may rage against us with overwhelming and merciless forces of destruction; and finally, from our relations with other men. The suffering which comes from this last source is perhaps more painful to us than any other. We tend to regard it as a kind of gratuitous addition, although it cannot be any less fatefully inevitable than the suffering which comes from else-where. [p. 77]

Roberta's sufferings from each of these directions were severe, deep, and lacerating. She was physically disabled, her face somewhat disfigured, although one came to see a certain beauty in it, and her left leg missing; she was hopelessly in love with Stone, who had abandoned her, although she didn't know it; she was in trouble on her job and threatened with economic catastrophe; she was subject to wild mood swings and seemingly inexplicable outbursts of rage; and perhaps worst of all, she was excommunicated from her religious community that was not only her support system, but virtually her only source of human contact. Nothing in Roberta's life was going well. Her artificial leg was out of synch and apparently no longer adjustable, and the orthotist was demanding cash up front, which she didn't have, to replace it. Stone had convinced her that she, as it turned out, like him, was manic-depressive, and her "lithium doctor," who ran a prescription mill and who couldn't remember her name, had lost her file. "Not single spies," indeed.

I called Tom Stone to thank him for the referral. He told me that Roberta had the worst life history that he had ever heard, that her rages were unbelievable, and that he could not talk to her because she was excommunicated. He went on to say that many of Roberta's experiences were uncannily like his, and he became progressively more nervous, finally hanging up abruptly. I never heard from him again.

Excommunicated? He had to be kidding. This was the twentieth century. The only excommunication I was familiar with was Spinoza's, from the Amsterdam congregation in the seventeenth century, and I considered that barbaric. Roberta's excommunication was less radical in that it was reversible. She was sort of temporarily excommunicated, but for the length of the ban, it was strikingly similar to Spinoza's; members of the community were prohibited from having any intercourse with her on pain of their being excommunicated. She was publicly disgraced by having her ban, with its delineation of her iniquities, read from the pulpit to the assembled congregants. Although she didn't have to wear a scarlet letter, she might just as well have. During the period of her excommunication, she could communicate only with her "committee," the group of elders who had handed down the ban, but this was strictly limited. Further, she was expected to attend religious meetings and services during the excommunication, if she had any hope of being reinstated. Of course, she could neither speak nor be spoken to at those meetings. Although excommunication (which, like an indeterminate jail sentence, could last indefinitely) was not conceived of as a punitive action but rather as a means of bringing a lost soul back to spiritual health, it inflicted intense pain. At one point, Roberta asserted that she would rather be taken out and whipped as in the days of old rather than be in a state of excommunication.

Countertransferentially, I had a great deal of trouble with Roberta's excommunication. It aroused intense feelings of repugnance and anger in me, which I needed to keep out of my interactions with Roberta, who accepted the tenets of her faith and its practices, although she felt that they had been misapplied in her case. What I saw as medieval cruelty, she saw as spiritual discipline. That didn't mean that she wasn't enraged by the elders' infliction of and maintenance of her ban.

Unlike Stone's other referrals, Roberta showed no signs of leaving, but week after week, she reiterated that I was sort of okay, but that she just didn't feel about me the way she felt about him. He made her feel alive, important, hopeful, while I did nothing for her. Why did she continue to come? It was useless. Forty-five minutes of being damned with faint praise — at best — is hard to listen to. I told myself that Roberta had nobody and was a very real suicide risk, so it was a damn good thing that she continued to come to tell me that, unlike Tom Stone, I aroused no hope, no self-affirmation, no excitement, no relief from her depression. Even worse, I offered her no consolation. Stone had told her how his sufferings paralleled hers, and that was consoling. I was starting to hate Tom Stone. Clearly, he was an asshole, and both an unethical and inept therapist, yet he had given this woman something she had never had before — he had made her feel lovable, and that had served as a consolation for all of her other troubles. Though I sometimes felt hurt and angry at Roberta when she relentlessly compared me unfavorably to Tom Stone, I was more concerned that she would drop out and literally have nobody than I was suffering from the real, but not very deep, narcissistic injury that she inflicted with her invidious comparisons. So I was pleased that Roberta continued her relentless barrage. Generally, "as long as they talk, they don't walk."

I didn't worry very much about my countertransferential feelings; I knew that I wasn't going to act out my hurt or anger by an injurious interpretation or a forgotten appointment. Countertransference has a narrow technical meaning: the therapist's

revival of the feelings attached to the archaic relationships of
infancy and early childhood in his relationship with his patient. It
is an unconscious repetition in exactly the same way that the
patient's transference is an unconscious repetition. Classical
psychoanalysis defines countertransference in this way. Countertransference in the broader sense is the sum total of the therapist's
feelings for the patient, whether induced by the patient or
emergent from the unconscious of the therapist. I use the term
countertransference in the latter sense. Beginning, and sometimes
not-so-beginning, therapists believe that they "shouldn't" have
feelings about and toward their patients, especially erotic or
angry ones. Of course, they do. The important thing is that they
be aware of them and try to sort out what is induced by the
patient and what is coming from them, without acting out or on
those feelings, whatever their source. I was certainly hurt by
Roberta's constant devaluation of me and was sometimes angry at
her. I parsed it out this way: she was angry at Stone but didn't
know it, so she had to devalue me, in a kind of displaced
transferential hostility, and even more saliently, she couldn't risk
caring about me after having been so deeply hurt by Stone, while
I was bringing my only child sensibility into the situation, not so
unconsciously wanting to be the most, the only, loved child.
Pondering my countertransference took most of the sting out of
Roberta's continuing devaluations, but left unresolved the question of how to "console" her.

Freud (1930) wrote, "My courage sinks to stand up before my
fellow humans as a prophet, and I bow before their reproaches
that I do not know how to bring them consolation—for that is
fundamentally what they all demand, the wildest revolutionaries
no less than the most conformist, pious believers." Few therapists
believe that they need to be prophets, although years of being a
supervisor have taught me that messianic yearnings are far more
common in therapists than their profession would allow; be that
as it may, the feeling that we must console, comfort, take away
the pain is well-nigh universal among therapists. Of course, we
cannot do it. Therein lies one of the deepest of therapists'

narcissistic wounds. We feel helpless. We feel impotent. We feel ashamed that we are so powerless. We feel enraged that we don't have the magic that our patients demand from us. If we happen to be working with a patient who consistently reminds us of how useless we are, it doesn't take long to begin believing it. The more we expect from ourselves, the more we set ourselves up for this kind of narcissistic wound. Of course, there are things we should expect from ourselves — integrity, sensitivity to the patient's communications, awareness of unconscious process, an attempt to bring to awareness and to understand the source of our countertransferences, but not the ability to make people feel good instantly or otherwise. In short, it is our grandiosity that sets us up for narcissistic injury as "useless" therapists.

These days, it isn't only disgruntled patients, or patients in negative transference, who devalue the therapeutic process: the slow accretion of insight and of the ego strength to contain impulses and delay their gratification. As someone once said, "The mature adult delays gratification and is miserable." Who wants to pay a therapist to be miserable? These days, it is also the insurance companies, the managed care networks, and the organicists who are telling us, the dynamic therapists, that what we do isn't worthwhile. Assaulted by the culture, by the drug companies, by the insurance companies, and by some patients insistently and all patients occasionally, is it any wonder that our "professional self-esteem" sometimes plummets, and self-doubt sets in? "Maybe I should go into plastics" must occur to every psychodynamic therapist from time to time. One of my supervisees treated a chronically mildly depressed man for years, with some improvement, but no real resolution of the patient's symptoms. The patient went on Prozac and was "cured." The supervisee became depressed — not to mention angry at me, although we had discussed referral for psychopharmacological treatment. The supervisee felt useless, powerless, worthless — she suffered a deep narcissistic wound. Interestingly, the patient did not hold the therapist responsible for not suggesting Prozac earlier and continued in therapy, which he apparently valued highly. It was the therapist who felt devalued. I suggested that the supervisee take up the issue with her analyst.

To return to Roberta. I certainly couldn't offer her the solace she wanted, but I didn't feel I had to. Well, that's not quite true. When somebody is as desperate as Roberta, we really want to do something for them. But where to start? I decided that the starting point had to be Tom Stone, or rather, Roberta's feelings about Tom Stone. This was closest to consciousness and the most disabling of the issues confronting her. It was also one that elicited the most resistance. Roberta had seen a therapist, Dr. M., before Stone who had played by the rules — no untherapeutic self-disclosure; strictly professional limitations to their relationship; dispassionate, objective interpretations; and all the sensitivity of a rhinoceros. Roberta's presenting symptoms at that time were her disappointment in romantic love and her despair at finding a partner, given her physical disabilities. The therapist, somewhat overstepping his stance of technical neutrality, said, "Even quadriplegics get laid." I suppose this was intended to shock the patient into awareness that her infirmities didn't preclude sexual love, but delivered with no context, it was merely a narcissistic injury. Roberta felt that the therapist thought of her as profoundly disabled. She became further depressed, more despairing about finding love, and shortly left therapy with Dr. M. I asked her if Dr. M. had explored her feelings about her disability, which being congenital, she had had to deal with as long as she had self-awareness, or her perception of how others reacted to her disability. He had not. Opening an issue without adequately exploring and ventilating, and, to use an old term, abreacting the feelings around that issue is not only antitherapeutic, it necessarily inflicts narcissistic damage.

The most bizarre therapist–patient relationship reported to me was reported by a middle-aged patient who was in pretty good shape when he decided to reenter treatment for fine tuning of some narcissistic issues — excessive self-involvement of which he was aware and that he wished to change. When I asked him as part of my standard intake if he had been in therapy before, he related his experience with a Dr. Smith. When the patient was in his early twenties, he suffered anxiety attacks for which he sought treatment. Interestingly, he had found Dr. Smith by searching the telephone directory, and entered treatment with him without recommendation of any sort. He soon formed a strong attachment to his physician, who was indeed able to help him insofar as the relationship provided security, and the patient's anxiety receded. However, things were not to remain so placid or positive. Dr. Smith had a secretary with whom the patient became involved. As he later found out, Margaret was not only Dr. Smith's secretary, she was his tenant, living in the apartment over his office; his patient; his mistress; and he was treating her estranged husband for paranoia manifested by excessive suspicion of his wife. The patient didn't (consciously) feel injured by Dr. Smith. As the patient put it, "Well, I was playing too; I didn't have to get involved with Smith's secretary. Besides, Norman, her husband, had a gun, and we acted a grade B movie scenario, with Norman chasing me around town in two-wheel-turn car chases. I loved it, and I now had so many reality problems that I didn't have time to be anxious." Surely one of the stranger "flights into health" I have come across. Needless to say, the oedipal and other implications of this triangle — quadrilateral — were not analyzed, and the patient dropped out of therapy, in itself an injury.

In the course of treatment with me, the patient came to see (and feel) that he *had* been injured by Smith, and that his regarding the whole thing as being a joke was both a defense and a manifestation of low self-esteem. When patients retell experiences, particularly negative experiences, with other therapists, I listen very carefully, trying to separate narrative from historical truth, which of course is not possible. Nevertheless, I tend to believe my patients. As far as I can ascertain, they rarely lie about matters of fact, and the business of therapy is to make conscious unconscious meanings and feelings.

To return to Roberta. She had certainly been injured by the first therapist. Of course he was "right," all sorts of people find sexual partners, but he was totally oblivious to where his patient was "at." Yet her relationship with Dr. M. was relatively sane, compared with her relationship with Tom Stone. I asked Roberta to describe her relationship with Stone in as much detail as possible. She told of how Stone had told her all about himself, about his manic-depression, when he had diagnosed her as a manic-depressive and sent her for lithium treatment; how he had invited her to his home and involved her with his wife and children, and invited her to come to feel a part of his family, which she did. But mostly, Roberta told and retold how Stone had made her feel. Finally, I said, "You're in love with him." Roberta laughed wildly, bounced off the chair, and said, "Dr. Levin, you're crazy, nuts." I didn't insist on the point. Clearly, admitting that she was in love with Tom Stone was more than the patient could do at that time.

An immediate problem to be addressed was her diagnosis as manic-depressive. I had my doubts. She didn't report any obviously manic episodes, although her rages could have been an atypical manifestation, and she was profoundly and dangerously depressed. Her lithium level had not been checked for a year, and it was possible that she might do better on an antidepressant. Stone diagnosed all of his patients as manic-depressive, so his diagnosis didn't mean much. As a nonmedical therapist, I was on dangerous ground, but I couldn't let Roberta sink further into depression when a change of medication might help her. From her description — and I had no reason to doubt it — her lithium doctor sounded like a total loss. In any case, she didn't want to return to her, yet she adamantly refused a psychiatric referral. "I'm not going to see another shrink. Oh, Dr. Levin, you must want to get rid of me."

The narcissistic issues here were complex. To admit the possibility that she was misdiagnosed or on the wrong medicine was to cast doubt on Tom Stone, and that Roberta would not do. It was possible that her idealization of him could cost her her life if it prevented her from getting the psychopharmacological treatment that might relieve her depression. Idealization is always an obstacle course for the therapist. As Kohut thought, the patient's idealization may sustain and stabilize the self, yet pathological idealizations are among the most pernicious of human behaviors — witness the idealization of such leaders as Hitler and the Reverend Jones. Again, that damned Stone. Clearly, Roberta's feeling for Stone had to be dealt with *before* she would accept a referral.

When a nonmedical therapist refers a patient to a psychiatrist for a medication evaluation, a transference–countertransference nexus is immediately set up. A dyadic relationship is disturbed. The patient may feel cared for, sloughed off ("Do you want to get rid of me?"), damaged, hopeful, or a multitude of other things. He or she may feel that the therapist is weak and inadequate, needing to refer to a "real" doctor, or on the contrary, may feel that the therapist is a wise, deeply caring professional doing his or her job. In any case, feelings are involved and *must* be elicited, uncovered, and expressed. In addition to dealing with the patient's feelings about being referred, the therapist must also deal with the patient's feelings about taking the medicine. Most psychopharmacologists do this, if at all, in a cursory manner. Needing to take medicine may be a narcissistic injury for the patient, who may resist because to need medicine is to have a defect in the self, which is inadmissible.

Roberta felt so hopeless that she saw no reason to accept a referral. She also had an at least subliminal awareness that her persistent devaluations might have elicited less than friendly feelings in me and contributed to her fear that I wanted to get rid of her. For some patients, referral for medication suggests that they are less than analytic material, and this constitutes a narcissistic injury. Roberta didn't have this sort of "sophistication," but had rather similar feelings. Additionally, she was suffering "therapist fatigue"; her first therapist had insulted her, her second traumatically abandoned her, her present psychopharmacologist didn't know who she was, and I was presumably better than nothing, but without much salience, and now I wanted to send her elsewhere. She refused. I thought of making accepting the referral a condition of treatment, but I thought she would quit, which would be life-threatening, and I am temperamentally adverse to coercion. What I finally did was to return to the possibility of medication helping her week after week until I wore her down, and she accepted my referral. As with her reaction to lithium, the effect of antidepressant medication was equivocal. It may have helped some, but its effects were not dramatic. The consulting psychiatrist did not think she was manic-depressive, which set off intense rage in her. Roberta was now furious with him and with me, insofar as we were separate persons, because we did not believe her to be manic-depressive. Tom Stone could not be wrong.

Our need to idealize is as primordial as our need to aggress. The need for perfect, all-powerful protectors is no more out-grown than our libidinal needs. All of our infantile wishes remain immortal in our unconscious. Idealization, of course, can be in the interest of control — "Because you are ideal, you will meet my expectations that you be ideal and use your infinite power to meet my needs." If we love the ideal, we need not deal with the real. The actual is ineluctably more recalcitrant than our idealizing fantasies. Frustration of our narcissistic needs, whether for mirroring or idealization, leads to narcissistic rage — the irrational pursuit of revenge (for narcissistic injury). Kohut cited Captain Ahab's mad quest for vengeance as a quintessential example of narcissistic rage. Injury to our ideals elicits just as intense narcissistic rage as injury to our core selves, and indeed, our ideal objects are part of us — self-objects — so injury to or separation from them is injurious to us.

Roberta reacted with narcissistic rage to the implicit criticism of her idealized previous therapist. She railed against Dr. P., the consulting psychopharmacologist, and against me for having sent her to him. I welcomed this openly expressed rage; it was better than her relentless devaluation, and infinitely better than turning her rage against herself. I figured that some of her rage was really toward Stone, but I didn't so interpret it. To do so would have inflicted yet another narcissistic injury and would have been of no use to her. Timing, or what Freud called "therapeutic tact" (he didn't always display it — see his case of Dora, 1905) is everything. Although Roberta damned psychiatry, reflecting real perplexity over the differing opinions of experts, she tried her new medication. Since the results were equivocal, Roberta continued to fulminate against the uncertainty of psychiatric diagnosis and the uselessness of psychiatrists. I acknowledge the realistic aspect of her complaints, but continued to delay interpreting the transferential determinations of her rage. Every time I thought the issue was dead, Roberta reasserted that she was a manic-depressive and that Dr. P. and I didn't understand her. Perhaps she was right, although she hadn't responded to lithium treatment. She continued to maintain that it controlled her rages.

My willingness to talk to her calmly and dispassionately about the difficulties and deficiencies of differential diagnosis and the sometimes empirical (trial and error) nature of psychopharmacological prescribing raised her self-esteem. I didn't criticize her rage, or try and take it away, or explain it away. I recognized her frustration, her desperation, her despair that nothing seemed to help much. For the first time, a therapeutic alliance started to develop. I presented myself and the consulting psychiatrist as less than perfect and less than omnipotent. On the surface, this lessened her opportunity to develop an idealizing transference to me, an opportunity Kohut believed to be essential for the patient, but I decided that Roberta had had more than enough of idealizing transferences, and that a bit of reality would do some good. It did. Our adversarial relationship around medication evolved into an alliance of two people trying to solve a problem with limited resources. She had never had such an experience, and she liked it. Our relationship started to change.

Franz Alexander (1943) spoke of a "corrective emotional experience" being the core of the curative power of therapy rather than the working through of resistance and transference. Kohut, who studied under Alexander at the Chicago Psychoanalytic Institute, always insisted that his self psychology was analysis, not a corrective emotional experience. I am not so sure. Psychodynamic therapy is both. Especially with patients whose early lives have been abusive and traumatic, revival of early relationships in the transference is purely negative, and revived feelings of rejection, injury, and humiliation are of dubious therapeutic value. On the other hand, it *is* necessary that the patient reexperience them, so a purely supportive technique equally misses the boat. I try to steer a middle course. In the course of time, Roberta became less interested in her diagnosis and quite willing to stick to a medication that gave her a modicum of relief, while she worked on the psychodynamic, psychological, and emotional determinants of her depression. I shortly learned her life history.

Roberta had been born with a congenital malformation of her nervous system, in which the peripheral nerves were impaired. This affected her vision, her facial musculature, and her leg, which was severely clubbed as well as imperfectly innervated. Her family had great difficulty accepting her. Her father, who was a character out of Dostoyevsky, was a "rage-aholic," tyrannical and cruel with his wife and children. Although he exempted Roberta from the routine beatings he inflicted on her siblings, he made it clear that he was ashamed of her and would have preferred that she had never been born. Roberta reported dreams in which she suffocated or drowned, and had a lifelong fear of water, which prevented her from learning to swim, a physical activity from which her disability did not bar her. As the psychopathic and perhaps psychotic nature of her father became progressively more clear, I realized that he had been capable of killing her. He had killed pets belonging to her brother, and ultimately was killed in the act of committing an assault.

I offered Roberta the construction that her father had tried to drown her. To tell a patient that a parent sexually abused her or tried to murder her is to inflict a severe narcissistic wound. If your parent so little loved you, or worse, hated you, you must be worthless, a piece of shit, and to be told by a therapist that that was the case when you didn't know it is awful. Freud advised the analyst to be like the surgeon, and to cut ruthlessly when cutting was called for. Freud valued insight and truth above all else.

Human dignity required it. If truth be painful, it is no less true and remains an absolute value. I do not disagree, although the analogy to the surgeon is an inaccurate and misleading one. I told Roberta that it was likely that her father had tried to kill her, because that made sense of the terror accompanying her dreams, of her chronic and sometimes suicidal depression, of her acting out, and of her anxiety. The narcissistic injury was unavoidable; however, as Aristotle said, "Men [and women too] by their nature desire to know." And knowledge ultimately heals.

The understanding that flowed out of my traumatic and injurious interpretation (made with less than conclusive evidence) convinced the patient that she wasn't "crazy." Roberta had always felt that her father, whom she deeply feared, had wanted her dead, so it was but a short step from that feeling to the knowledge that he had probably tried to carry out his wish. This interpretation gave Roberta a chance to put her rage where it belonged, and to begin to express rather than act out or internalize that rage. Nevertheless, she was deeply hurt to discover that her hateful, violent father had actually—in all probability—tried to kill her. She now felt free to hate him, which she had long known she did, without guilt. I took the risk of lowering her self-esteem when I offered my construction. We therapists take more risks than we usually acknowledge. Our choices often aren't good. We inflict pain in the hope of lessening it, yet we are never sure to what extent our hurtful interpretations are driven by unconscious sadism or countertransferential retaliation for injury, real or imagined, done by the patient to us. Guilt is intrinsic to doing therapy.

I have told a number of patients that their parent tried to murder them. I suspect that infanticide is more common than we would like to admit. In each case, the patient was deeply wounded and self-esteem plummeted dangerously, and in each case, the patient's experiential world came to make more sense, particularly the affective aspect of that world; and that understanding ultimately increased the patient's self-esteem. The problem is the dangerous period, with its risk of suicide, immediately following the construct. It is vital that the therapist help the patient ventilate (or sometimes communicate) rage toward the murderous or, as is more common, incestuous parent.

Roberta never recovered any actual memories of her father attempting to drown her, although both of us came to believe with near certainty that that was the case, however, she did recover many memories of violence and assault in her home. Her father was not alcoholic in the usual sense, but his reaction to alcohol was pathological. His chronic, barely contained rage would become overt as he beat his wife or children, smashed things, kicked in walls, or got into fights. Roberta grew up in constant fear.

When she was about 6, both of her older brothers raped her. The rapes were both anal and vaginal, and were initially extremely painful. Her brothers continued to have sex with her until she reached puberty. She had never told anyone about this until she told Stone. Roberta also reported an aversion to fellatio, the thought of which violently nauseated and disgusted her, which suggested that she had been forced to suck somebody's penis. She had no memory of doing so to her brothers, and I hypothesized that her father had forced her to fellate him. Classic psychoanalytic interpretation of her violent antipathy to fellatio would be that it was a reaction-formation to a forbidden wish, and indeed that may have been a component of her aversion. Premature sexual activity with an adult is traumatic for many reasons, among them the fact that the child's fantasies and unconscious wishes are now realized, so that along with the pain and the rage is guilty pleasure. Roberta came to experience such guilty pleasure in her sexual relationships with her brothers. This was barely conscious. In terms of technique, to interpret Roberta's aversion to fellatio in terms of it being a reaction-formation to a hidden wish, although partially true, not only misses the point but would increase the patient's guilt, lower her self-esteem, and further injure her. The salient point, and that which must be interpreted first, is that the aversion flowed from having been forced to perform fellatio, an experience that had initially been traumatic and the memory of which was now repressed. Roberta was a compulsive overeater, and her compulsive overeating may have been, among other things, an unconscious acting out of a fellatio fantasy, but it is far more likely that her violent father had sexually abused her, and that her repugnance stemmed primarily from that. Roberta remembered her brothers' behavior very clearly, but her memories of her father were patchy; many were recovered in the course of therapy, especially through dream analysis, so it made sense that it was her father rather than one of her brothers who forced her down on him — if that, indeed, was the case.

Roberta had great guilt about her relations with her brothers. Although she never remembered finding it pleasurable or stimulating, it is likely that she did, and that was the basis of her guilt. In another hurtful interpretation, timed so it was tolerable, I told her that. In addition to feeling guilty, she was deeply ashamed. Her guilt and shame were acted out in a variety of self-punitive actions — baiting the leader of her religious movement resulting in excommunication, compulsive overeating, outbursts of rage at work. Her near-suicidal depression was also, in part, a self-punishment. The more she talked of her guilt and shame, the less she needed to act them out. She had run up to the leaders of her sect and told them that she became sexually excited when she read the Bible. When they expressed shock, she replied, "I'll stop reading it." That incident foretold her excommunication. It was a typical example of how her shame drove her to provoke others into punishing her.

Children who are abused, physically or sexually, blame themselves, as do children whose parents divorce. This is conventionally understood as the egoism of childhood and as an identification with the aggressor, and it is both of these, but preeminently, it is a pathetic unconscious attempt to retain some control in a situation of powerlessness. The child unconsciously reasons that if it (the beatings, abandonment, sexual abuse, separation) is because I am so bad, then it is possible that I can change and become good so Mommy or Daddy won't beat, abuse, abandon me. Self-blame offers hope, while if there is nothing I can do to change Mommy's or Daddy's behavior, then there is no hope, and I am lost. (One wonders if Freud, who hated helplessness above all else, was unconsciously motivated by precisely this mechanism to place the "blame" inside the child rather than in the parent when he revised his seduction theory.) Of course, idealization also plays a role here, and self-blame protects the ideal object, who must be all the more ideal the more dismal the real.

Roberta had certainly blamed herself for her father's and her brothers' behavior, for all the above reasons. I interpreted her shame and guilt repeatedly, as consequences of the defense of self-blame. In using it, the child gains the *illusion* of having the power to change things, when in reality he or she has little or no such power; unfortunately, this illusory and unconscious comfort is attained at the cost of being "bad" and of believing that you are "bad"; and that that badness must be eradicated by self-punishment, usually of a savage nature. Roberta had set up her excommunication for complex reasons, one of which was to punish herself for her badness, sexual and otherwise. Among the other reasons she set herself up was that it was the only way she could leave an organization she had more and more doubts about; her unconscious need to rebel against oppressive authority; and her need to express the enormous unconscious rage she felt at the sect and the people in it. Transference, repetition, and here-and-now stuff were so thoroughly intermixed that it took years of therapy to disentangle them. Roberta's excommunication was not entirely the product of an unconscious setting up of a punishment; some of the behavior that brought it down on her was compulsive for reasons other than the elucidation of punishment.

When I told Roberta, bolstering my argument with a detailed recital of her many provocative actions, that she had set herself up for excommunication, she was shocked and disbelieving. That interpretation too was narcissistically wounding. "Dr. Levin, you think I'm really crazy." Even after she came to see that I was on target, the very fact that I understood something about her that she did not was narcissistically wounding; most interpretation, in fact the entire analytic situation, is intrinsically narcissistically wounding. An adult puts him- or herself in a position in which he or she becomes as a child, being told what he or she feels by an adult, who was not long ago a stranger. I lessened this hurt by universalizing it: "We never see ourselves clearly if we are in the picture." Trite but true, and it helped. Comments like this lessen the pain of the therapist understanding things about the patient which the patient understands not. Being all-too-well understood is both a consummation devoutly to be wished and an intrinsically invasive and devaluing act. In seeing how she set herself up, Roberta was forced to intellectually acknowledge, and then feel, the enormous hatred and hostility she felt toward her sect.

A few years after the rape, Roberta was sent off to an institute for "crippled children." Being sent off even from a home as barbaric as hers was traumatic. Her mother, however terrified of her father and unwilling or unable to protect Roberta from him, nevertheless tried, however imperfectly, to nurture her. The adult Roberta was enraged that her mother went back time and time again (there were many separations) to the hated father, whom she (the mother) loved. Roberta felt rightfully that her mother loved her monster father more than she loved her, but she also felt that her mother had loved her. This conviction, apparently based on reality, that her mother loved her, "saved" Roberta from the back ward of the state hospital or from suicide. The institution Roberta was sent to was run like a concentration camp. Visiting was prohibited; discipline was strict; painful surgeries and restrictive appliances tormented her; affection was considered antitherapeutic; and as a sort of gratuitous humiliation, the children were given frequent large-volume enemas, which terrified Roberta. She was yelled at for not being able to retain more enema fluid, and this experience was yet another source of her aversion to water.

Roberta felt deeply ashamed of having been given the enemas. At first she referred to them as "all that water," not wanting to use the word enema. She unconsciously experienced them as a repetition of her brothers' anal rape. Both were painful intrusions; the hot, soapy, white enema solution was all too like her brothers' hot, white semen; and the enema experience, with its build-up of tension leading to an explosive discharge, was all too orgasmic. These experiences eventuated in a fusion and confusion of pregenital anal and genital impulses, and of a similar fusion and confusion of sexual and aggressive drives. Just as in her traumatic sexual experiences with her brothers, there was a secret pleasure in receiving enemas. There was also a deep sense of shame — shame in being violated, shame in the explosion of smelly feces.

THE METAPSYCHOLOGY OF SHAME

For Freud, shame is a reaction formation. It always masks and is derived from an ontogenetically or phylogenetically prior sexual pleasure. Freud ties shame to the sense of smell. Animals go on all fours and enjoy sniffing feces. With the assumption of upright posture, olfactory pleasures diminished and there was a reaction-formation against our "animal" inheritance. The reaction to Darwin was, in part, driven by this denial of and distancing from forbidden olfactory pleasures. Vision replaced olfaction as the primary vehicle of sexual attraction and pursuit. Yet for Freud, nothing of the past is ever really given up, and he points out that we all think that our own shit doesn't smell (bad).

I am sure that Freud is right in pointing out the instinctual basis of shame as a reaction-formation to forbidden anal and genital olfactory pleasures, as well as other instinctual pleasures, particularly sadistic ones, but this is not the whole story. The metapsychology of shame is importantly object relational whatever its instinctual basis. Shame differs from guilt in being primarily interpersonal rather than intrapsychic. Guilt is the superego's punishment of the ego for indulging in or wishing to indulge in the forbidden. Shame is the fear of being seen by another in a position of exposure or vulnerability. What we fear the other will see in shame may be something that we are doing, but it can equally well be something that is being done to us or to those we love. For me, the central feeling in shame is the feeling of worthlessness induced by being treated worthlessly, accompanied by terror that others will find out that we are treated, perhaps deservedly, contemptuously. The link between the Freudian and the object relations views of shame is the feeling that we are a piece of shit that shame experiences induce in us. The link between shame and guilt lies in the internalization of the other. From this analysis, it would appear that shame is the earlier, primordial affect and guilt its derivative. Erikson (1969) makes a distinction between the moral and the ethical. The moral is compulsive, shame-based, and irrational, being driven by reaction-formation and a savage, primitive superego; while the ethical is based on rational judgment by the ego. When we suffer narcissistic injury, we lose our capacity to function on the ethical level and revert to the irrationally moral.

As an adult, Roberta gave herself medically rationalized enemas, although she did this only occasionally during periods of particularly strong stress. It was an attempt to master a trauma through repetition. Whatever sensual pleasure she experienced was unconscious. The metapsychology of the repetition compulsion is complex: its many components include identification with the aggressor, attempting to work through a trauma (which never works), and an unconscious attempt to turn a passive experience into an active one. Turning the passive into the active is usually understood as doing (actively) to others what was done (passively) to you, and that happens frequently enough. However, far more central to the pathological side of turning the passive into the active is "choosing" to do to yourself what was done to you without choice. Even though this entails inflicting pain on the self, the pain is secondary to the choosing, to gaining control over what once you had no control over. This is the most powerful mechanism driving the repetition compulsion.

Physical pain, emotional coldness, impersonality, and separation from the mother by whom she felt loved all contributed to the traumatic nature of Roberta's stay in the institution. In spite of this, she didn't want to go home when the time for discharge came. In spite of the inhumanity of its deliverance, the medical treatment helped her and increased her functional capacity. Roberta spent two prolonged periods at the institution. Shortly after her second discharge at age 12, her mother committed suicide. Stone had been right. Roberta did have the worst history I could recall.

The experience of the hospital with its traumatic separation and equally traumatic returns to her home, which of course entailed separation from the hospital to which she was now attached, was a sort of parodic mockery of the rapprochement substage of the developmental process of separation-individu-ation (Mahler et al. 1975). Instead of emerging from the stability of a secure bond with Mother, or her substitute, to explore an exciting albeit dangerous world with the assurance that there is a safe place to retreat to in a symbiotic merger, or more safe relationship with Mother, Roberta oscillated between the treach-erous atmosphere of her home and the unloving, certain pain of the hospital. Two weeks after her return from her second hospital stay, during which she, like the other children, only got to see her family from the balcony of her dormitory as the families stared up from the lawn below, her mother walked in front of a car, after fleeing from home during a violent altercation with her father. Whether the mother was so distraught that she didn't know what she was doing, or chose to end her life, was never definitely established. Whatever actually occurred, Roberta ex-perienced her mother's death, at the time and during therapy 30 years later, as a suicide, as a deliberate abandonment of her children to her sadistic and probably insane husband. Who could feel lovable with the parent they experienced as loving them, loving them so little that she chose to leave them in hell? Roberta's level of self-esteem could not be other than abysmal, and her need to punish herself for her "badness" knew few limits. Of course, that already catastrophic dynamic was exacerbated by her turning her rage, or a good part of it, against herself. How Roberta survived the rest of her latency and adolescence with a modicum of sanity is almost beyond comprehension, but she did. It was an experience of continual terror. Roberta's father became progressively more irrational; her brothers left the house, and she spent her high school years alone with a withdrawn, now noncommunicative, volcano that never erupted into violence toward her, but which continually threatened to do so. Roberta functioned in spite of her burdens, conscious and unconscious, of fear, rage, and depression. She graduated high school and moved in with a family as a sort of combination nanny and maid. She regarded herself as a member of the family, and when it became clear that that was not the case, she once again experienced traumatic rejection. Whether she had misperceived the situation from the start, or the family turned on her, or some combination of the two, never became clear during our work together, but that she experienced excruciating pain and bitter disappointment was clear. At that point, she landed the civil-service job she still had when she came for treatment. Because she was intelligent, conscientious, and competent, her sometimes testy personality and occasional temper outbursts were tolerated, and she settled into a middling, but self-sustaining career. At that point, Roberta encountered the religious fellowship, which became her family, her support system, her belief system, her source of validation and valuation, her social nexus, her spiritual sustenance — in short, a self-object that sustained, nurtured, and mirrored. It "saved her." Without some such affiliation, Roberta would probably have succumbed to despair and committed suicide. With the security of membership in an organization of spiritual healers, Roberta was able to decide to have her nonfunctional leg amputated, and to learn to walk with an artificial limb. This increased her mobility and greatly improved her life.

IDEALIZATION AND COUNTERIDEALIZATION

Kohut's concept of the self-object has become a familiar one in psychoanalytic theory, but is often misunderstood. He himself is terribly unclear as to what he means. When he is speaking developmentally, the self-object appears to be an internal representation in which the self is experienced as an extension of the (idealized) object, or the object is experienced as an extension of the self. The first type of self-object experience Kohut called an "idealizing transference," which can and ubiquitously does occur outside of therapy in the ordinary interactions of everyday life. It is a state in which we experience ourselves as a part of some larger whole, be that a person, a belief system, or a group. The second, Kohut called the "mirror transference," which is a state in which the object, whatever its nature, is experienced as under the omnipotent control of self. This makes psychological sense, since the object is but an aspect of, an extension of, the self. Being omnipotently controlled, the object mirrors, reflects whatever we wish it to, affirming our wonderfulness, value, uniqueness, and glory. The object affirms our exhibitionistic grandiosity and values it. According to Kohut, all of this is developmentally normal, occurring in the stage he calls the stage of the omnipotent, archaic, bipolar, grandiose self. Although self-object relating and experiencing matures into forms less counter to fact, it never disappears. So here, Kohut is speaking metapsychologically, and he is talking not about interpersonal relations but about the internal world and how it and its representations are experienced. Such a metapsychological state, of course, would affect interpersonal relations, but the concept here is not interpersonal; it is intrapsychic. However, elsewhere Kohut seems to be speaking of self-objects as people rather than as cognitive-affective structures — people who perform the self-object functions of modulating anxiety, giving cohesion and continuity, maintaining self-esteem, and enjoying and validating the self. According to Kohut, we need such self-objects all of our lives.

Roberta's affiliation with the religious fellowship provided her with a self-object in the latter sense. It was an ideology, a belief system, a set of rituals and structures, and a nexus of people that affirmed, mirrored, provided self-cohesion and continuity, raised self-esteem, and in general provided narcissistic sustenance.

Intrapsychically, the organization was experienced not so much as an extension of self (although it was that) as an ideal object with which Roberta could fuse. That is, her transference to it, although it had mirroring aspects, was predominantly an idealizing transference. At the manifest level, the religious fellowship had what Kohut calls, critically, a "maturity morality," and condemned narcissism and "self-centeredness," while in giving its members an opportunity to "join" with an ideal object, it actually provided powerful narcissistic nurturance — infantile grandiosity was transferred from the self to the group where it found (or did not find, according to the observer's value system) socially useful expression. Roberta had been told by her parents that she was disabled and deformed because "God willed it," presumably as a punishment for some kind of badness — disabled persons often believe and find much social support (Wright 1960) for the belief that they are disabled because they are bad. Now Roberta had a loving God who could certainly chastise, but who had not "punished" her by causing her affliction. All of this importantly sustained and supported Roberta. It made her feel lovable for the first time. It increased her self-cohesion, making her less prone to regressive fragmentation, and enormously increased her self-esteem. For the first time, she was happy. Of course, organizations, including religious organizations, are composed of people, and therein lies the rub. Initially, the possibility for interpersonal relating in the fellowship was a purely positive thing, and for the first time, Roberta had friends. But people aren't really self-objects; they may be intrapsychically, but Kohut notwithstanding, they aren't interpersonally. Eventually, Roberta began to experience traumatic disillusionments as one member after another of the fellowship "let her down." Whenever they failed to perfectly "mirror" her as a self-object should, Roberta was narcissistically injured. As Kohut has taught us, the response to narcissistic injury is narcissistic rage, and Roberta, who already carried more rage than she could contain, did not restrain herself as conflicts, hurts, battles of various sorts ensued. Whether the "fault" lay in Roberta's "unrealistic expectations," or in the callousness of her fellow members, pain was the result. Rightfully or wrongfully, Roberta felt that she was often used to meet other peoples' needs while hers were ignored. I am certain that there was some truth in this, and that she often lived beyond her emotional means, giving too much in desperation to be loved and accepted, while both consciously and unconsciously resenting it. Her response was fury. This fury, and her "gluttony" (impulsive overeating), was to lead to her excommunication.

There is another way to look at the improvement in Roberta's psychic state in life after she entered the fellowship. Paul Tillich (1952) speaks of two types of anxiety: *neurotic* (or Freudian) *anxiety* stemming from unconscious conflict between desire and con-science, id and superego, along with the anxiety induced by the superego for unconscious, forbidden wishes; and *ontological anxi-ety*, the anxiety that is intrinsic to being human, and which comes in three forms — the anxiety of finitude, the anxiety of meaning-lessness, and the anxiety of condemnation. The first is the anxiety flowing from our mortality, from our limitations and vulnerabilities and of the certainty of our final termination and the pain caused by the awareness of this; the second is the anxiety of having no ultimate ground, of being subject at any moment to gnawing doubts that anything we do has any significance or purpose; while the third is the anxiety consequent on the ineluctable, realistic, as opposed to neurotic, guilt that comes from engaging in the struggles and conflicts, the vanquishing of other beings, intrinsic to life. Repression, denial, our failure to come to terms with ontological anxiety, exacerbate neurotic anxiety. Joining the fellowship reduced Roberta's anxiety about finitude, powerfully reduced her anxiety about meaningless-ness — now she had a purpose, spreading the message of her faith and winning converts, as well as the intrinsic meaning of living the prescribed life of her community, and gave her a mechanism for dealing with ontological and, to a lesser extent, neurotic guilt. All of this increased her sense of well-being.

The years went on, and Roberta muddled through. Constantly threatened by the return of the repressed, particularly her repressed rage, she derived a modicum of satisfaction from life with the support of her coreligionists and her belief system. She fell in love several times, but her relationships remained unconsummated and essentially unrequited. Although she wasn't conscious of it, each frustration resulted in yet another accretion to her already vast repository of repressed rage. Her hurt was more conscious. The fellow she had cared about the most turned out to be homosexual, which allowed her to rationalize his rejection of her. Unfortunately, this did not completely prevent her from turning her rage against herself. "How could I have been so stupid as not to have known?"

Roberta did succeed in finding a circle of friends within the fellowship. Their activities together mostly centered around food — cooking, eating, talking about food, going to restaurants, seeking out exotic spices — a motley mixture of healthy and compulsive orality. Roberta's circle of friends had fun together; they giggled about sex, about life, about other people. In many ways, Roberta experienced, lived through, a delayed adolescence. On the whole, it was an adaptive, creative remediation of developmental deficits, and I told Roberta so. She remembered her friends talking about sex, which excited both her envy and her desire. She was confused by her erotic desires and felt somewhat guilty about them, a guilt she was to act out in various self-punitive maneuvers. On the whole, she (consciously) enjoyed the sex talk, but felt disgust and repugnance when her friends giggled over mostly fantasized fellatio. As the years went by, the fantasies turned into reality as her friends found boyfriends and married. Although Roberta was included in social gatherings of the new couples and families, she felt left behind and progressively more isolated. Her feelings had a basis in reality. More hurt, more anger, more repression, more tension, more anxiety.

There were other complications in Roberta's social relations. Her fellowship attracted many troubled people who were difficult to connect with, and who sometimes acted out their conflicts in ways injurious to Roberta. This constituted a difficult situation, which was exacerbated by Roberta's tendency to idealize people.

She suffered one traumatic disillusionment after another. As Kohut (1971, 1977) has taught us, idealization is both a developmental stage and a lifelong need. The phase-appropriate idealization characteristic of the developmental stage of the archaic, bipolar, nuclear self is a primitive one. It is direct, unmediated, driven, and totally without the perspective that an observing ego can contribute. This is contradistinction to the idealizations of healthy maturity, which are just as emotionally powerful yet mediated by a modicum of reality. Falling in love always entails idealization. Roberta's idealizations, often of more than averagely humanly flawed people, were totally without benefit of perspective. This idealization of often seriously disturbed people set her up to be exploited, used and discarded, traumatically disillusioned, and profoundly narcissistically injured. Her relationship with Tom Stone was the culmination of a long-standing trend. Roberta, of course, had had no opportunity for phase-appropriate idealization. Her need to do so was frustrated, and frustration points, just like points of excessive indulgence, are fixation points. Roberta was fixated at the point in development of the archaic self, where idealization is normal. Since the drive to idealize comes from within, the child does so even if the human environment provides no suitable objects for such idealization. Roberta's environment did not. In normal development there is a gradual, progressive, nontraumatic disillusionment that leads to what Winnicott calls the destruction of the ideal object and its replacement with real and now differentiated objects. This had not occurred in Roberta's case.

Idealization is also a means, however pathetically unrealistic, of controlling other people. We idealize people, in part, because if you are so wonderful, then you will do all sorts of wonderful things for me, and by my participating in your omnipotence and omniscience, the good things of life will be mine. Perhaps most importantly, you will love me uncritically and unconditionally. Roberta's expectations of the people with whom she affiliated were often highly unrealistic, and the many wounds she received in these relationships flowed out of an interaction of her unrealistic expectations and the tendency of people to use those to make themselves available to be used — and Roberta was sure available.

Idealization as defense, as manipulation, as psychic fixation, as means of control, and as means of fulfilling unmet childhood needs is not restricted to patients; therapists are also prone to it. Although there is a vast literature on countertransference and counterresistance, there is a paucity (I know of none) of discussion of *counteridealization*. Therapists, like everyone else, use idealization in their lives, but that is not our present concern. They also idealize patients, and this is rarely confronted or discussed in supervision. I first became aware of counteridealization in listening to an analytic candidate present his control case. Although his idealization of his patient was blatant and patently unrealistic, neither supervisor nor discussants commented on it. I have since observed the same behavior in many supervisees and therefore have reason to believe that it is widespread and not noted. This is unfortunate because counteridealization can be a major impediment to successful therapy or analysis. It leads to unrealistic expectations of the patient on the part of the therapist, and to missing aspects of character pathology or lesser symptomatology that the patient needs analyzed. Further, such counteridealization constitutes a narcissistic injury, experienced not necessarily or even usually consciously, because the patient's real self, which desperately needs affirmation, is not addressed, while the therapist's idealized fantasy of the patient is. Counteridealization arises both from the therapist's fixations and the therapist's narcissistic need for famous, brilliant, insightful, "special" patients. This need is understandable, but it disables the treatment and needs to be addressed in supervision. Counteridealization also exposes the therapist to a very real risk of narcissistic injury through traumatic disillusionment or from an explosion of rage from the "wonderful" patient who inchoatively senses that he or she is being mistreated and reacts. Sudden and completely baffling terminations sometimes result from the patient's unconscious realization that he or she is not being treated as a "real" object, as him- or herself. Such terminations are excruciatingly painful for the therapist struggling with his or her own narcissistic issues. To rub salt in the wound, it is only the healthiest patients whose unconscious figures out what is going on and who then terminate. Thus, the counteridealizing therapist loses his "best" patients.

The therapeutic task of helping Roberta sort out what was unrealistic expectation and what was plain rottenness on the part of others was a delicate task. It was so easy to hurt her further and exacerbate her tendency, so powerful as to be almost a reflex, to turn anger against herself. I chose initially to largely ignore the ways in which she set herself up through unrealistic expectations (this was not entirely a psychodynamic matter; it was, in part, a skill deficit, she having grown up in such a pathological environment [since the phrase "dysfunctional family," like the phrase "neurotic person," is redundant, I avoid it] that she had little opportunity to learn normal social expectations and often expected to be treated as a member of a family when she was in fact a friend), and to concentrate on putting her in touch with her anger and helping her express it. Alleviating her depression had to take precedence over all else; understanding how she set herself up could (and did) come later. Once her rage at a friend, for typically using her as a confidante and confessor and source of uncritical support and then spurning her when she looked for similar support, was surfacing—made conscious, verbalized and expressed in an atmosphere of acceptance of all of her feelings, including the raging ones—the antecedents of the painful rebuff could be looked at, and Roberta's contribution to the action made conscious. In general, this is sound therapeutic procedure with all but rage-aholics. The narcissistically injured are all too self-critical, and the indubitably essential insight that they are, as by primitive idealization, sealing their own doom can come later. In the long term, the gradual strengthening of the self, or ego if you prefer, makes the fantastic expectations consequent upon primitive idealization unnecessary. Goodness is seen to repose within, as well as without, and more satisfying, because more realistic, relationships become possible. Winnicott said that God is the repository of our projection of our inner "goodness," to protect it from our inner "badness," or fantasized inner badness. There is a profound truth here; it is not only God but people and ideologies and institutions that are so experienced to the detriment of the people projecting their goodness. Therein lies a process that explains a good deal of human mischief and misery. The result can be tragic, at the individual no less than the collective level. Both the patient and the culture must reclaim their goodness, as well as the badness they project onto devils of all sorts. Boundary problems compound the difficulty, since the objects on which we project both goodness and badness are often self-objects. Once we project our goodness, our need for powerful protectors keeps us hooked into our own myths. Roberta participated in all of the above dynamics, and my job, among other things, was to facilitate their unfolding in the transference so they could be worked through.

The projection of the good and bad discussed above entails *splitting*, the division of the self and world into two distinct entities, the good self (-representation) and the bad self (-representation), and the good object (representation) and the bad object (representation), respectively. Projection and introjection of both the split self and split object radically complicate the representational world, by providing for a rich array of permutations and combinations. Splitting as a defense is to be distinguished from what has been variously called the paranoid-schizoid position (Klein 1975), the preambivalent stage, and the third stage of object relations development (Kernberg 1975) in which the separation of good and bad aspects of self and object is phase-appropriate, normal development. It is the normal mode of being before the integration of the depressive position. A developmental arrest at this stage (Kernberg's second stage of object relations development) results in the predominance of splitting as a defense and a borderline personality disorder. However, splitting is a universal phenomenon; witness the ubiquity of gods and devils in politics, in international relations, in religions, in intellectual and ideological controversy, in interpersonal relations, and in the history of psychoanalysis with its schisms and anathematizing. Such splitting is not the result of fixation to the developmental stage preceding integration of the representative world—at least not primarily so, unless all of us are so fixated—rather it is a regression to a primitive defense. Daniel Stern (1985), on the basis of infant observation and experimental research, denies that the representative world of the infant is one of pure whites and pure blacks. Instead he sees a kind of averaging of a continuity of experiences ranging from pure frustration (by a bad object) to pure gratification (by a good object) with the infantile object representation reflecting that averaging. The Sternian infant lives in a more subtle, more complex world than does the infant depicted by traditional psychoanalytic theory, be that theory classical, ego, or object relational. However, Stern does not challenge the clinical evidence for splitting as a defense. It may not be intrinsic to the first years of life, but it exists. Perhaps splitting, rather than being initially the product of an innate template, requires a certain level of cognitive development to become manifest. Be that as it may, splitting is widely employed and plays a prominent part in the clinical situation. Stern similarly denies the existence of a symbiotic stage, though he does not doubt that adult patients have merger fantasies and experiences. Roberta had her problems with both splitting and merger. Idealization, of course, is one way to create a good object with which one can, among other possibilities, merge. The good object of idealization all too readily transmutes into the bad object of traumatic disillusionment. The metastability of the transference in cases where the patient puts the therapist on a pedestal only to deprecate and savagely denigrate that same therapist for the slightest lapse of empathy is notoriously difficult to manage. Countertransference reactions including bewilderment and deep hurt are common. The best protection from such injury is understanding the patient's developmental level and dynamics. That way you take it less personally.

MARRYING THE "GOOD MOTHER"

There is another sort of splitting, an adaptive one. Freud (1940) first talked about splitting of the ego for the purposes of defense in his discussion of the dynamics of fetishism, in which there are two egos (selves), one of whom knows that women don't have penises and one of whom believes that they do, the fetish serving as a substitute penis. Here splitting does not refer to the division of reality into all-good and all-bad, but rather to the splitting of the self (ego) in order that instinctual pleasure may be pursued without the risk of castration. This is an adaptation that sacrifices reality for the sake of a psychic gain. I would like to suggest that splitting is often adaptive and makes possible a higher level of functioning than would otherwise be possible. I have in mind, in particular, the adaptive nature of not integrating good and bad parental (usually maternal) representations in cases where the real experience of the child with the parents was predominantly "bad." I, like most analysts, have often been baffled by the level of adaptation, the psychic and emotional strength, and level of functioning of patients with horrendous life histories. Native endowment, the awesome resiliency of the human spirit, and sheer courage all play their part, but I have come to believe that the persistence of splitting, which allows the preservation of the good object by keeping the "good enough" mother of early infancy uncontaminated by the "not good enough" mother of later childhood, permits some patients to feel lovable and worthwhile in the face of later disconfirmation of that lovableness and worthwhileness by traumatic parental failure. Integration would overwhelm the goodness with the badness that predominated in reality, while splitting preserves it. Such splitting sometimes facilitates the realization of a level of object relations that the history does not predict, and allows some patients whose models of marriage are uniformly dreadful to have remarkably healthy relationships. (See Sally in Chapter 3.) I call that phenomenon "marrying the good mother." Roberta's affiliation with the religious fellowship was such a marrying of the good mother. Although it ultimately went sour, this affiliation provided Roberta with a stable sense of self-esteem, with a feeling of being loved, and with a sense of the worthwhileness of life for many years. The best of her interpersonal relationships were also marriages with the good mother. There were aspects of suppression, repression, and reaction-formation in all of Roberta's (good) relationships, especially the one with the religious fellowship, but they weren't only that. The preservation of the good object, by whatever means, is necessary for mental health. Unless we feel somebody loved us, we never feel lovable. Roberta certainly didn't feel very lovable, but she had enough residual self-esteem to persist in her search for health and to turn from the agony of Stone's rejection to therapy with me. Classical theory (Freud 1914a) holds that self-love comes from the reservoir of narcissistic libido left after our investment of libido in objects. Narcissistic libido is primeval, while object libido is derivative. I do not doubt this, but it is not explanation enough. The drive for self-preservation is doubtlessly innate, and the self-love necessary to bringing it about equally innate, but the kind of self-love that makes possible a satisfactory and satisfying adult life is only possible if there are memory traces of being thought valuable, estimable, by somebody else. Self-esteem and the capacity to maintain it at a reasonably high and reasonably consistent, even level is the product of internalization. In spite of the dreadful shape she was in when she presented herself for treatment, Roberta had some self-esteem or she wouldn't have been there. Other facets of her life echoed that strength that shouldn't have been there. To take nothing away from her or her courageous struggle, they derived from a good enough mother of the first 3 years of her life experienced as totally disconnected from the mother who failed to protect her from her father, brothers, or the institution, and who abandoned her through suicide. I did *not* see the task of therapy as integrating this walled-off good mother with the bad mother of her more conscious memories. At least, that would be a task, if necessary or desirable at all, for the last stage of therapy. Overzealous beginners, and sometimes more experienced therapists, some of whom I have supervised, often interpret the patient's "unrealistic" experiencing of the parent as virtually two parents, without realizing the psychic function of the patient's disconnection. The adaptive function of any behavior, symptom, or psychic mechanism must be understood before it is confronted or interpreted, lest great damage be inflicted on the patient.

There was a side of Roberta that I saw little of in the early stages of therapy, although there were glimmers of it now and then. It is difficult to characterize; the best way I can put it is to say that she had charm. That charm manifested itself mainly through humor, which was often based on a power of acute observation that didn't jibe with her usually distorted interpersonal perceptions; it was sometimes healthily self-deprecating, and sometimes barbedly witty. She had a flair for pungent expressions, and her considerable intelligence manifested itself in her verbal facility. I didn't mind being the respondent of her sharp wit; she did it with grace. I came to admire her tenacity, and although it took a while to see it, there was something wonderfully likable about this woman.

ENTHRALLMENT TO A DEMONIC THERAPIST

By the time she consulted Tom Stone, Roberta's relationship with the religious fellowship had deteriorated; the "elders" were on her back for her "gluttony." They viewed her by-now-chronic depression as a symptom of alienation from God. Feeling, partly realistically, exploited by her fellow congregants, she fought with most of them, and it was mostly the now explosive nature of her interpersonal relationships that led the elders to suggest that she seek help from Stone. When the elders suggested help, they had in mind prayer and consultation with them, but going to Stone was an acceptable alternative, delaying any action by them against her.

Roberta bonded with Stone immediately. Her need was strong, and he had charisma. She didn't know it, but it was love at first sight. As with all falling in love, there was something old and something new. With uncanny instinct, she had refound her mother — both the split-off good mother of infancy, and as the night follows the day, the mentally ill, grossly inadequate, nonprotecting, abandoning bad mother of later childhood. (Stone also had aspects of the raping brothers and the sadistic father.) Freud (1905b) wrote, "Every object finding is a refinding," (p. 222) and he was right. On his part, Stone used all of his charisma seductively. However cruel or unethical, he made her feel loved and lovable, alive and worthwhile. It was exciting. Her relationship with Stone was certainly a repetition, but it wasn't only that — it was both the same as and different from her relationship with her mother. She had found something old and something new. Does the wedding ritual of something old, something new, something borrowed, something blue unconsciously give recognition to the fact that every marriage is both a refinding and a new adventure? I wonder.

Stone was the great love of Roberta's life, yet she didn't know it. My confrontation of her with that love had brought only denial and ridicule. "Oh, Dr. Levin, you don't mean that." Where to go from there? To continue to confront Roberta head-on would have been useless, and it might have driven her out of treatment. Sometimes resistance must be respected; it is there because the pain of relinquishing it is too great. So I backed off, but the seed had been planted. In a split similar to the fetishist's splitting of the self into a part on the side of reality (women don't have penises), and into a part on the side of fantasy (women do have penises — my fetish proves it), Roberta believed both that I was "crazy" and that I was right. Over the next 2 months, Roberta spent her sessions talking about Stone. I accumulated evidence of her love, and gently returned to the topic. This time there was less resistance, and soon afterwards, in a tear-filled session, Roberta "confessed," more to herself than to me, the depth of her love for Tom Stone. We were on our way. Her pain poured forth like pus from a lanced abscess. I did everything I could to keep the wound open and draining. I did that by saying injurious things like "You must have really loved him if you did that for him," "that" being counseling his depressed wife, reassuring him, taking care of his children, and much else. I slowly introduced the notion that Stone had violated his professional, not to mention human, obligations, and had treated her abysmally. Once again, I increased her pain. The whole trick was to correctly dose my interventions. How much reality could she take? By now we were working together, the therapeutic alliance had been established, and I rarely heard how I was inferior to Stone. Finally she asked me, "You think he was a bastard, don't you?" The analytic response would have been silence, or "What do you think?" But Roberta was too alone for that; she needed an ally, a confederate in rage in order to experience that rage. So I said, "Yes." It is necessary to remember that all during this period of our work together, Roberta was excommunicated, and literally could not speak to a single person who mattered to her. Her hurt switched to rage, and a mourning process was initiated. It was long and agonizing, but successful. Eventually, Roberta's mourning for Stone and all he represented came to an end.

Mourning is of the essence in the treatment of narcissistic injury, but mourning cannot commence until the narcissistic injury is acknowledged and experienced. Although the circumstances of Roberta's denial of the injury done to her by Stone are unique, such denial is exceedingly common. To admit that one has been narcissistically injured is itself narcissistically injurious, and often avoided, disavowed, fended off, or repressed. So the first task in the treatment of narcissistic injury is to make it as vivid, real, and emotionally alive as possible. That's what I was doing in my low-key and sometimes delayed but persistent insistence on Roberta's love for Stone and her deep hurt at his having rebuffed and abandoned her. Timely confrontation *and* analysis of the resistance are what works. As Freud said, "Nobody is really hanged in absentia," and mourning is only possible when loss is palpable.

I spoke much more about Stone than is my wont when patients talk about their relationships with others. Roberta's reality testing in this area was poor, and she needed that. I validated the ways in which Stone had helped her, and speculated that he might have initially really cared for her—as a professional trying to help—but that, as his illness (manic-depression and apparently a character disorder) relapsed, he had regressed and traumatically failed her. It was important for her to know that she hadn't been merely crazy in trusting him—many others had as well—and that there was a germ of health in her attraction to someone who initially made her feel good. That lessened her pain and self-blame. Besides, it was true. I held off on transference interpretations of her relationship with Stone until the mourning process was well underway. Only then could insight into the repetition of her experiences with Mother, with Father, and with her brothers in a relationship with Stone be mutative.

The injury inflicted by Stone healed only slowly, but heal it did. However, that didn't lift Roberta's excommunication. Here there was no necessity to uncover her rage; it was all over the place. I encouraged its ventilation in therapy, while trying to help her contain it in her outside life—a tricky task for therapeutic tact—on one hand, the suppression or repression of that (narcissistic) rage could result in suicidal depression, and on the other hand, its uncritical and unanalyzed acceptance deprived Roberta of an opportunity to understand its transferential, compulsively repetitive aspects and to gain insight into her role in provoking her excommunication. The treatment of narcissistic rage—the ineluctable concomitant of narcissistic injury, the inexorable reaction of the "insulted and injured"—is complex. Narcissistic rage differs from mature aggression in having as its goal destruction of the offending object. Aggression is instrumental; we aggress in order to obtain something—food, status, wealth, love, whatever—and when we have achieved our goal, we have no interest in harming anyone. We might kill in the pursuit of our goal, but that killing would be incidental, not intrinsic, to the aggression. Not so with the narcissistically injured; they seek destruction of those who have, or are imagined to have, injured them. Those in the thrall of narcissistic rage have not learned that "living well is the best revenge." In his discussion of narcissistic rage, Kohut cites Captain Ahab and Nazi Germany as his examples. Narcissistic rage is extremely dangerous; it not only fuels revenge obsessions like Ahab's and Hitler's; it may be turned against the self, resulting in suicide or less radical forms of self-destruction. Kernberg understands such rage differently, conceptualizing it in terms of the traditional psychoanalytic psychosexual stages as oral rage and anal-sadistic rage. He zeroes in on oral rage, the murderous reaction of the Doberman deprived of the bone, or a human infant of the nipple. Kernberg seems to consider the potential for primitive oral and anal rage as innate, and postulates that some borderlines have so much constitutional rage as to be virtually untreatable. From the life histories of my borderlines, I have my doubts about innateness. They seem to have more than adequate justification for their rage. That doesn't make it any more functional.

In treating narcissistic rage, the first step is to make it conscious. In Roberta's case, her rage at the elders was conscious, while her rage at Stone was not. Once the rage surfaces, it must be felt, verbalized, and expressed in the empathic, uncritical receptivity of therapy. Critique and understanding come later. It is very easy to close down a narcissistically injured patient like Roberta who is all too skilled at repression and turning against the self. The best situation is not to be enraged; the worst is to be enraged and repress or turn it against yourself.

It is easy to mistake repressed rage with the absence of rage. This can be a fatal mistake. There is a difference between isolated seething or fuming alone, and expressing angry feelings in the presence of an empathic other. The first goes on endlessly and often feeds on itself; the latter often leads to a discharge and diminution of the rage. The very anchoring of the therapeutic alliance diminishes anger. The stage of uncovering and expressing may go on for a very long time; however, sooner or later, the historical origins of the rage must be uncovered, and the present anger connected to past anger. That is the job of interpretation. Narcissistic rage comes from narcissistic vulnerability; the more vulnerable, the more early hurt; and the more early hurt, the more easily injured. So the final stage in the treatment of narcissistic rage is the lessening of narcissistic vulnerability by raising self-esteem, increasing self-cohesion and continuity, and strengthening the ego. The entire therapeutic process contributes to these ends. In Kohut's terms, "transmuting internalization" increases self-cohesion and remediates self-deficits. Transmuting internalization is a gradual, grain-at-a-time, so to speak, internalization of the functions of the self-object therapist through his or her nontraumatic failure to mirror the patient, a failure that inevitably occurs in the process of working through a mirror or idealizing (i.e., self-object) transference. I will have more to say about this process when I discuss Roberta's transference to me. With remediation through transmuting internalization, the self is changed and becomes more capable of modulating anxiety, self-soothing, and companioning itself so it is less vulnerable to the slings and arrows of outrageous fortune. To review the treatment of narcissistic rage: make it conscious; help the patient express it in the context of an empathic relationship; interpret both its current precipitants and its historical antecedents (i.e., its genetic meaning), and its relationship to narcissistic vulnerability, exploring the source of that vulnerability and its exact nature in terms of deficits and conflicts; and finally, reduce the patient's narcissistic vulnerability by increasing self-cohesion and strengthening the ego. I am aware that I cross realms of discourse, sometimes using the language and operating within the conceptual realm of Kohut's self psychology, and sometimes within the realm of classical and ego psychology. I do this deliberately because neither school gives us an adequate account of clinical experience or human life (cf. Pine 1985). Their synthesis does. Kohut (1977) wrote, "All worthwhile theorizing is tentative, provisional, and playful" (p. 237). I agree.

Back to the excommunicated Roberta. If helping her experience and express her rage was the salient task in helping her deal with her feelings for Stone, helping her contain her rage at least enough so as not to further alienate the elders and thus guarantee that her excommunication would not be lifted, was the salient task in helping her deal with her feelings about that excommunication. Technical neutrality would not do here. Left to her own devices, Roberta would have continued to rage at the elders. For her, that would have had devastating consequences. My opinion of her religious fellowship and my analysis of her reasons for wanting to be a member of it were irrelevant. She had spent her entire adult life as a member of that community, had no ties to her family, and no friends apart from it. It was the only game in town. To destroy the road back into it was to destroy herself. If a person who happens to be a therapy patient is about to walk in front of a speeding truck, for the therapist not to shout "Stop!" is to allow the patient to sustain a serious, even fatal, injury; it is irresponsible. Of course the patient may not stop, and the warning may be futile. It often is, but that is no reason not to try. I was directive with Roberta, and by now I had enough clout for my direction to be efficacious. I told Roberta to lay off the elders and to express her rage at them to me. What about unconscious motivation, compulsively driving patients into all sorts of self-destructive behavior — the voice of reason, assuming you have it, won't do a thing. That is often true, but sometimes the patient wants to be stopped and willingly allows the therapist to act as an "auxiliary ego." That happened this time. A savagely punitive superego may not allow the patient to act in his or her best interest, but the self that doesn't deserve to give itself good things, including prudent restraints, may be able to accept them from the outside. That way the patient isn't being good to himself, merely following orders. The palliative nature of such interventions is apparent, but they buy us time until the patient is in a position to work more psychodynamically. I recall a supervisor screaming at an overly rigidly classical psychiatrist who refused to hospitalize an actively suicidal patient because what was needed was interpretation of the transference, "You can't do dynamics with a corpse!"

Roberta ranted against the elders but no longer directly accosted them. I began to analyze Roberta's ambivalence toward the fellowship, and the father transference she had to the most punitive of the elders. She listened. We strategized together, considering ways she might get reinstated. We analyzed the personality and motivation of each elder, and when the time came, Roberta was able to write a letter that pushed the right buttons. I figured she needed an ally more than anything else, and became one. At the same time, I kept pressing my interpretation that part of her had wanted to break with the fellowship, and that she had accomplished that in the only way she knew. Eventually, I scored and was rewarded with Roberta's highest accolade. "Dr. Levin, you're weird (said with a characteristic giggle)." The therapeutic alliance had been forged. After 2 years of total isolation, Roberta was reinstated. Six months later, she confronted the elder who had treated her most cruelly, calmly telling him how angry she had been at his personally motivated humiliation of her, although she accepted the part of his behavior that was motivated by his doing his job as he understood it. She also pointed out how unjust the length of her excommunication was, relative to the treatment of other offending members. Amazingly, she was heard, and her confrontation contributed to the spiritual (or if you prefer, emotional) growth of that elder, who subsequently treated people more humanely. The confrontation was a major growth step for Roberta, immensely decreasing her fears of people, especially those in authority, and raising her self-esteem.

As Roberta's self-esteem increased, she took a much more aggressive stand with her orthotist, and he agreed to replace her deficient prosthesis. Her physical pain abated, and her mobility increased. Not being in physical pain and no longer feeling victimized lessened her rage. Roberta showed me her stump and explained how her artificial leg worked. My acceptance immeasurably strengthened our bond. Roberta no longer felt alone. After an initial period of euphoria, her return to the fellowship proved not as wonderful as she had hoped. Nevertheless, it gave

her a community, and we were able to analyze the unrealistic
expectations, fear of closeness, transferential distortions, and
sometimes near paranoid misrepresentations that plagued her
interpersonal relatedness. I always acknowledged the realistic side
of her difficulties; to not do so would have been both inaccurate
and narcissistically injurious.

As her reality situation improved, Roberta started having
nightmares that clearly stemmed from her childhood. Much of
the history related above was obtained in analyzing this material.
The security afforded by our relationship permitted her to do so.
Herein lies another principle of general applicability in dealing
with narcissistic injury. Those patients who have sealed off,
repressed, denied, disavowed, or isolated the affect attached to
the memory of narcissistic injuries know what they are doing (this
is not to deny the deleterious consequences of these defenses);
they do so because they cannot stand the pain ineluctably
concomitant with working them through (or even attempting to
do so), but pain shared with an empathic other is pain trans-
muted, perhaps no less painful but pain now tolerable and
meaningful rather than merely gratuitous. Put more simply, this
work cannot be safely done until a firm therapeutic alliance and
a positive transference have been established. Looked at in
another way, old object relations, however tormented and tormenting, cannot be relinquished until they are replaced. A bad
object is better than no object. All therapy is "about" such a
process but is particularly salient in the treatment of narcissistic
injury with its attendant shame and rage. The shame leads to
isolation and denial to self and others of how badly one has been
treated. Who wants to acknowledge that they were treated like a
piece of shit, and came to believe that they were one? Who wants
to acknowledge that a parent wanted them dead, as in Roberta's
case? The shame can only be faced and worked through in the
context of a safe relationship. As all the great theorists knew
(even Freud, for all his emphasis on insight, stressed the necessity
of rapport) that relationship cures. Just as the shame cannot be
faced alone, the rage is too dangerous to deal with alone. To do

so is to risk destructive acting out or turning against the self in a vengeful self-hating suicide.

Roberta did indeed go through a depression of suicidal intensity as we worked through her historical narcissistic injuries. Each recovery of a repressed memory, each reconnecting of affect with an already conscious memory of horror, loss, abandonment, and violation, set off weeks of tormented sleep, new episodes of gluttony, extended bouts with despair, and devastatingly deep feelings of futility. An unexpected contact with one of the brothers who had raped her accelerated the process. Once the door opened, an avalanche of pain cascaded through the opening. A period of intense mourning ensued. Rage alternated with despair. I encouraged the expression of both—the rage was by now minimally acted out—mostly at work where it was tolerated (and frequently triggered by the insanity of the department she worked for). Once again, I acknowledged the realistic side of her response, even as I interpreted the displacement and reenactment. Slowly, ever so slowly, her rage, so long repressed or acted out, diminished and her anger became more and more appropriate here-and-now stuff. As her rage diminished, so did her compulsive overeating—what her excommunication called her gluttony. I see fat as *solidified rage*. Most often, it is. Her binge eating being relatively innocuous, I rarely commented on it beyond connecting it with an attempt to self-soothe and not feel the emptiness of which she was now acutely conscious, especially as we worked through her mother's abandonment. In other words, I stressed the adaptive function of the binges. Roberta was only too skilled at beating herself up and didn't need my help to continue to hate herself for the binges. Only later came interpretation of her binges as savage acts of aggression, of trying to shred, tear apart, destroy the good breast turned bad, devouring her dangerous father and brothers so they would be safely under control within her, and the self-punishment for that aggression through the deleterious consequences, especially pressure on her stump, of her binging. Roberta proved to be an intuitive Kleinian. Although she often commented, "Dr. Levin, you're weird," or "Dr. Levin, you are so smart," meaning both intelligent and a smarty, a wise-guy, my interpretations of primitive aggression resonated with her. To have stressed the aggression before the adaptation would have been injurious. She would have heard that as "You are bad."

Interestingly, Roberta had made remarkably good adjustment to and acceptance of her disability before she came for treatment. I doubt that I could have dealt so effectively with so incapacitating a disability. That didn't mean that there wasn't more work to do in this area. Kohut commented on Freud's observation that Kaiser Wilhelm II's withered arm did not constitute a narcissistic injury to him; his proud mother's rejection of him for that arm did, and Wilhelm's attempt to compensate for that narcissistic injury was one of the efficient (in Aristotle's sense) causes of World War I. Mutatis mutandis; that was true of Roberta. Fortunately, her mother had been accepting of her disability and had done everything possible in her strained circumstances to give Roberta whatever rehabilitative potential medicine had to offer. She was less able to help the little girl deal with her feelings about her condition, but she listened and accepted, and that made Roberta's relatively good adjustment to life possible. All her life, Roberta had been marrying that early good mother. The rest of the family, like Wilhelm's mother, scorned and rejected her, the father even wishing—and possibly having tried—to eliminate her. During treatment, Roberta reexperienced the profound depression of her childhood as we brought to consciousness her experience of her father's murderous hate and her mother's traumatic abandonment.

The closest to bitter I'd seen Roberta was when she discussed her lack of a mate, which came up again and again, especially in relation to the excommunication. She differed from other excommunicants in having no spouse or children to cushion her banishment, hence suffered more than other excommunicants. The elders' failure to acknowledge this infuriated her. Roberta had suffered social and sexual deprivation because of her disability; nevertheless, it was true that as her first therapist, in his

bull-in-a-china-shop manner, had said, "Even quads get laid." I
began to suggest that her rages and "gluttony" might have
something to do with her failure to attract a mate. Interpretation
of the need to distance and protect herself from abandonment
fitted this rubric. I was careful not to arouse false hope. Roberta's
odds, with her mild but real facial disfigurement, and other
disabilities, along with her being long accustomed to being alone,
made it unlikely that she would find a mate or even a companion
in middle life. But it was not impossible. If arousing false hope is
cruel, giving no hope at all is even crueler. Both are narcissistically injurious. You could argue that the therapist's job is
neither to give nor not give hope, and that is true. Yet we always
do one or the other through our attitude, and in a thousand
subliminal, mostly unconscious ways. Better to be aware of this
dimension of hope/despair present in all therapeutic relationships
and think through what stance you want to take and how
explicitly you want to carry out that stance. I am a tempera-
mental optimist and must discipline myself against arousing false
hope.

Roberta's characteristic mannerism of referring to me and
others as "weird" or using one of her other favorite words,
"peculiar," was among other things a self-referent. It was she who
was "weird" and "peculiar." It was a long time before I told her so.
A good part of the art of psychotherapy is learning to keep your
mouth shut. Making me an honorary "weird" was her way of
assimilating me to her, of making me more like her, which
enabled a reciprocal identification with me and my function as an
auxiliary ego (and auxiliary, benign superego).

Just as our work was in one of its most productive phases,
Stone resurfaced, calling Roberta for "help." This set off a
precipitous, albeit short-lived, regression. It turned out to be an
opportunity. This time around, she was able to experience the
full depth of his betrayal of her, mourn his loss, and move on.
Her last comment on both was, "He's really pathetic, isn't he?
How could I have been such a fool as to fall for him?" I pointed
out the unique role he had played in her life, with its initially

positive aspect, which lessened her self-criticism and facilitated her letting go of him.

What about the transference? Was there any, with all of my "active" nonneutral interventions? There sure was, although the establishment of a secure therapeutic alliance was even more vital. Roberta's transference to me was essentially a "good mother" transference, and as such, needed to be protected from her "negative" feelings toward me. Another way of looking at it was so say that after a prolonged period of testing and comparing, Roberta settled down into an idealizing transference. Kohut discovered (created) what he first called the narcissistic and later the self-object transferences. He did so while analyzing a group of patients who were neither psychotic nor classic psychoneurotics. They were subject to what he called "temporary regression and fragmentation." That is, they became psychotic—lost it—fell to pieces, from time to time. Roberta did that, particularly in her rages. Kohut saw his patients five times a week on the couch for analysis; I saw Roberta once a week, face to face, for psychodynamic psychotherapy. There was bound to be more "real relationship" and a "shallow" transference. Kohut found that his narcissistic patients either related to him as if he were an extension of them—the mirror transference—or as if they were an extension of him, experienced as omnipotent and omniscient—the idealizing transference. He understood the mirror transference according to the degree of separation of self and object. In its most primitive form, there was a virtual merger, with little reality awareness of separation; such transference characterized borderline and psychotic, as distinguished from narcissistic, patients. Kohut considered merger transference unanalyzable. At a developmentally higher level was the "twinship" transference, in which the analyst is experienced as separate but the same as the analysand, who was experienced as the patient's identical twin. Roberta's attributing "weirdness" to me was, among other things, an attempt to create a twinship, which facilitated bonding. Finally, there is the mirror transference proper, in which the patient wishes the analyst to reflect his or her specialness and wonderfulness, and to take pleasure in the patient's phase-appropriate infantile grandiosity. Kohut sees this as a normal developmental phase, which needs to be relived and the fixation to it eventually remediated through transmuting internalization. Although there is a realistic awareness of separation in the mirror transference proper, the analysand acts as if the analyst existed only to fulfil the patient's need for mirroring. The patient demands omnipotent control of the analyst, who, being an extension of the patient's self, should (from the patient's point of view) be under such control. Failure to so control results in narcissistic rage. Kohut cites, as an analogous experience, the stroke victim's rage at not being able to move a paralyzed limb that should be under control of self. Roberta displayed little of a classic mirror transference with me. Although I did my share of mirroring, I did not interpret the mirror aspects of her transference to her; however, it was evident that traumatic failure of her self-objects, such as Stone and the elders to whom she did have strong mirror transferences, resulted in narcissistic rages. Her way of telling me that she was in a narcissistic rage was to say, "I was *wild*, Dr. Levin, *wild*." I wondered who had told her that she was "wild."

Kohut's language—*self-object*, *mirror transference*, and *idealizing transference*—depersonalizes what are intensely personal relationships. What we are talking about are father and mother transferences, and it is well to keep that in mind. That is, not only do narcissistic transferences have the structural characteristics so clearly delineated by Kohut, but they are also recapitulations of relationships with real people. Kohut tends to lose the historical genetic dimension in emphasizing the structure and the working through of the structure, rather than the revival of the historical relationship in the transference. Kohut speaks of the potential for regression in narcissistic patients whom he sees as being fixated in the developmental stage of the archaic, nuclear bipolar self. That is the stage in which a centered (nuclear) cohesive but fragile (archaic) self, characterized by the bipolarity of grandiosity and idealized parental imagoes, has come into existence but is in danger of regressive fragmentation. Since regressive fragmentation — going to pieces, falling apart — is terrifying, it leads to panic dread of psychic annihilation, dissolution of the self, which must be defended against at all cost. Roberta's rages were, in part, a defense against, as well as a reaction against, such fragmentation, although ironically it was a defense that exacerbated the fragmentation. So were her eating binges. Her disability and amputation increased her fears about bodily intactness and self-cohesion. This having been said, she was remarkably intact, with a fairly developed sense of self as continuing, cohesive, bounded, and capable of initiative. Perhaps that is why she did not develop a primarily mirror transference.

What about confronting and working through an idealizing transference? Kohut thinks that it is extremely important to sit still for an idealizing transference and to let it unfold and develop, while Kernberg believes that idealizing transferences are setups to control, and must be confronted early in treatment. In a way, this is a new version of the old argument about whether or not the positive transference should be analyzed. The standard resolution is that the positive transference is analyzed in analysis but not in psychotherapy. I think that the dispute between Kohut and Kernberg on the management of the idealizing transference is more apparent than real. They are talking about different groups of patients, or about the same patient at different stages of the treatment. Kohut's patients are the narcissistically wounded, while Kernberg's patients are the narcissistically exploitive. We refer to both as narcissistic personality disorders, and any particular person suffering from a narcissistic personality disorder will have aspects of both; however, one or the other — the injury and the depressive defenses against it or the injury and the exploitive defenses against it — will predominate. Roberta's idealization of me was far less primitive or uncritical than her idealization of Stone had been. She had learned something from that one. Nor did I feel controlled. The therapist's countertransferential experience of being controlled or not controlled is the therapist's best guide in deciding how to deal with an idealizing transference. If the idealizing transference is primarily in the interest of control, then Kernberg's early confrontation technique is appropriate; *per contra*, if the idealization is primarily in the interest of securing an ideal object to stabilize the self, then Kohut's recommendations are salient. All idealizing transferences have some controlling and exploitative aspects; however, in the Kohutian patients, it is a minor chord in a recapitulation of a developmental stage. Kohut points out that unless we are particularly grandiose, we know, at least in our saner moments, that we are neither so wise, so loving, nor so powerful as the patient believes us to be, and that such idealizations make us uncomfortable. Nevertheless, he believes that it is extremely important to allow the idealizing transference to unfold without prematurely offering reality corrections. I essentially agree with him. To prematurely disillusion the patient is to inflict a narcissistic injury. It is a parent telling a small child who looks up at him or her that he is really a schmuck unable to fulfill any of the child's dreams. Disillusionment, in life and in the transference, is inevitable; it is a part of normal development, so there is no need for a contrived or premature disillusionment, which is inevitably traumatic. On the contrary, such disavowing interpretation of an idealizing transference is catastrophic. Kernbergian idealizers are best treated differently, but Kohutian idealizers, like Roberta, are best left alone. The exception is extremely primitive and totally unrealistic idealization, which must be understood before it is interpreted. Eventually, Roberta's idealizing transference will work itself through. For now, she continues in treatment. I continue to be "weird," and she continues to grow.

3

ACOA: A Special Kind of Narcissistic Injury

ACOA means Adult Child of an Alcoholic. Growing up in an alcoholic home does strange things to people. Alcoholism being, on its psychodynamic side, a regression-fixation to pathological narcissism (Levin 1987), the alcoholic parent is too self-involved to meet the child's needs. That is the best-case scenario. Frequently, there are parental sins of commission, as well as parental sins of omission: active as well as passive injury. Quarrels, fights, family dissension, and angry withdrawal are all common, and far from uncommon are overt sexual and physical abuse by the alcoholic parent. Incest and alcoholism are bedfellows. Compounding the various levels of neglect, disregard, inconsistency, and overt abuse is the shame. "Don't tell the neighbors; make excuses for Daddy; take care of Mommy, she has a headache." Cross the street when you see Daddy stumbling home when you are with your girlfriends; blame yourself when Mother slaps you in a drunken rage. I could go on. Subtly or grossly abused, children growing up in a home where one or both parents are alcoholic (or drug addicted or psychotic) suffer repeated narcissistic injury. Being tough, children can absorb an amazing amount of less than optimal care (cf. Winnicott's concept of the "good enough" parent). Good enough doesn't have to be all that good, but alcoholic parents, even if their underlying love for their children is great, simply can't be good enough. The alcoholic family literature describes a variety of roles—the scapegoat, the mascot, the "lost" child, and the hero (also known as the parentified child)—that children in such families assume or are cast into. Heroes are particularly prone to become therapy patients. They are classic Alice Miller (1981) narcissists, often outwardly successful, particularly in academic or intellectual pursuits, perfectionistic, inwardly empty, suffering from feelings of meaninglessness and dissatisfaction, and usually having trouble in their interpersonal relations. Heroes, among other things, have a deep need to be in control and often defeat themselves trying to control others who rebel against that control and desert them or retaliate against them. At another level, they are in a desperate struggle to control their underlying rage, which is largely unconscious. Heroes or nonheroes, ACOAs are abysmally narcissistically vulnerable. How that vulnerability manifests itself is individual and highly varied but basically takes either of two forms: the Alice Miller child syndrome described above, or the overtly depressed, poorly functioning, crushed and angry, obviously damaged type of patient.

REPRESSION OF SHAME

Children of alcoholics have to contend with massive amounts of *shame*, shame that is often denied, walled off, or repressed. That shame comes from two sources: the child's being treated shamefully, and the child blaming himself or herself. As is well known, children blame themselves for all sorts of disasters—parental divorce, parental death, parental desertion, parental abuse, and parental illness, including alcoholism. Children blame themselves because it is less painful to think that they are bad than that their parents are hateful or don't love them. Self-blame is a way of preserving the idealized object and of preventing (denying) the loss of the object or the loss of the love of the object. Freud (1926) postulated a developmental scheme in which anxiety is transformed from fear of annihilation, to fear of loss of the object, to fear of loss of the love of the object, to castration anxiety, to fear of the superego, to social anxiety with massive, unmodulated panic dread developing into signal anxiety. Better that I am bad than that Mother or Father doesn't love me. The only problem with this unconscious defense, strangely, is that I am ashamed of my badness and develop what John Bradshaw (1988) calls shame-based behavior. It also has the disadvantage of not being true. At the most basic level, the child blames himself or herself because that offers the possibility of control—if I am the cause of these catastrophic events, then if I change (from bad to good), they would cease to be. Of course, this unconscious feeling of having control of a traumatic situation in which one is totally without power is illusory. Self-blame not only makes control possible, it also gives one a way of understanding an irrational situation. It provides explanation and cognitive structure, and that turning of the irrational into the rational reduces anxiety, albeit at the cost of lowering self-esteem. The mechanism of turning a passive experience into an active one is similarly driven. Therapists usually think of turning the passive into the active as doing to others what has been painfully done to us, and indeed this is one meaning of the term. But the turning a passive experience into an active one can also mean doing to yourself what has been done to you. In this sense, it is part of the dynamic of the repetition compulsion. The issue once again is control, and avoidance of, or better transcendence of, helplessness. Better to choose than to have done to you, even if the chosen is painful and injurious. We also repeat because we hope the outcome will be different, and probably because evolution has stamped in adherence to the familiar because on the whole, that behavior has greater survival value than seeking the novel. We also return to the traumatic in the hope of mastery of the overwhelming feelings engendered by the trauma through repetition, now from an active, that is, self-chosen perspective rather than a passive, that is, inflicted-upon-one perspective.

Be that as it may, ACOAs, like all of us, tend to repeat their early object relations in adulthood so that every object-finding is a refinding, with all too often disastrous consequences. If you are repeating or seeking to repeat early experience with alcoholic parents, you cannot help getting yourself into one mess after another.

Children are resilient and absorb many slings and arrows without suffering serious personality disorder. We all suffered occasional trauma and, for the most part, assimilated it. Not so with what Masud Khan (1974) called "cumulative trauma," the repeated experience of narcissistic injury, and that is precisely what occurs in an alcoholic home. Alcoholism, like any addiction, is the same shit over and over again. Some folks give up active addictions because it becomes so damn boring. Children in alcoholic homes aren't shamed occasionally; they are shamed chronically, and the resultant cumulative trauma asserts its baleful effects over a lifetime. Khan was thinking of the accumulation of relatively minor injuries; here we have the accumulation of not-so-minor ones.

Children of alcoholics have received a great deal of attention in the last decade. There is a plethora of popular books addressed to them. There is a "Twelve Step" self-help group modeled on AA called ACOA, which has been highly successful—certainly in attracting members if not in "curing" them. And there is a glut of "shopping lists" of traits and characteristics of ACOAs in both the pop-psych and the professional literature. Most are so broad that, like the fortune teller's prognostications, they can apply to virtually anyone. I do not wish to add to this literature, and given the fact that literally millions of people are children of alcoholics, they are bound to show considerable variability. The problem is exacerbated by the necessary distinction between those ACOAs who are themselves alcoholic and accordingly manifest the stigmata of alcoholism, and those children of alcoholics who are not themselves alcoholic. Having said this—and I abhor the facile oversimplification of the ACOAs' situation—I have to, in a way, add to the ACOA shopping list supply. However, my list is simple, consisting of the belief that it is not possible to grow up in an alcoholic family without suffering profound narcissistic injury with its concomitant shame and rage. This is true for both those ACOAs who are themselves alcoholic and those who are not. The vexed question of whether or not alcoholism is a disease, and the role of genetically transmitted neurochemical vulnerability to (or predisposition to) that "disease," if there is one, need not concern us here. In either case, the children must deal with the effects of the parents' alcoholism on them and their emotional development. Understanding and conceptualizing the parents' behavior as a disease is a double-edged sword; it reduces guilt and shame by giving an alternate explanation of the parents' behavior—"It wasn't because I was bad or unlovable; it was because Father was ill." This dynamic is complicated by the possibility of the guilt and shame being unconscious or acted out, as it frequently is; but it also makes it more difficult to experience and express repressed rage—"How can I rage against a poor, sick woman, my mother, who couldn't help what she did?"—thereby paradoxically increasing guilt and shame by illegitimizing the rage he or she has to feel. Thus, our interest is in the patient's beliefs about alcoholism being an illness or not being an illness, rather than whether or not it is one. (My own belief is that it is a complex bio-psycho-social phenomenon [cf. Levin 1990, 1991]). ACOAs are not cut out with cookie cutters, nor do they conform more than other human beings to the list of characteristics ascribed to them, but they do inevitably suffer serious narcissistic injury, which manifests itself in a wide variety of ways. Many psychotherapists are Alice Miller children, using their highly attuned sensitivity to the nuances of others' emotional states, originally developed for defensive purposes in an unsafe environment in an adaptive way. They are especially vulnerable to countertrans-

ferential narcissistic injury. Some of these Alice Miller therapists
are ACOAs. Enough of theory and general observation; it's time
to turn to case material.

Sally was the most terrified patient I have ever treated.
Looking cadaverous, she cringed in the waiting room, flattening
herself against a wall as if she wished to be absorbed by it. Hands
turned, palms against the wall, this nearly anorexic-appearing
woman radiated sheer terror. My office is a flight above the
waiting room. When I would call her in, she would go up the
stairs half-twisted to keep her back against the wall, not relaxing — if moving from terror to tension and anxiety can be
called relaxing — until she entered the office and I closed the door.
In her mid-thirties, she was potentially attractive, given a 20-
decibel reduction in her tension level and a 20-pound gain in
weight, but her distress made her no more appealing than a
frightened animal. Not only her movements and her body
language, but her eyes radiated her fear. Although I wouldn't
have described her as fragile, her tension was so great that I
feared she might break, even shatter. I mean this not metaphorically, but concretely — bodily. It took some time before the basis
of her fear, guilty secrets and terror of her alcoholic and abusive
father, became apparent. As she sat rigidly on the couch, the
tension in the room was palpable. It made me anxious. I figured
that I wasn't going to be able to be very helpful to her unless I
could reduce my anxiety level, but this proved elusive — I couldn't
do it. It was as if the terror were contagious. Perhaps I too
believed that her father would kill me. I think I also sensed the
infinite rage behind her fear, and that too frightened me. Some
sort of *projective identification* was occurring. A concept originating
with Melanie Klein (1955), projective identification is the notion
that infants project unacceptable aspects of themselves onto the
environment in order to protect their inner goodness from their
inner badness — essentially it is projection of the death instinct
and its derivatives. Once the projection is in the environment, it
takes on an object characterization and becomes a persecutory
object. The persecutory object is then reintrojected because it is

too dangerous in the environment, and a whole sequence of introjection and projection ensues. More contemporary understandings (Ogden 1979, 1990) view projective identification as a process in which a child or an adult patient rids himself or herself of an unacceptable feeling by engaging in behaviors that will induce the very same feeling in someone else, in this case the therapist, where ideally it is processed; that is, the projected affect or state of being is contained and tamed. Projected, not now by Klein's mysterious phantasizing process but rather through a behavioral inducement, the affect state is now present in the therapist, who has more mature resources to handle the feeling, and in that sense, processes it in such a way that it is tamed. The projector, in this case the patient, is now able to identify with that which he or she has projected, which is now in a more benign state, so it's his stuff, but his stuff in a more handleable form, and now through identification, is able to take it back in, where it will now be more easily handled by the person who originally projected it. In this version, there is nothing mysterious about projective identification. It's about behavior-induced affective states in both the projector and the recipient of the projection; the recipient of the projection doing something with it, which the projector was unable to do, which now induces a behavioral state in the one who originally projected it, so he or she can easily identify with it.

Something like that seemed to be going on with Sally and me. Like most people, I get anxious about being anxious, and a vicious cycle sets in. Being in that state lowers my self-esteem; I like myself less—although I also know (at least cognitively) that there is nothing wrong with my being anxious; I am entitled—and that liking myself less constitutes a narcissistic wound, albeit a shallow one. Of course, I didn't want to appear anxious, and my social fear of being perceived in a way I didn't want to be perceived added to my discomfort. Since I was functioning in a professional role, my concern there was not purely psychopathological; it had a real social referent, and there were reasons not to appear anxious, which would only make things worse for Sally. I started to dislike my new patient for "making" me so uncomfortable. I dealt with this by mulling it over and trying to understand it, as well as by turning my attention away from myself to Sally. That sounds contradictory, even paradoxical, but it isn't. My bit of self-analysis included her and her projections, and the objectification calmed me and turned me away from my subjective discomfort so I could more easily focus on her, which in turn further reduced my anxiety by making my self-perception closer to my ego-ideal of the dispassionate understanding of others, at least in my professional role. Other ways of understanding my countertransference: Was it induced by projective identification, as speculated about above? Was it truly transferential — echoing and arousing similar affect states in me by putting me in contact, albeit unconsciously, with terrifying experiences of my own? Or was it an unconscious attempt at understanding through identification with, and empathizing with, Sally?

PROJECTIVE IDENTIFICATION REVISITED

Projective identification is a vexed, complex, multiply-meaning concept that has been understood in a bewildering variety of ways. Some redundancy may be helpful here. For our purpose, I am going to take the term in its implicit and most concrete meaning, one that doesn't require belief in the projection of internal objects or object states from one mind to another. It involves three steps: first, behavior of some sort, usually highly emotive, by the projector, which is driven by an unconscious wish to induce a usually but not necessarily disruptive and painful affective state in the recipient (the affect as well as the wish may be unconscious). Second, the induction of that state in the recipient, who is usually puzzled by the subjective experience he or she is undergoing. The recipient does something with the induced change in his/her state of being to broaden it from a relatively clear-cut feeling; this is usually referred to as containing and processing the feeling. Third, the projector now becomes cognizant of the processed state of being and identifies with it, such identification leading to a reintrojection or internalization of the state of being, which is now manageable. Step three takes place with various degrees of awareness (consciousness), but usually what the original projector experiences is a change in state of being which is mostly a change in affective state. This too need not be entirely conscious.

There are several problems here: although we speak of "stuffing feelings," or repressed affect, it is not at all clear how or where repressed affect could be stored. Affect always has a somatic component, which is either present or not present and doesn't lend itself to storage in the unconscious. It makes more sense to conceive of the process of repression of affect as a repression of ideation that would release the affect, so with derepression a thought, image, concept, or memory triggers the feeling. But thought doesn't travel through or between minds without being verbalized; hence, projective identification seems impossible. But not so; the affect state induced in the recipient becomes associated with the recipient's ideation, which may be more or less similar to the projector's, and this is what is, to varying degrees, processed beneath awareness. Freud wrote that identification precedes object relating, and is a kind of psychic cannibalism, an almost literal oral incorporation. The boundaries and sense of separation needed for object relations are lacking. Hence, projective identification is a primitive process, and its very archaicness induces anxiety in the recipient. That is, Freud says that identification is more archaic than object relating in that there is no separation; identification is in essence oral incorporation. He speaks of an object relation regressing to an identification.

Part of my anxiety with Sally came from this primitiveness. As Ogden (1990) points out, there can also be projective countertransference, which is particularly likely to occur when the therapist is working with highly regressed patients. If a projective identification/counterprojective identification is proceeding without awareness, that is, is unanalyzed, the result is confusion for both parties and frequently pain. This confusion and pain can be narcissistically injurious to both patient and therapist and can easily lead to premature termination of therapy.

To return to Sally, certainly part of the anxiety I felt in her presence was the result of projective identification. Accordingly, how I dealt with the portion of my anxiety so induced would be highly determinative of how the patient would do. She needed me to contain and process the anxiety that was overwhelming her in some way that soothed it without denying it, so that she could in turn internalize that at least somewhat tamed anxiety. I also had to look at whatever (counter) transference this woman was inducing in me. I could not immediately identify any. She simply didn't resonate any important figure in my life. That didn't mean that I wasn't having any countertransference in the narrow sense, but for the moment, it wasn't in evidence. Not so countertransference in the broad sense. Being around anxious people sometimes makes me anxious, and Sally sure did. How about the third possibility that I was simply feeling what she felt so I could better understand her? (To be more accurate, I certainly wasn't feeling what she was feeling, only a highly attenuated version of it.) Perhaps, but that didn't seem particularly salient. Projective identification can simply be a communication, an attempt to make another feel what we are feeling, so they can better understand us. Some such mechanism is the basis of all empathy. No doubt Sally wished to be empathized with, otherwise she wouldn't have been there, and her unconscious doubtless did what it could to obtain that empathy, but that wasn't mostly what was happening to her and between us. On the contrary, she was simply terrified, and her terror was so extreme for an outpatient office setting that I was shaken and discomfited.

The question of diagnosis arose. Of course, I knew nothing about her, but her appearance, demeanor, and behavior suggested that she was crazy. As I get older, I have a harder and harder time seeing psychopathology. What I see are human beings struggling to deal with their lives in ways that make some sort of sense when viewed from their vantage point. I find it harder and harder to judge them as pathological. I see shades of gray rather than black and white. All sorts of patched-together arrangements, making do, compromises get people by, and who am I to judge them? Nevertheless, diagnose I must. Some conditions are correlative with neurochemical anomalies and require referral for their remediation; some conditions, such as active addiction, require direct confrontation, while other diagnoses also have implications for technique. So I diagnose but do so tentatively, aware that I may be missing something or just plain wrong. I didn't yet have a working diagnosis for Sally, but she seemed pretty disturbed. Diagnoses objectify, and that objectification, necessary as it may be, is often the source of a deep narcissistic wound for the patient, who feels like an insect impaled on a dissecting stage. One patient said to me, "I feel like the postage stamp mounted in someone's stamp book. The only thing about me that matters is that I be placed in the correct position on the correct page." Much of the work we do is helping people with problems in living, hardly diseases, but we don't like to admit it; it gets in the way of third-party reimbursement — insurance companies don't pay for personal growth — and far more significantly, it makes us feel less important, less scientific, less professional. To relinquish diagnosis is to lower our self-esteem, to narcissistically injure us. Somewhere in the course of our work together, I flirted with many diagnoses for Sally. Why don't you diagnose along with me as Sally's story and treatment unfold?

Sally's anxiety level was so high that it was almost impossible for her to speak. She sat rigidly, not quite trembling although threatening to, and said little. Her initial communications made little sense. She told me a garbled account of triangles, squares, and circles, which evidently had special (magical?) meaning for her. Try as I did to understand their significance, I could not. Did they have some sort of sexual symbolism? Triangles could represent both the male (penis plus two testicles) and the female (pattern of pubic hair, two breast and vagina) genitals. The circle — the breast? And the square? This sort of analysis was a dead end; it went nowhere. Eventually it became clear that the geometric shapes represented modes of confinement, of being imprisoned within them, but for the moment, they seemed to be representative of the magic world of the schizophrenic. Was my patient schizophrenic? I began to think so. She was unemployed, terribly worried about finances, and struggling to find work. She was able to talk about this with difficulty. I also learned that she was married, but not much else.

I usually do an "intake" — another potential source of narcissistic injury in treatment. Badly conducted intakes can really batter: they make the patient feel not just interrogated (which of course is happening) but interrogated as a detective might interrogate a suspect (which need not happen). What should be the beginning of a rich interpersonal experience is turned into another instance of being processed, categorized, pigeonholed, quantified, just as if the patient were a loan applicant at a finance company. The patient feels objectified, turned into an object — scrutinized for weakness and flaws, and perhaps rejected, the loan turned down. I figure that I can always obtain a systematic history later, and although I prefer to conduct a structured intake, I do not insist on it. If an intake is done, it must be done sensitively; aspects of the patient's life relevant to the treatment elicited in such a way that the patient feels the inquiry is part of the treatment, as indeed it should be — not the filling out of forms antecedent to it. Perhaps the key is empathy — discovering with, rather than voyeuristically finding out about, the patient. In Sally's case, conducting a standard intake would probably have driven her out of treatment, so I deferred it. In retrospect, that was the correct decision, but it put me at a disadvantage, and I resented her for it.

We did manage to reach a "contract," in which time and fee were set. She agreed to twice-weekly sessions, to say what came to mind, while the fee would be paid by her husband's insurance — her circumstances made treatment impossible without that third-party payment. The fee is *always* a narcissistic injury. Nobody expects to pay for Mother's milk. Too often we forget this, and do not sufficiently uncover the patient's feelings about the fee. Even with the patient who feels important because he pays a high fee, the flip side is, I shouldn't have to pay this—this guy is an emotional whore—he only cares about me because I pay him. This inflicts a narcissistic injury on us, the therapists. It's true, sort of, or too true for comfort.

Terror and hesitant speech were our mode of being together for some time, until Sally asked, "May I sit on the floor?" adding, "I'll feel more comfortable there." Without really thinking, I nodded, and she did so. In retrospect, I wonder where I was coming from. With almost any other patient, I would have "analyzed" her request. "Tell me more about wanting to sit on the floor." "What does sitting on the floor bring to mind?" "I wonder why you are asking me that now?" I think I nodded unreflectively because I wanted a tension reduction at almost any cost. I wanted the impasse broken. Sally needed to control something, and where she sat was one thing she could, perhaps, control. Though I was proceeding on unconscious "intuition," it is true that to have analyzed her request would have increased the distance between us, further reducing her self-esteem and increasing her fear. The longer I practice, the less I say. If I don't get in the way, most patients cure themselves (cf. Anna O.'s "talking cure" and "chimney sweeping" [Freud and Breuer 1895]). Sally immediately moved to the floor; once there, she looked up at me imploringly, yet with the first manifestation of warmth I had seen in her, and asked, "Will you join me here?" Sensing nothing seductive in her request, I did. We sat silently for a long time—she was no longer terrified—then she said, "I used to sit like this with my mother, eating the cookies we baked together or just playing." After that, the therapy, hitherto frozen, exploded.

A TRAUMATIC DEREPRESSION

What followed was the most rapid derepression I have ever witnessed. A series of hitherto inaccessible memories flooded the patient. The earliest concerned physical abuse by her mother; throwing her against a wall and throwing her out of the way. This abuse was apparently episodic and rare. The way it came to consciousness was interesting. Sally had been to a chiropractor who had discovered that she had a cracked coccyx. He had treated her kindly, and she had had a strong attachment to him. His kindness had reminded her of the warm side of her mother, and when I sat on the floor with her, the transference to her chiropractor, which was a good-mother transference, transferred to me, and feeling safely and firmly held by the "good mother," she was able to tolerate memories of the "bad mother." The recovered memories of being between her parents, her father throwing her aside (was she getting in the way of his sexual advance, or of a physical assault on the mother?), and of her mother throwing her against the wall disorganized her. In frozen terror, she became hysterical, or nearly so. Her father's hostility was not news, but her mother's was. Devastating news. Here we have two narcissistic injuries: the original was inflicted by the mother, and the second inflicted, in a sense, by me, who had facilitated the discovery that the parent who seemed to love her had not always been loving. A child needs a good object, and lacking one, uses the best material available to create one. In a sense, Sally's good mother was more of a transitional object than one-half of a split, although she was also that.

The transitional object is a concept of Winnicott's (1951) in which he postulates that the child's infusing of his or her blanket or stuffed animal with symbolic meaning as a substitute for the mother is the basis of all human culture. The most familiar example of the transitional object is Linus's blanket in the comic strip *Peanuts*. It is not the animal or blanket but the meaning the child gives it that makes it a transitional object. Patients often make therapists their transitional objects, assigning them meanings as substitutes for parents, much as a child does with a blanket or toy.

It was as if a "good mother" transference established by our "making cookies on the floor" provided the security and safety needed to experience the bad mother. This transference and the derepression it enabled were facilitated by Sally's positive experiences with her chiropractor; her rapport with him (or, if you prefer, positive transference to him) accrued to me before she even walked in my door. Without it she would have been too afraid to enter psychological treatment. Transference often works that way; rather than being a recreation of an early object relation, it is a carryover from a previous adult experience with a teacher, physician, or previous therapist, or another authority figure. All therapists know this, yet there is little note of it in the literature. Of course, the previous relationship was also a transference, but the intervening relationship modified the transference in crucial ways that powerfully influence the patient's relationship with us. Transference as usually understood is a "reenactment instead of remembering," (Freud 1914b, p. 150) but that does not adequately account for what happened between Sally and me. Freud said that in the transference, the patient acted instead of remembering. That is, instead of remembering the traumatic events of childhood, he or she enacts them in the relationship with the therapist.

Here a reenactment of the "good mother" transference enabled Sally to get in contact with the traumatically bad mother, without the split; historically and developmentally in the patient's life, as well as contemporaneously in the transference, neither the degree of health the patient had achieved nor the facilitation of further growth through treatment would have been possible. Not only is splitting developmentally normative, its defensive elaboration, although usually viewed as pathological, is often highly adaptive. ACOAs grow up in chaotic environments, where Jekyll-and-Hyde — sober and drunk — parental behavior is the norm, so alternation of good and bad mothers and fathers is reality. This reality is reflected in and reinforces developmentally normal and defensive splitting, and may be the only way the child can experience love and goodness. The problem lies in the deeper reality that the two parents are in fact one person, and far more fundamentally that, as Melanie Klein (1946) pointed out, you can't split the object without splitting the self, so ultimately integration must occur for the self to be experienced as a centered whole. But that integration lies in the future, after the therapeutic work that can only be accomplished while the split is operative has been done. Although many disagree with me, I don't believe that therapy is possible unless the positive transference predominates. In ACOAs and many others whose early experience was horren- dous — cumulatively traumatic — the reenactment of those horrors in the transference, if that be possible, only further lowers self-esteem and reinforces narcissistic injury. Patients who were abused as children need to feel loved by their therapists, and good-mother or good-father transference makes that possible. Syrupy as that may sound, there is nothing sentimental about it; it is simply true. The difficulty is that these patients feel neither love nor lovable, and that makes the establishment of a thera- peutic alliance and/or a positive transference extremely difficult. A good deal of the skill in their therapy lies in facilitating its development. None of this prevents the patient from reliving and working through painful experiences in the transference, but this comes *later*, after the splitting has given the patient some sense of safety. In Sally's case, the central trauma of her life was reexperienced transferentially, fortunately only after a powerful bond had been built. As my first analytic supervisor, Claude Miller, used to say, "You have to build the trampoline before you can jump up and down on it."

The chiropractor had a nontransferential impact on Sally's recovery of the traumatic repressed. He told her that her X-rays showed an old fracture of the coccyx. Had she been injured? This information — the existence of a fracture — became operative within the safety of her transference to me. We were sitting quietly on the floor when Sally's face turned wooden; contact seemed broken as she retreated inward; then she started screaming — the screaming was brief, followed by prolonged, broken, haunting sobbing. I said nothing. Her convulsive sob- bing continued. Gradually quieting, she cried herself to exhaus- tion. Tears became whimpering, and then ceased. After an interlude, Sally said, "She broke my back." Over the next week, Sally recalled how her mother, in an uncontrolled fury, had picked her up and smashed her against a wall. She was about 5 when that occurred. The remembrance was devastating. Mother had been the stable, caring parent, while Father, nightly drunk, had been cold, uncaring, hostile, withdrawn, and sometimes violent. The threatened loss of Mother as a good object was almost unbearable. Was the broken coccyx a screen memory for many such happenings? A screen memory is a memory that acts as a screen and conceals as much as it reveals. Freud suggested that they be analyzed much in the same way as a dream, with the patient free-associating to each element of the screen memory. Sally's memory didn't appear to be a screen for multiple abuses. The mother of Sally's infancy, toddlerhood, and latency had been remarkably caring in a home of persistent hostility and violent arguments. That love had been interrupted by a small number of brutalities (additional widely separated similar episodes were uncovered).

Having little history, I knew nothing at that time of her parents' drinking. After about 3 weeks of alternating disbelief and all too convincing belief that her beloved mother had so mistreated her, Sally stopped talking about her mother's abuse, risking cutting off her feelings (we seemed at an impasse), and began talking about her parents' drinking. She had perfect recall of most of this, and she proceeded to relate how her father, who always worked and who used his status as a "good provider" to justify doing anything he damn well pleased, drank every single night. He "held it well," meaning that he rarely slurred or staggered. What he did do was scream and argue, virtually continuously. Utterly self-centered, Father could not tolerate not having his way. When he could not dominate, he ranted. Sally's memory of the "baseline" status of her childhood home was of parental fighting; loud, vulgar, occasionally physical, and always terrifying. The terror she had exhibited in the waiting room, trying to disappear into the wall, was the terror she had lived with night after night as a small child. The attempt to disappear was a re-creation of her earlier attempts to disappear, which was her way of coping. She literally hid in the closet, under the bed, and when older in the woods in back of the house. Constant fighting meant constant terror. Sometimes Sally's mother interposed her, "literally frequently, and metaphorically constantly" between herself (the mother) and the father. Sally was Monkey in the Middle with a vengeance. Her mother's use of her as a shield was totally repressed until these episodes flooded back during the period of traumatic derepression in therapy. They too were traumatically disillusioning. Sally was tossed around — pushed aside by her father, and sometimes flung across the room. Although not quite explicit, it was clear that what the mother was using Sally to protect herself from was, at least sometimes, sex. Sally was almost literally fucked by her father as he thrust toward her mother. "How could she? I thought she adored me," sobbed Sally in a thousand variations. Children need to idealize their parents — clearly her father was not idealizable, which left Mother. Disillusionment is inevitable and normal — nontraumatic, gradual disillusionment. This was not possible for Sally. Being thrown against a wall so hard that her coccyx was broken, and being put between Mother and her enraged father, could not be integrated with Mother, the loving baker, so instead of phase-appropriate, gradual deidealization through nontraumatic disillusionment, Sally maintained a pathological, albeit adaptive, conscious, primitive idealization and repressed unconscious reservoirs of traumatically disillusioning memories. Early in treatment, this defensive structure, stable for 30 years, disintegrated with startling rapidity, leaving Sally nakedly vulnerable.

When Sally was thrust in front of Mother, Father was not physically violent toward her. Rather, his attitude was one of scorn, rejection, hostility, and barely repressed rage. He had contempt for "girls." Her older brother, although hardly well treated, was more accepted and later sent to college. Sally, in what was one of the most damaging of the many injuries inflicted on her, was not. Father didn't believe in education for girls, which was a waste, since they soon married anyway. Needless to say, this highly intelligent woman's being deprived of higher education had reality consequences in terms of her earning power and inability to find meaningful and satisfying work that went far beyond the already indelible psychological damage that her father's dismissal of her as insignificant had inflicted.

There was an exception to the father's not hitting her outside the sexualized fighting between the parents. When Sally was trying to disappear, she sometimes had temper tantrums. Her rage had to have some outlet. When she was 4, she had a particularly intense prolonged one. Her father came, pulled down her pants, put her across his knee, and spanked her with a strap. Her conscious memory was of the experience being humiliating and enraging. Yet as an adult, she sometimes found being spanked in exactly the manner her father had spanked her highly sexually exciting. This was one of her most guilty secrets. In addition to that which was a secret to herself (the repressed), Sally had a number of guilty secrets that she had confided to nobody. Her pleasure in "erotic" spankings was one of them — she blushed scarlet when she finally told me about them (they didn't play a major role in her sexual life, being an occasional behavior). Sally was ashamed of the pleasure she gleaned from being spanked. That shame was threefold: it seemed perverse; it had first occurred in an affair she was deeply ashamed of; and most saliently, the idea that the original spanking by her hated father had been sexually stimulating was repugnant, violently unacceptable. Yet it almost certainly had been, the pleasurable (or, better, the stimulating) effects having been repressed. Sally tried to detach her pleasure in erotic spanking from her father, saying that a reddening of the skin of her buttocks was physically stimulating and had no psychological meaning (my wording). I didn't believe that was the case, but I didn't interpret the genetic source of her pleasure for years. Children who are severely beaten do not find spanking erotic, although they may otherwise seek to repeat their experiences. (Freud interpreted shame as a reaction-formation to sexual pleasure. Sally's shame over pleasure in spanking was partly exactly that.) To have told her this would have been premature, and would have inflicted needless narcissistic injury. Sally would have hated herself for "enjoying" anything "sexual" with her father. She had more than enough self-hatred. This was knowledge she didn't need yet. Eventually, we did discuss it, and I pointed out that her temper tantrums were states of high arousal from which the spanking, which had not been so painful for the pain to override the pleasurable cutaneous stimulation of the spanks, had brought a resolution, a sort of "climax." Sally's temper tantrum had put her in a high state of arousal; the spanking, with its affective discharge, was in effect a detumescence. That episode was also one of the few times in which Sally's father had paid much attention to her, so for a few moments he was intensely engaged with her, rather than ignoring her contemptuously. At a more unconscious level, sex-play spankings were an eroticization of a terrifying, traumatic experience in order to gain mastery. The pulling down of her pants, the father's attention, the father's sexual excitement, her own state of arousal, all fixated this experience in her mind so it was one she returned to in adulthood with intense, highly guilty pleasure. Further, the pain that did exist was a trade-off for the forbidden pleasure and sufficiently reduced guilt for her to experience it. Sally then said, "My father got an erection when he spanked me. I think I can remember feeling it. That's why he stopped." I said, "He stopped because he came." I went on to suggest that it was no accident that she had first experienced this form of eroticism in a relationship with a man who was in many ways like her father.

I return to Sally's parents' drinking. As the years went on, the parents' fighting intensified. The father's alcoholism was stable in the sense that he continued to drink in the same way, with the same effects of sullenness, barely contained rage, and contempt. He often repeated that he had never wanted children, and that they were a burden he couldn't wait to get rid of. When Sally was in her early teens, her mother started to drink heavily. She did not drink well. Unlike the father, she staggered, vomited, slurred, and was a public humiliation. Her drinking hastened her premature death from a series of strokes. Sally's parents finally separated and divorced when she was in her late teens. At the time Sally came to treatment, her father was dying of cirrhosis of the liver and other somatic complications of his alcoholism. Surely, you say, what went on in Sally's home was psychopathological, the result of her father's extremely narcissistic, virtually sociopathic personality disorder, and of her mother's inability to cope with his pathology. True, but don't underrate the impact of alcoholism alone. Narcissistic regression, if narcissistic fixation doesn't already exist, is the ineluctable psychodynamic concomitant of alcoholism (cf. Levin 1987), and narcissistically regressed/fixated parents cannot but help inflicting narcissistic injury on their children. Sally's mother would have been "good enough" if it wasn't for her alcoholism, and Sally's father, although unlikely to have been "good enough," would not have engaged in the constant fighting if he had not been drinking. Further, parents' drunkenness is *always* a source of shame, self-blame, self-hatred, humiliation, and injury to the self, all of which *always* engender rage, which is frequently turned against the self, inflicting further narcissistic injury. Alternately, it is acted out in self-destructive ways which also eventuate in harm to the self. Even as a best-case scenario, being an ACOA is no bed of roses. Another patient recalled walking down the street in a small southern city with her high school girlfriends and seeing her father, now separated from the family and in the last stages of alcoholism, stumbling along, looking every bit the Skid Row bum he had become. Indelible shame permeated her body and soul. Cringing, she hid herself between the other girls and got by her father without being recognized or greeted. The thought that her friends would have known that that was her father was more than she could bear. Twenty years later, her shame overwhelmed her as she recounted what didn't even, but only threatened to, occur. She felt as worthless as she felt her father to be. Yet another patient remembered running, at about the age of 6, with his brother to greet his father getting off the bus upon his returning from work. Thrilled that his Daddy was home, Tom ran eagerly to greet him.

Daddy, although not staggeringly drunk, had drunk enough to react irrationally and cruelly. He shouted, "You're mocking me — running up to jump on me with your shoes untied," and slapped Tom across his face. Daddy had a thing (a pathological thing) with neatness, and in his paranoid alcoholic rage, thought his children were deliberately making fun of him. Again the patient never forgot, and never fully or unself-consciously loved again.

The narcissistic injury from growing up in an alcoholic home need not be so blatant. Kelly's father never cursed, ranted, fought, or abused. He simply got drunk every night and discussed deep philosophical issues with his drinking companions. Kelly, although her physical needs were all met and her father treated her in a superficially affectionate and kindly manner, might just as well not have been there. Her injuries were not as debilitating as were Sally's or Tom's, but neither were they slight. I could go on, having treated scores of ACOAs, but shan't. You have the idea.

Sally's account of her mother's alcoholism allowed me to offer her a reconstruction — a reconstruction that allowed her to regain some self-esteem and proved vital in her rehabilitation. I told her, "Your mother must have been drinking, even drunk, when she threw you against a wall, and when she interposed you between her and your furious father. You remember her alcoholism as developing in your teens, but it is highly unlikely that she started drinking then. She went downhill too fast. It is far more likely that she had drunk episodically for years and was ashamed of it because she could hardly drink and object to your father's drinking in the way she did. She must have drunk secretly, and it was when she was drunk that she involved you in their fighting and broke your coccyx."

"Do you really think that is so?" she asked pathetically, pleadingly, so strong was her need to make sense of her mother's behavior and to feel loved by her. "Yes," I said. "I can't be sure, but it fits, makes sense. Why else would your loving mother, who usually protected you from your father, act in that way?" Sally's relief was enormous; it was her mother's alcoholism, not her hatred, that injured.

This brings us to a need to understand alcoholism. I believe that it is a disease—a bio-psycho-social disorder with complex determinants (Levin 1987, 1990, 1991), and I tell my patients so. I do that in a rather didactic way, not very differently than I would deliver a classroom lecture. I explain the constitutional, neurochemical, genetically transmitted predisposition to alcoholism, the evidence for such a factor, the sociocultural determinants of alcoholism, and how emotional factors (psychodynamics) enter into pathological drinking. I do so succinctly and try not to get into a position where my presentation of the disease model seems to judge the patient's negative feelings toward the drinking parent(s). As a great slogan of pre-Hitlerian Austrian Liberalism had it, *"Wissen macht frei,"* "knowledge liberates." Didactic interventions can be woven into psychodynamic work very nicely. In Sally's case, I wanted to give her a rationale for her mother's behavior without blocking the emergence of her rage toward her father by "dismissing"—explaining away—his brutal rejection of her. Later, much later, after fully experiencing and expressing her rage at him, she would be able to see that he too was ill, and to quote Erikson, "accept the inevitability of the one and only life one has lived." Having to do so prematurely would have been catastrophic, preventing her from externalizing the rage now turned inward.

During this period of derepression, Sally's behavior and demeanor altered abruptly and totally. One minute she would be engaged, in the room on the floor with me; the next minute she would "leave," either freezing in terror, or going into a cold withdrawn, immobile rage (not experienced as rage) reminiscent of the catatonics I encountered in my psychiatric hospital days. Her utterly frigid rages were unnerving. I tensed when she went into them, sometimes for reasons that I could not discern, and sometimes in response to some slight disturbance in our relationship—the phone ringing, or my being 2 minutes late, a failure of empathy on my part. These withdrawals, with their psychotic quality, were frightening. I worried that she might not come out of them; they were too close to psychosis, and regression is sometimes irreversible. They also angered me; I don't like to be cut off, and I felt punished. To the best of my self-scrutiny, nobody significant in my past or present life had treated me that way, so I figured that my reaction to Sally's withdrawals was here-and-now stuff and that her interpersonal impact on other people was being gauged pretty accurately by my response. When she spoke again, sometimes not until several sessions later, she often spoke of not wanting to live or, more actively suicidal, of wanting to die. I did not doubt that she did and that her rage was quite capable of being enacted in a suicide. I felt threatened and controlled, both of which enraged me. I calmed myself by telling myself that none of this was personal—it wasn't—and that helped; nevertheless, the situation remained intrinsically scary. A highly disturbed patient was, as a result of my interventions, undergoing overwhelmingly intense emotional experiences, and discovering intolerable things that might well make her feel so hopeless that that hopelessness, if not her rage, might very well kill her. It was a high-risk situation, and I knew it.

I had had patients suicide before. I suspect most therapists, if they work with the seriously pathogenic at all, have lost patients. Losing a patient to suicide is one of the worst narcissistic injuries that a therapist can suffer. Of course, one's reaction to an event such as suicide of a patient is not fixed, and the therapist could respond to the suicide of a patient without experiencing it as a narcissistic injury, but I would question whether that reaction was not a defense against the awareness of injury. Therapists, one hopes, are highly invested in their work and seek to enhance their patients' lives rather than see them end—patients suffering from chronic, painful, terminal illness excepted. To have a therapy patient suicide is to fail, fail oneself and fail one's patient. Feelings of failure are accompanied by feelings of shame, lowered self-esteem, and self-hatred. We feel angry at that those who contribute to our failures. So here are rage, shame, and feelings of humiliation—the triad of emotions associated with narcissistic injury.

There is a phenomenon called postschizophrenic depression. In it, the patient recovering from a schizophrenic episode goes into a profound depression and, all too frequently, suicides. Such depressions are usually understood as manifestations of the depletion of available catecholamines, norepinephrine, and serotonin following the neuroleptic treatment of a schizophrenic episode, and as the patient's reaction to the realization that he or she has a chronic relapsing and highly disabling disease. All of that is true. Yet, there is another way of looking at it. In Kleinian and object relational theory in general, there is a developmental sequence in which the infant goes from the *paranoid-schizoid* position, which is a stage of preintegration of good and bad, into the integration of the *depressive position*, in which the child realizes that the good object and bad object are one object, and that his or her aggression in part created the bad object. This is the stage in which guilt is developed, or in Winnicott's (1963) terms, there is a development of the "capacity for concern." It is extremely important developmentally, and makes possible human empathy. However, the guilt experienced in the depressive position is a primitive guilt, and the superego that drives it is an archaic, savage superego. I would suggest that part of the etiology of postschizophrenic depression, with its suicidal potential, results from the rapid integration of preambivalent, good and bad split self- and object representations into more complex, unsplit representations enabled by pharmacological treatment through neuroleptics, and that the patient is overwhelmed by the primitive guilt of this chemically induced progression into the depressive position before he or she has the resources to cope with the new experiential world of the postambivalent depressive stage.

The first patient I lost was a severely borderline woman who had just been released from her second hospitalization. I had arranged for her to attend a day treatment program, and when I met with her the day she suicided, she was future-oriented, talking about her expectations of that program. Only hours later,

she swallowed pills and died, after having jumped out of the car
as her parents rushed her to the hospital. Looking back on it, I see
that she clearly wanted to die, seeing herself as having a career as
a mental patient to look forward to. She just didn't want it. I don't
want to sound like Ludwig Binswanger (1944), justifying the
death of Ellen West, but I doubt if any intervention would have
kept my patient alive. But I didn't know that then, and suffered
greatly, questioning my judgment and ability as a therapist. My
professional self was profoundly shaken. Some of that was
healthy; I wouldn't want to be the kind of therapist who wasn't
upset by a patient's suicide. The consulting psychiatrist who had
discharged the patient felt even worse. What is needed in such a
situation is peer support and consultation. I sought both, and
they helped. I learned that my powers are limited, that my
illusion of omnipotence was just that, an illusion that needed to
be relinquished, and that hospitals can't always do the job either.
Relinquishing some of my omnipotence freed me up to be a
better therapist, not to mention making me less vulnerable to
narcissistic injury. Recovering from the narcissistic injury of
Julia's suicide didn't lessen my feelings of sorrow at the waste that
her life had been. The lessening of grandiosity always lowers the
risk of narcissistic injury.

Another patient I treated who suicided videotaped his suicide
for the benefit of his wife. I was so enraged at this sadism
inflicted by the patient, who had refused psychiatric referral and
dropped out of treatment, that I felt only anger. My last
experience was with a Donald Mann–type situation, of a man
who had been hospitalized thrice after three attempts and clearly
preferred death to indictment. I had scant relationship with him
and felt no guilt.

Three were more than enough for me; I didn't want Sally to
suicide. Neither did I want her to limp through life terrified and
half-alive. Therapy is a serious and sometimes dangerous business. All therapists take risks and expose themselves to injury. If
they are never on the edge, they aren't doing their job. On the
other hand, failure to protect our patients as fully as we can is

inexcusable. What to do with Sally? Hospitalize her? Not if I could help it. The narcissistic injury of hospitalization is profound, and in her case, would have been experienced as a violation of the tenuous trust we had established. Naturally, I would rather lose the case than lose the patient, but damn it, I didn't want to lose the case. Things were happening, and Sally just might go far if she could live through the violence of traumatic derepression. So I decided not to recommend, let alone insist on, hospitalization at that time. It was a decision that cost me no little sleep.

The question of the diagnosis that I preferred not to make reoccurred. Was Sally psychotic? Were her catatonic-like states more than transferential repeats of her rage at and flight from the traumatic disruptions of the self-object relationships of her childhood? I decided probably not, and that the intensity of her reactions to "minor" disturbances in our relationships were reflections of her intense need for all of me and all of my attention and understanding for her to feel safe enough to do the work that she was doing. As it turned out, she reacted as she did largely because any lapse in my self-object ties to her meant that I could no longer protect her from her father's vengeance, which would be to murder her. But I didn't know that then. If not psychotic, what then? For quite a while, I thought that I was working with a multiple-personality disorder. So rapid and so total were the shifts in her state of being that I considered consultation with a multiple-personality specialist. Her third-party payment diagnosis was dysthymic disorder, which was true enough. In retrospect, Sally came very near to fragmenting (in Kohut's sense) in this stage of therapy, but that fragmentation was not so total as to preclude communication between alternate states of being.

Just as things seemed to settle down, Sally was hit by — and that was what it seemed — another wave of derepression, this time of sexual abuse by her father. This was possible only after my interpretation of her mother's violent behavior toward her as being an early manifestation of the mother's chronic alcoholism, which helped Sally feel loved and protected by her mother once again. After that interpretation, an interlude of relative serenity was certainly welcomed by me and must have been by her. However, that interlude was brief, and Sally's extreme terror returned. She spent several sessions rigid and far away. There was little communication, and I could not seem to make contact with her. In the fourth such session, I was sitting worrying that she might be slipping into psychosis, when Sally erupted in convulsive, prolonged sobs. When Sally sobbed in that way, which I had seen before, her face reflected all the pain of a heartbroken child. As her tears poured forth, the triangle formed by her eyes and nose seemed to regress inward, so that her face split into two planes, much like a crushed cardboard box. At first I thought my visual impression was hallucinatory, and to some extent it was, but I now believe that her musculature actually changed her physiognomy. After about 15 minutes, Sally started speaking through her sobs, and her face regained its normal contours.

"He tore me; he's going to kill me for telling you. When I was 3 and 4 and 5, Mother worked nights as a waitress, and he would baby-sit me. He hated it, taking care of kids was woman's work. When he put me to bed, he would lie beside me and hold me very tight. At first I liked being held; it made me feel secure, but then he would hold me too tight, very tight. It hurt, and I was scared. He would rub up against me and I would feel something hard. I guess he would come; maybe I partly liked it. I don't know." (More convulsive sobbing, during which Sally again retreated far inside herself.) "One time — one time — one time." (Silence.) "One time," I prompted her. "Oh, it hurt, it hurt. He tore me. There was blood. Then he took my panties and threw them out, telling my mother I had wet them. I think that happened. I know the rubbing did; I'm not sure about the rest — oh, it hurt."

During the ensuing month, Sally's terror reached an apogee. Her petrification against — into — the walls of my waiting room became continuous unless she was sitting on my floor. She moved only her head, searching for danger.

I told her I thought that the events she remembered were real, that they had actually occurred. Could I be sure? No. But here is a problem that has vexed psychoanalysis from the beginning. Were the confessions of Freud's hysterics about childhood seduction true? (Seduction is an odd word for what is sometimes rape and always involves an extreme power differential, which already says something about the need of adult theorists [of childhood sexuality] to exculpate adults.) Or were they fantasies? Historical truth or narrative truth? Although Freud himself abandoned his seduction theory, he never denied that adults sexually abused children and that such abuse is traumatic and etiologically powerful in the formation of neurosis. On the other hand, there is currently an atmosphere of near hysteria in which any physical affection expressed by an adult toward a little girl is suspect. I do not wish to contribute to that hysteria and make no general statement judging the veracity of accusations by children, or by adults remembering childhood, of sexual abuse. However, I am inclined to believe my patients, at least without evidence to the contrary. In Sally's case, her father drank heavily every night and was certainly near drunk when he "baby-sat" her, and we know that sexual abuse is highly correlated with alcoholism. Sally's father was in a constant rage because his wife was "cold," and Sally was involved in their violent quarrels over his sexual demands. Further, the way Sally "remembered" this "seduction," and the emotionality accompanying that remembering only made sense if her memory was a memory of a real event. The only possible alternate explanation is that she is crazy, and/or that her remembered father is a projection of her own pathological rage. Do I believe that? No way. I was there, and Sally's struggle to *not* remember was at least as powerful as the affects that accompanied that remembering.

Sexual abuse of children by drunken adults isn't confined to girls. Mark's story has many parallels to Sally's: a father who had been alcoholic and an indifferent father throughout Mark's life. There was constant fighting between the parents. His mother, who had initially been loving and warm in early childhood, eventually joined her husband in heavy drinking, becoming alcoholic herself. After that, the parents would go to the tavern together, come home blind drunk, and violently quarrel. From the age of 11, Mark and his two-years-younger brother would get between the parents who were too drunk to resist and lead them to separate beds, the younger brother remaining with the father while Mark slept with the mother. One such night, he awoke to his mother playing with his genitals, trying to induce an erection. Mark's sexuality was permanently inhibited by that incident (which was probably a screen memory for many such instances), and he "chose," if that's the right word, a celibate life. When I treated him for panic attacks 40 years later, he had cognitive memory, but no affective memory, of that "seduction." Only when he experienced and expressed the rage he had been afraid to feel for 40 years did his panic attacks subside.

I concluded that Sally wasn't crazy, but I was concerned that she was becoming so. Maybe she just couldn't handle knowing that both parents had so little loved her that they had each violently attacked her. Even more ominous, she remained convinced that her father, now old, seriously ill, and 2,000 miles away, was going to kill her in my waiting room. That did seem near psychotic. I asked her if he had threatened to kill her if she "told." I was convinced that he had, but Sally couldn't remember such a threat, only that she had always been terrified of him. I tried reassurance and supplementation of her reality testing, to no avail. I wondered if a need for punishment was fueling her delusional fear, if it was delusional — her father sounded pretty crazy. Was he capable of coming north and killing her, if he knew of her "betrayal" of him? Did she need to be killed because she had enjoyed the pre-tear rubbing? Did she have other (conscious or unconscious) guilty secrets? I was soon to find out. Sally was poorly differentiated. During the first years of treatment, she would relate incidents that I interpreted as incidents in which she lost her identity in merger with casual acquaintances, in which she would be overwhelmed by their misfortunes. It was as if she became them, especially when they shared great pain with her. As

Freud would have said, her object relations all too easily regressed to identifications. Was her lack of firm boundaries contributing to her terror? I asked her if she thought her father could read her thoughts. She replied, "I don't know." My telling her that he couldn't did not help. Confessing her "guilty secret" did.

For Freud (1915a), an identification is a regression to a pre-object relations state of being; that is, to a state before the separation of subject and object. It is both a regression and a defense. If you can't have the object or the object's love, then you can become the object. Alternately, Freud describes this process as an internalization of the object. We have already looked at the mechanism of projective identification and the mechanism of introjective identification, in which there is no projection but simply the taking in of the object. So in identification, we become the object, and in introjective identification, we somehow put the object inside us and identify with it. Identification is also used in a less technical way in ordinary speech, and in the ideology of the "Twelve Step" programs. In them, identification is seen not as a regressive state, but as a powerful mechanism through which guilt is deliquesced, and denial and resistance broken down through identification with those who are further along the process of recovery. In the Twelve Step setting, identification is all of the things Freud said it was, but it is something else as well, whatever the underlying mechanisms. Perhaps the best way to put it is that identification can be not only a regressive defense but also a highly adaptive mode of intrapsychic functioning, which is the ultimate basis of empathy.

Like so many ACOAs, Sally had married an alcoholic. In the early years of their marriage, he was daily drunk, frequently unemployed, and totally irresponsible. In a sense, she had traded down; at least her father had consistently worked. (She had also traded up, as we shall see. Hank wasn't only an alcoholic, and Sally's "object finding being a refinding" was complex, being simultaneously a refinding of her father and a refinding of her "good" mother.) Sally and Hank recapitulated her parents' arguments. Finally, she emotionally detached, threatening divorce if he didn't stop drinking.

At that time, Sally was working for a physician as a sort of all-around assistant office manager and untrained nurse. Outwardly, he looked as different from her father as possible, a nondrinking educated professional. Needless to say, she became his mistress. He too was unhappily married. (As someone once said, clichés are clichés because they are true.) Sally became friendly with the wife, and was quickly monkey in the middle, just as she had been as a child. Further, Steven turned out to be a dominating tyrant who used the power differential (employer-employee, upper middle class–working class) between them to exploit her sexually and otherwise, sweating long hours and demanding total devotion. Steven did give her something in return: he taught her a great deal about medicine. For Sally, grievously hurt by her lack of education, this affiliation was, among other things, an attempt at remediation. It raised her self-esteem and gave her vicarious if not real status. Steven, whatever his character defects, was masterly at his profession, and Sally adored that. At first the sex had been mutual and highly gratifying. Then Hank stopped drinking to save his marriage, and Sally grew close to him. The sober Hank was remarkably different from the drinking Hank; loving, considerate, responsible. Sally no longer wanted sex with her employer. He pressed her relentlessly, demeaning her and belittling her—"Who else would employ you?"—and she usually gave in. When she didn't, he would grab her in an empty examining room and push her head down on his penis; when she swallowed his ejaculate, which she enjoyed doing and then was sexually aroused in spite of herself, he ranted, "That was disgusting," and that only whores swallow cum. She came to hate him, yet couldn't break with him. Now that she was in love with her husband, Sally's guilt knew no bounds. Finally, she quit her job, but her guilt never left her. Her guilt was exacerbated by her naïveté and lack of caution in agreeing to go for a ride with her podiatrist, who raped her. He threatened to kill her if she told, and fear of him added to and was displaced onto her already great fear of her father. Sally continued to have lunch with her physician ex-employer, hating it but not knowing why she did so.

Confessing to her affair and discussing the rape somewhat lessened her terror, one source of which was her fear that she would confess to her husband; telling me obviated that need and removed that component of her terror. Sally didn't connect Steven with her father. I made the connection for her, going on to give her one of my passive-active interpretations (I see so much pathology driven by that mechanism, which can be understood as a futile attempt to remediate [heal] a narcissistic injury by enacting power rather than experiencing powerlessness, that I frequently use it; patients readily understand turning passive into active — it resonates), saying, "When your father forced himself on you and tore your vulva, you had no choice. You were powerless. When you found Steven, who as employer was a father of sorts and who shared your father's domineeringness, self-centeredness, and ruthlessness, you unconsciously repeated your relationship with your father, but you were now choosing instead of having it inflicted on you. Your relationship with Steven was an attempt to master a trauma by repetition." That was the most I had said for months. My interpretation was instantly understood, and the response to it was profoundly emotional. Neither Sally's terror nor her guilt left her, but the intensity of both abated.

In the next session, Sally arrived with a large paper bag, blushing beet red. "Can I show you something?" I nodded. Whether or not she was a multiple personality, psychotic or whatever, I had by now come to trust Sally's drive for health, and let it direct the treatment. After all, she had opened things up with her move to the floor, had bonded with me to enable her to experience and integrate her childhood traumas, and had told me that which she feared she could destructively blurt out to her husband. Out came Charlie — a large and obviously well-loved teddy bear. Sally, looking about 2 years old, cuddled Charlie. At last, she felt safe. One didn't have to have read Winnicott and his theory of the transitional object to understand Charlie, and Sally's relationship to him. In one creative act, an illusion if you prefer but a transmuting illusion, Sally had provided herself with a reliable object, one who cared and loved, and could be cared for and loved. She was doing as an adult in treatment what she hadn't been able to do for herself in childhood. Few of my patients have had Sally's gift for creative, restitutional, healing regression. We spent many sessions talking about Sally's relationship with Charlie. I offered no interpretations. It was during this relatively serene period of our work together that Sally revealed other sources of her strength — her love for nature, and her reading of Norman Vincent Peale.

We stopped "doing therapy" and talked about hiking, woods trails, and mountains, and how the power of positive thinking had prevented her suiciding during her giving in to Steven's sexual demands. Should I have told her that both nature and Peale were transitional objects? Analyzed instead of shared? No way. You don't take away before replacing. Triangular relationships in psychoanalysis don't usually refer to patient, therapist, and teddy bear, but this particular triangle bore fruit. Did I enjoy regressing with Sally? You're damn right I did. Is such regression on the therapist's part dangerous? Sure, but therapy is a dangerous business. The trick is to have binocular vision; to regress and not regress simultaneously. I decided to risk being too tolerant of my and my patient's therapeutic regression, rather than to risk distancing myself and inflicting a narcissistic wound by making her feel foolish. So to speak, I chanced turning (on my side) an object relation into an identification.

Charlie enabled Sally's next, and vital, "confession." Out of the blue, Sally said, "I don't know how to tell you this, but I'm addicted to amphetamines. I get them from Dr. X., my diet doctor. If I get fat, I'll kill myself. I can't stand being fat. I went off them once, but I got so depressed I nearly suicided. I've never wanted to live, and I'm afraid if I go off, I'll kill myself." Sally's fears of suicide were all too realistic. I was taken aback. I shouldn't have been. So many ACOAs themselves become addicted to alcohol, perhaps partly on a genetic susceptibility basis, or marry alcoholics that such behavior is expectable. Addiction to other drugs or to compulsive activities is also extremely common among ACOAs, yet I had totally missed Sally's addiction. Looking back, I could see that her extreme tension, bodily rigidity, fear, near anorexia, runaway anxiety and near psychotic ideation, whatever their psychodynamic determinants, were pathognomic of amphetamine addiction. I'm an addiction specialist, and should have (Horney's right about the "tyranny of the shoulds") spotted it. Here was a place where diagnosis *was* important. I felt stupid—my professional self-concept was being threatened, and I was narcissistically wounded—I felt shame, lowered self-esteem, and rage at myself. If—if I had taken a standard intake as I almost always do, I would have inquired into Sally's alcohol and drug usage. If I had done my job more thoroughly, in all likelihood she would have lied and felt so guilty that she would have had to quit, so maybe my error wasn't such an error. Rationalization? Perhaps, but in any case, no harm was done, and the facts were now on the table. Sally's diagnosis was becoming clearer. She was an ACOA and amphetamine-dependent.

ACOAs who aren't addicted to some substance are usually addicted to perfectionism and "people-pleasing"; nevertheless, their treatment is importantly different from the treatment of chemically addicted (or alcohol-addicted) ACOAs whose addiction must be confronted and arrested before their narcissistic injuries and deficits can be worked with. In Sally's case, we were working in the reverse order. Sally had told me that she had smoked pot a lot in the past, and sometimes drank too much, but had minimized this, putting it all well back in time. She felt ashamed not only of her addiction, but of having "lied" to me through minimalization and omission. Addiction, to anything, is *always* searingly narcissistically injurious. Something else has power over the self; feelings of shame, humiliation, and guilt are ineluctable. That's saying too little. The self-hatred of the addict is the essence of his problem. Feeling powerless, he or she can only recover through a paradoxical admission of powerlessness—powerlessness over the addictive substance or activity. I borrow that from AA and the Twelve Step movement because it is true. Some form of " surrender" (Tiebout 1949, Levin 1987), which is simultaneously narcissistically injurious and narcissistically sustaining, is required. The paradox lies in the relinquishing of the reactive and compensatory grandiosity that the self-object (simultaneously idealizing and mirroring) transference to the substance of abuse confers in return for a slight but real gain in self-esteem. Sally wasn't ready to surrender; she was too scared. Amphetamine, a "good mother" psychodynamically and an antidepressant pharmacologically, seemed to be something that she couldn't live without. She also couldn't live with it—not anymore—the guilt and shame and self-hatred were too great. That's why she "confessed" her addiction.

Here was the missing piece of her terror. Her need for punishment for her addiction was handily projected onto her all too terrifying father. Of course, he would kill her; she deserved to be killed. Her use of pills and, as it turned out, more than a little pot, also contributed to her poor reality testing and her tendency to confused mergers. "Can't live with and can't live without it" is the terminal point of all addictions. It is a dangerous point always. Suicide is an ideal way out for any addict at this point, and Sally had long been suicidal. I again considered hospitalization, deciding against it. Instead, I kept her talking about her shame, her need to lie and evade, her constant fear that her husband would find out, her need to play money games for her supplies, her fear that Dr. Feelgood might cut her off. She repeatedly tried to cut back, always failing. The more we talked about drugs, the more she wanted to be off them, but could not do it—her fear being too great. Now I discussed rehab, but she would have none of it: Hank would find out she had been deceiving him, at least about her drug use, if she went into one. Unlike an alcoholic at a parallel stage of the "disease," her physical health was not immediately threatened, nor was she pharmacologically regressing in such a way that therapeutic gains were swept away and meaningful relationship was impossible. Her consumption was stable. For several months, we were at an (apparent) impasse.

A CREATIVELY CURATIVE REQUEST

Then Sally made another one of her creatively curative moves. She came to session more frightened than I had seen her for a long time. With trembling lips and shaking voice, she asked, "May I pray?"—a request no patient had ever made. I was taken aback, although I don't think I showed it. I nodded. Speaking now in a low but increasingly firm voice, she prayed, starting, "When two are gathered together in My name" (which made me, being neither a Christian nor a believer, vaguely uncomfortable), and went on to ask God "to help Dr. Levin help me get off of amphetamines." At her final Amen, I almost cried. That prayer was what Leston Havens (1986), borrowing from the English philosopher John Langshaw Austin, calls a "performative utterance," a use of language not to denote, connote, or emote, but rather to act. Such speech is an action. Sally's petition was clearly self-fulfilling. The act of asking God to help me help her, released her, even if not entirely, from her paralyzing fear; it was also a commitment at a deep emotional and psychic level to getting off drugs. I knew at that moment that Sally would soon be drug-free. It was her "surrender," her admission that the two of us were powerless over her addiction. For her performative utterance to be efficacious, I too had to surrender—admit my powerlessness, thereby becoming a participant in her sanctifying and enabling ritual. It was humbling, and that was good. If, in her surrender, she relinquished a grandiose illusion of control in order to transfer that control to an idealized self-object, God, then I too relinquished a part of my grandiosity and transferred my illusion of control to an idealized self-object, the anabolic forces of the universe manifest in the therapeutic process. It was a healing moment for us both.

We were not yet home free. I tried to send her to a psychiatric consultant to determine how much amphetamine she was on and propose a safe withdrawal schedule. Sally resisted this referral, not wanting to tell anyone else of her addiction. Finally, I sent her pills to the consultant, who identified them and worked out a detoxification schedule without actually seeing her. I was angry about this, but she was adamant. Psychiatric referrals by non-medical therapists are frequently experienced as narcissistically injurious by patients, and not all that infrequently by therapists. Both halves of this must be addressed. Generally, if you talk through the patient's feelings about being sent to a "shrink" — that usually means that they must really be crazy — and deal with your feelings about the patient's feelings that someone has more magic than you do, such referrals go well. Not so in this case.

Fortunately, we got by that, and Sally started cutting down. All went well until we approached ground zero. At that point, Sally panicked and upped her dosage. We went around that merry-go-round several times. I was then doing a lot of analyzing and interpreting. I pointed out as many meanings of her addiction as I was aware of— starting with the unconscious identification with her mother's and father's addictions, and ending with amphetamine's role as an idealized, magical object that would soothe, satisfy, thin, and mood-elevate. I told her that contrary to her expectations, she would feel better "off" the drugs—her self-esteem would get a huge boost, and her self-hatred diminish. I was very active, very didactic, and very firm in my assertion that things could only get better for her if she were drug-free. It finally worked, and there she was feeling bereft, naked, more vulnerable than ever, after I had reassured her that she would feel better without the drugs. She was as angry as she dared to be with me. I repeatedly urged her to go to NA (Narcotics Anonymous) meetings, and/or to an ACOA meeting. She resisted but finally went. Sally never became a deeply committed member of the Twelve Step (so-called for AA's Twelve Steps of Recovery) movement, but her intermittent, rather tepid involvement significantly helped. It reduced her shame and lessened her social isolation.

Sally dealt with her fear of people by superciliousness and contempt, which kept her socially isolated. Of course, her fear that people would "know" that she was an addict and adulteress made matters worse; fortunately, neither was now nearly as salient, and NA provided her with a first socialization experience in an alcohol- and drug-free environment. She was still too troubled and struggling too hard to ward off depression to become socially involved outside of NA, but a seed had been planted, and she became less defensively contemptuous of others. A year later, she started having lunch with fellow workers, and developed some friendships with women, but that was yet to come. For the present, she had only Hank and me.

Psychotherapeutically, "curing" an addiction always involves a transfer from dependence on a substance (seemingly much safer) to dependence on people. Relationship cures. Therein lies both the opportunity and the problem. Sally's transference to me was so overwhelming (for both of us) that the slightest deviance on my part (e.g., being a few minutes late) threw her into a panic, and she responded to a perceived narcissistic injury with narcissistic rage, punishing me with catatonic-like withdrawals (which were also self-protections), suicidal threats (not experienced as threats), and frantic calls at all hours of the night and day. I understood her desperation, yet felt enraged and controlled. I did not for a long time point out the aggression (narcissistic rage) behind much of this behavior; she would not have understood such an interpretation. Instead, I set such limits as I needed to function and otherwise remained tolerant of and empathic toward her need to cling, control, and position. That behavior diminished only slowly. Even more troublesome, Sally lived in dread of my going away, which inevitably would occur.

At this point, her fear of her father returned. Now I pressed for and encouraged her to express her rage toward him. Fearing fatal retaliation, this was very difficult for her. However, our bond was now so strong (confining and infuriating as I sometimes experienced it to be) that she was able to do this work.

Her most characteristic defense was turning against the self. I actively intervened when she would tear into herself. During a particularly virulent orgy of self-deprecation in which she insisted on her "worthlessness," I said, "It isn't you but your father who is worthless." That opened things up. Once begun, her rage at him was poured out volcanically, yet her fear didn't abate. She oscillated wildly between wanting to kill him and wanting to kill herself. (I pointed out this confusion.) She asked me if she should call him and express her feelings. Technical neutrality would have been disastrous; Sally needed to actively experience and express anger to her father and not be killed. I actively and strongly encouraged her. Technical neutrality refers not only to the analyst's noninvolvement in the patient's life but also to the analyst's neutrality, equidistancing, between id, ego, and super-ego. It is a technique of extraordinary power and efficacy when used appropriately. This simply was not such a situation.

After several weeks of "I will," and "I can't," (confront Father), Sally came in and said, "I called him and told him I hoped that his prick would fall off, and hung up." I shook her hand. Sally fully expected to be murdered, but the longer nothing happened, the less fearful she became. Several months later, her father died. His death was a liberation for her. Probably, for the first time in her life, Sally wasn't terrified. What she feared may have been an introject, but the death of the objective correlative of that introject dislodged it, and so to speak, it was expelled. Sally felt no guilt, or at least none I could detect, and I probed for it. Her only regret was not seeing him buried, so that she could be absolutely sure he was gone. I wondered if she would have driven a stake through his heart if she had been at the funeral.

The momentous events following Sally's ceasing to take amphetamines were largely adaptive. However, she certainly experienced a "postwithdrawal crash depression." Amphetamine withdrawal is dangerous because of the rebound depression; such depressions can and often do lead to suicide. Hence, my making myself as available as possible during that period. Whatever nonpharmacological form of psychodynamic determinants her behavior had at that time, it was powerfully psychopharmacologically driven, and her "clinging behavior" was the clinging of a drowning person to a life raft. In other words, it was necessary and restitutional.

THE LIBERATING POWER OF HATRED

If love and forgiveness can liberate and cure, so can hate. We don't give hate its proper place in the restoration of the self. Sally's hatred of her father, a well-earned hatred, derepressed, experienced, and expressed, was the single most potent force driving and enabling her recovery. I deliberately say "hate" and not "rage," for it was truly hatred. Therapists, generally identifying themselves with the angels, are generally uncomfortable with hatred, especially hatred of parents. It goes against the grain of our professional self-images as healers and restorers of harmony. Some things can't and shouldn't be fixed, and some families and some parents are toxic. We need to help our patients hate them, and use that hatred in the service of separation and individuation. Sally's boundaries firmed up once her introjected father ceased tormenting her; of course, being off of amphetamines also helped her differentiate. The pills, which she literally internalized, ingested, were, along with being an all-powerful, loving mother, also her hateful and hating father—safer within her than without—yet, like him, tormenting and persecuting her. Part of her fear of giving up the pills was a fear that he, no longer symbolically within, would be even more dangerous without. I told her all of this while she was still struggling for abstinence, and warned her that she would suffer a rebound depression—a rebound crash—which would be neurochemical, intensely painful, but self-limiting and without emotional (psychodynamic) or symbolic meaning.

After a prolonged working through, all went well until my

vacation grew closer; Sally regressed to near psychosis. Her phone calls became more frequent, and increasingly unmanageable. I now found them invasive and intolerable. Sally's voice assumed the same remoteness that her face expressed during her quasi-catatonic withdrawals. Glacial, dead, astral, were some of the adjectives that came to mind listening to her calls. She seemed to be a different person. Was she indeed a multiple who split, perhaps to prevent complete and total fragmentation when her anxiety reached panic proportions, when faced with disruption of a life-sustaining self-object transference, by abandonment by the self-object—me? Sally constantly threatened (she didn't experience it as a threat) to return to her old friend, her previous self-object, amphetamine.

In *Inhibitions, Symptoms and Anxiety* (1926), Freud described a developmental sequence of anxiety, starting with fear of annihilation, followed by fear of loss of the object (separation anxiety), fear of loss of love of the object, castration anxiety, and social anxiety. In his revision of his anxiety theory, Freud moved from his earlier view that we are anxious because we repress—that anxiety is a somatic product caused by a toxin, the degeneration product of bottled-up libido—to the opposite view, that we repress because we are anxious, in which anxiety is more psychological and communicative than somatic, although Freud never entirely abandoned the belief that anxiety had some sort of somatic basis. In the revised theory, anxiety is a signal, a signal of an external or internal danger that calls forth defenses. However, the move from fear of annihilation to *signal anxiety* is a developmental achievement, subject to regressive loss. Sally had reached the level in which anxiety is a signal, but her development was tenuous and insecure. Kohut offers an alternate explanation of the same phenomenon when he speaks of "regressive fragmentation" to panic terror of the loss of the (archaic nuclear) self, in response to loss or disruption of a self-object transference. They (Kohut and Freud) offer alternate and complementary ways of conceptualizing Sally's anxiety.

My impending abandonment threatened the ultimate narcissistic injury, destruction of the self. That threat was being defended against by going away, by not being there, and by the cold, murderous fury of narcissistic rage. That narcissistic rage could easily prove fatal. This time, I was fully convinced that Sally was capable of killing herself as the ultimate way of not being there—of avoiding annihilation, and of punishing me for my abandonment. An eye for an eye, a tooth for a tooth. I was abandoning her; she would abandon me. We were in deep shit. This time I decided to make hospitalization a condition of treatment, if things didn't change before I left. Now I interpreted the aggression—narcissistic rage—behind her frantic calls and suicidal ideation; she couldn't hear it, although much later she did and was able to use it. I went back to empathizing with her terror, saying in more emotive and personal terms what I said earlier about Freud's and Kohut's understanding of anxiety. I emphasized that it felt *as if* she would shatter, but that it wouldn't happen. It worked. Sally now asked, in a less enraged, albeit still desperate, way, "How can I survive your vacation?" She then had another one of her creatively curative breakthroughs. She asked, "Can I come and sit in your waiting room (which was shared and accessible) during the times we would be having our appointments?" I was relieved that the hospital, which would have been narcissistically shattering for her, wouldn't be needed. I spontaneously went her one better and said, "I'll give you the key to my office, and you can go in and sit in the usual place, at our regularly scheduled times." She now had her self-object back, and panic terror of annihilation turned into more ordinary forms of separation anxiety. It's just as well that I don't need the approbation of the "classical school." Eissler (1958) spoke about *parameters*—deviations from analytic technique as a temporary expedient in the course of the analysis. "Parameters all right, but isn't this ridiculous?" The classicist would say, "This isn't analysis; this is unvarnished gratification. Allowing Sally to use your office has to arouse memories of the primal scene, anal invasion, and oral incorporative fantasies that will remain uninterpreted." Not so, say I. First things first, as they say in the Twelve Step programs, and the first thing was to get this patient through my vacation without her either suiciding or having to be hospitalized. Of course, being in my office did have all of the above meanings; it had to, but they were secondary. The salient meaning of being able to sit on the floor in my office while I was away was that Sally would spend my vacation baking cookies with her mother. Another way of conceptualizing Sally's problem is to say that she had failed to develop *evocative memory*, a prerequisite to *object constancy*. Evocative memory is the ability to get in touch with object representations when we need them. Lacking this ability and regressing in the face of great anxiety, Sally needed the concrete sensory stimuli of my office to conjure me (and what I represented). Safe in the womb, if you want to see it that way, she could feel connected with me, although I wasn't there, even though she lacked object constancy — the ability to libidinally cathect (to revert to the language of drive theory) an object (representation), even in a state of need and deprivation. Of course, I did encourage Sally to explore all of her feelings about being in my office and interpreted some of them *after* the vacation (or to be more accurate, after many vacations).

The security of knowing that she would be able to stay in my office stabilized Sally. And she had a dream, the associations to which led her to one of the most traumatic events of her life. This wasn't really, strictly speaking, repressed, but it had never come up, and Sally didn't connect it to her present panic. When she was 12, her mother, by then far advanced in her alcoholism, stated, screaming, "I can't stand you fucking kids anymore. I'm leaving." And she did. She got in her wreck of a car and drove away, not returning for weeks, and only then because she couldn't make it on her own. Sally was devastated. She was abandoned, on the verge of adolescence, to the mercies of her drunken, sexually obsessed father whom she lived in fear of. The weeks her mother was gone were sheer hell for her — all security and safety, however meager, vanished. Nothing dramatic happened during her mother's absence, and the incident was never talked about. Life, such as it was, slowly returned to the status quo ante, but things were never the same for Sally again. It was Mother's second traumatic failure: a broken coccyx, and a broken heart, strange legacies from a good mother. (Of course, there was a good mother, not entirely of Sally's creating, but the degree to which she had defensively and adaptively idealized what was idealizable about Mother was now clear.) The primary meaning of my leaving was now apparent. I, like Mother, was abandoning her to Father, who would kill her horribly, sexually, mutilatingly, if she didn't kill herself first.

A wall had been breached; Sally's frozen, furious withdrawal was no more. Now sorrow and fear, rage and fury, poured forth. I pounded away at the transferential link. Time and time again, I took her back to Mother — also pointing out that I wasn't Mother (which in her near psychotic transference, was not always clear to her), and that Father was dead. Much was accomplished before I left. As the date of my departure neared, Sally's fear, as to be expected, escalated again. I insisted that she see a covering therapist, as well as sit in my office. With surprisingly little resistance, she agreed. Ensuing vacations were almost equally traumatic for her, but each was a little less traumatic than the last, and as the years went on, Sally steadily improved. It took her several years to be completely comfortable without amphetamines or pot. She knew few people who weren't into drinking or drugs, but as her defensive devaluation of people subsided, her social anxiety (really fear of rejection and fear of a consuming and annihilating merger) abated, and she made new connections. Her self-esteem rose, and her anxiety level fell, as she progressively individuated.

An enduring current narcissistic injury was lack of meaningful or fulfilling work, a constant source of pain that I could do little, beyond empathizing, to alleviate. (I shall refer again to this in Chapter 5.) She came to terms with her father ("I don't forgive him, yet I understand him more now. He never wanted children and resented us. If there is an afterlife, perhaps his punishment could be helping me now — he owes it to me, and I deserve it.") and experienced more and more rage toward her mother. She did a lot of mourning work (her mother had died of complications of her alcoholism), and it paid off. Sally's rage seemed to separate her from her mother, her bond to me giving her the security to do so. She was becoming more and more her own person.

My next vacation approached. Sally as usual was upset, but this time she was more nervous than terrified. Just before I left, she said, "I'll miss you." That wasn't transference. That was here and now, "real" relationship stuff. Leston Havens says, "If there is one moment without transference, the patient is cured." I don't know that there is any moment completely without transference, and I doubt that any of us is "cured," yet something was profoundly different. I said, "You are going to miss me because you are you, and I am I, and you like being with me, but I will be away. You used to think that you would cease to exist if I went away because you could not be, except as a part of me. Now you are secure in your own identity, as evidenced by your growing interest [here I exaggerated the evidence of Sally's growing individualization] in intellectual activities, hiking, and bicycle riding. And you don't need me in the same way. Your missing me isn't about your mother; it's about us. You used to get confused with your mother. You weren't sure what was you and what was her, but the more we talked about her dying and your feelings about her dying, and of her earlier leaving, the less confused you became [here I cited the evidence in several dreams of her progressive separation-individuation] about who you are and who she was. You knew perfectly well that Mother wasn't you in the sense that you had separate bodies and were separate people, but in your mind, you had images of you and your mother that were blurred, confused, and merged. Now those images in your mind are clearly demarcated. When you get very upset, they may temporarily blur again, and when that happens, I will point it out to you; however, you have moved on to a different space, a different way of being, and that achievement is indelibly yours. It was only after you separated, in your mind and heart, from your mother, finally felt her loss, experienced her as a whole person, good and bad, loving and hating, there for you and not there for you, that you yourself could become a full person, loving and hating, joining and separating, joyful and sorrowful, fearful and secure, and it was only after your mourning allowed you to experience your mother as separate and whole, forever gone and forever a part of you, but not to be confused with you, that you could experience yourself as separate and whole with all the feelings you have about that separation and wholeness; that you became able to experience me as separate and whole, as there and not there, as focused on you and as having my own needs, as magnificently capable of helping you and as frequently flawed and sometimes inadequate. It is you, the separate, individuated, and whole Sally who will miss me as a separate, individuated, and tired therapist. I will miss you too, but not so much that I won't have a hell of a good time."

Sally wept a little, but she was not fearful. "I hate your going away, but I hope you have a good time, if you know what I mean." I did and said so.

4

Unrequited Love — Transferential and Otherwise

In his essay "On Narcissism" (1914a), Freud wrote, "We must love or grow ill." In the same essay, Freud adumbrated the impoverishment of the ego, the precipitous fall in self-esteem correlative with unrequited love. The shame, rage, and humiliation of rejection that companion the victim's remnant of self-regard are pathognomic of narcissistic injury. To love "not wisely but too well" is to fall into melancholy. In contemporary terms, it is to suffer from "codependency." In "On Narcissism," Freud described a developmental sequence from a preself autoeroticism (love of isolated body parts and sensations) to narcissism (love of the ego or self) to object love (love of others). Self-love, the libidinal cathexis of the ego, is primordial, and Freud called such self-love *primary narcissism*. At that point in the development of his instinct theory, he postulated two complex instincts, complex in the sense of being composites of component instincts: libido and the ego instincts. Reminiscent of Spinoza's *conatus*, the desire of every living creature to continue living, Freud's ego instincts are innate and self-preservative, and he sometimes conceptualizes

153

primary narcissism as the libidinal component of the instinct for self-preservation. When he so conceptualizes narcissism, he says that the ego instincts are anaclitic on (leaning up against) the libidinal instincts. He here anticipates one difficulty in his structural model where the ego lacks a source of energy and must somehow "borrow" it from the id. There is confusion in this metapsychology of the instincts, but the notion of self-love being primordial makes sense; a more serious problem with this early view of a dual-instinct theory is that Freud, like Spinoza before him, has trouble accounting for self-destructive behavior, suicide in particular. Both the ego instincts and libido have an aggressive component, so he can account for aggression, but with self-preservation and love as his only driving forces, aggression against the self is unaccounted for. Freud soon rectified this. In 1920, he published *Beyond the Pleasure Principle*, in which his instinct theory, still dualistic, now pits Thanatos, the death instinct, against Eros, the love instinct. Before the Great War, Freud wrote of self-love; after that war, he wrote of self-hatred and destruction. Certainly that was no coincidence.

In the original version of the instinct theory, primary narcissism flows outward to cathect objects in the world, and ego libido becomes object libido. However, not all of the libido of primary narcissism is invested in the world. A reservoir remains that sustains our self-regard. Normal narcissism is a libidinal cathexis of the prestructural ego (the self) by that portion of ego libido that is not converted to object libido—is not invested in the world. Yet, to not invest a portion of our primordial libido in others is to fall ill. Pathological narcissism causes narcissistic injury as our uninvested energies go sour and poison us, engendering anxiety and melancholia, or lead to megalomania and delusions of grandeur. So love we must. Yet here we easily become impaled on the other horn of this Freudian (and human) dilemma. If we love too much, too uncritically, too delusionally, we soon deplete our reservoir of primary narcissism and become impoverished. Now all of our energy is focused on the beloved, who possesses every virtue and every attribute worthy of love. The lover experiences him- or herself as unworthy of the beloved. Freud uses the simile of the manometer—U-tube—filled with mercury. In egomania, libido is wholly in the left arm of the tube—the self. In health, it is in both arms, and in unrequited love, totally in the right arm—the beloved—leaving none behind to provide a source of self-love. Kohut criticizes the manometer simile, maintaining that self-love and object love are parallel developmental lines, and that more of one does not entail less of the other. Perhaps true in mutuality, but Freud's image accurately reflects the experience of unrequited love.

Freud's second simile, for the libidinal cathexis of objects, is the pseudopodia of the amoeba, which reach out into the world and cathect, occupy, grab hold of objects. The aggressive element in loving comes to the fore in this representation of the theory, and narcissistic injury seems less a risk than injury to the object. It is only in his notion of *secondary narcissism* that narcissistic injury becomes prominent. According to Freud, when the ego experiences traumatic disappointment in the world of objects (there having to have been a prior fixation of libido on the ego), the ego retracts its libidinal investment in the world and once again, invests all of its libido in the self. This according to Freud, is the basis of the psychotic delusion of the end of the world—a world I no longer love does not exist for me. With all of my emotional—libidinal—energy concentrated on me, I become megalomanic and delusional. A world bereft of emotional significance is unlivable, and the aridity of a world without meaning, no matter how grandiose my delusional self becomes, is intolerable, so I create a world that "never was on land or sea," this process being Freud's metapsychological explanation of the "symptoms"—the delusions and hallucinations—of some kinds of psychosis, which are in fact restitutional, or at least an attempt at restitution, and these symptoms are mistaken for the disease, which is actually the withdrawal of libido from the world.

So we must love, but not love too much. Is all being in love pathological? In Plato's *Symposium* (1961b), Socrates describes the lover as frantic, self-neglectful, reckless, and more than a little mad in his pursuit of the beloved. Shakespeare tells us that "the lunatic, the lover, and the poet/Are of imagination all compact" (*A Midsummer Night's Dream* 5.1). The romantic poets equated love and death, and indeed there is a loss of self amounting to death of the self in the lover's absorption in his beloved. Wagner's *Tristan und Isolde*, that peerless evocation of the universal urge for symbiotic union with the mother, thinly but effectively disguised as a symbiotic merger of the lovers, ends with a "love-death." At best, love is a risky business. Tristan and Isolde are requited, yet nevertheless die; suicides of the unrequited occur daily.

Temporary insanity at best, yet humankind has always known that life without love is a dismal business. "Better to have loved and lost than never to have loved at all." Psychodynamic psychotherapy is primarily about love; in fact, Freud called psychoanalysis "the cure through love." The essence of the treatment is the patient falling in love with the therapist. A love, one hopes, that is unrequited. Being loved has its own difficulties. It sets up obligations, and the idealization ineluctably concomitant with love sets up a set of expectations that the lover cannot possibly meet. We therapists cannot possibly be what our bewitched patients believe us to be, and the discrepancy between their idealization and what, in our saner moments, we know ourselves to really be is often painful for us, that pain constituting a mild narcissistic injury. What if the patient doesn't love us? That hurts too. There is a pathetic letter from Freud to Lou Andreas-Salomé (1966) in which he writes, "There is no transference, she does not fall in love with me. I am too old." For a man as narcissistic as Freud, his patient not falling in love with him must have been exquisitely painful. On the other hand, nothing is harder to handle than an intense erotic transference. That too can be wounding, not only to the patient but also to the therapist.

Every therapy case is about unrequited love. We have all been jilted. The great narcissistic injury of the oedipal phase is that the beloved parent loves someone better, or at least differently, and that our love cannot be satisfied. The alternative to narcissistically wounding oedipal rejection is sexual abuse, clearly a worse outcome. Later episodes of unrequited love echo and recapitulate that first unrequital, and the evocation and recapitulation of that archaic pain, consciously or unconsciously, intensifies and may make intolerable and unmanageable our current injury. Our early love may be further unrequited through the arrival of a more loved — in reality or in fantasy — sibling(s). Then there is the indifferent universe's failure to reciprocate our awe and love of it, a rejection and narcissistic injury usually handled by denial and the projection of "loving parent(s)" onto the cosmos in the form of a loving god. This belief, or if you prefer, fantasy, shields and protects, increasing self-esteem and allaying fear. Any threat to it arouses terror, and the threatened narcissistic injury instantly evokes narcissistic rage, as does any threat of loss of love. Savage retaliation against those who threaten belief systems, and thereby threaten the narcissistic injury of unrequited love, has driven many of the most horrendous episodes in human history. From the medieval burning of heretics, to the condemnation of Galileo, to the death sentence against Salman Rushdie, narcissistic rage defends by murder the particular illusion of love of the believer. The narcissistic rage shadowing all narcissistic injury makes unrequited love all the more dangerous. Projected outward, it can and often does provoke murder; turned inward, suicide. So important is loss of love in inducing psychic pain that Freud (1926), in his hierarchy of anxieties, places it, at least developmentally, before castration anxiety — his hierarchy of anxieties being fear of annihilation, fear of loss of the object, *fear of loss of love of the object*, castration anxiety, and social anxiety. Notice the intimate connection of fear of loss of love to separation anxiety.

Religious experience not only gives us the believers the certainty, however illusionary, of being loved; it equally importantly provides an outlet for love. To love is as necessary as to be loved. One of the most magnificent coming to terms with unrequited love is Spinoza's (1677) notion that the highest value is the "intellectual love of God." Spinoza's God, or Nature, is the totality of that which is, not a person, and not a lover or source of love. It is intellectual love as the dispassionate understanding of the necessity of the causal laws that are the sinews of the universe. In understanding the nature of Nature, and the mathematical relations of its forces and components, one comes to see that what is, must be, and learns that "freedom is choosing the necessary." Not only does the philosopher pursue truth, he loves that truth, and the Nature or God that embodies it. This is strictly a one-way street, Nature or God does not love us. Spinoza knew unrequited love: three mothers died, a father rejected him, and a community expelled him. His highest good, his intellectual love of God, although it doubtless conceals depthless narcissistic rage, is a creative and courageous sublimation. They do not love me; that is all right. They do not need to; I will love them, is a dynamic projected onto the universe. Poor Spinoza, loving that which does not love, and making that love his highest value. Or is it poor Spinoza? Freud in his relation to *anake* (necessity) holds a very similar position.

Plato wrote that philosophy was a meditation on death, but he also said that the philosopher was a lover, a lover of wisdom. Socrates presents himself as an expert on only one subject—love. The modern psychodynamic psychotherapist has succeeded the philosopher as the expert on love, but there is a mystery and a paradox in the therapist's expertise in love. His expertise is an expertise in transference love, and transference love isn't "real." So our expertise is about an illusion. Freud wrote that the transference was a "playground" in which conflicts and emotions could be "harmlessly" enacted. It ain't true. Transference as a concept is a way of attenuating and denying the all too real intensity of "transferential love." The same is true of counter-transferential love. It too is all too real. Freud's notion of transference was, among other things, a way of cooling things off. When patients are in love with us, they are "really," not merely "transferentially," in love with us. One of the worst narcissistic injuries therapists inflict occurs when they tactlessly interpret the patient's love as something else. "You aren't in love with me; you're in love with your father—the father of your childhood." What a cruel brush-off. The patient is in love with us. Transference interpretation denies the reality of this. The same is true of countertransference love.

Mrs. Breuer knew that transference love was real. When in the course of the Ur-case of psychoanalysis (Freud and Breuer 1895), Anna O. fell in love with a therapist, Josef Breuer, who was paying her three house calls a day, Mrs. Breuer abruptly transferred him off the case and took him out of town on a second honeymoon trip. Anna O. took this abandonment hard, danger-ously relapsed, and became an implacable foe of psychoanalysis, detesting analysis and analysts for the rest of her life.

Harold Searles says that he falls in love with every patient, and I suspect that something like that happens in every successful analysis. If "every object finding is a refinding," all love is transference love. This is not to say that transference isn't a "real" phenomenon. On the contrary, most human troubles come from "unanalyzed" transference, but it is to say that the notion of transference has a self-protective aspect for the therapist and that insensitive transference interpretations of a patient's love for us are often self-serving—getting us off the hook—and deeply injurious. There is no more difficult task in psychotherapy than correctly "handling" an intense erotic transference.

MARY: AN UNMIRRORED CHILD

Mary was beautiful. She was also sexy, not in any obvious or overtly seductive way, but in a simple, tastefully sensual way. She had youth and vitality, and it was appealing. She projected an openness, enthusiasm, and innocence that turned out to be both real and deceptive, not that she had set out to deceive. She believed that she was what she presented. I was instantly attracted to her, which at that point was not a problem. I like to work with patients I feel positively about. It is said that the patients we like the most get the worst treatment because we miss some of their "pathology," their hang-ups, their "character defects." This may be true, but on balance, it is better to be fond of patients than indifferent toward them. Although having no formal education beyond high school, Mary came across as a slightly undertweeded Seven Sisters student. In reality, she was a depressed secretary in her late twenties with an unhappy marriage. Her depression was not such as to seriously dampen her natural energy; rather it manifested itself in vague feelings of unhappiness and frustration. It wasn't hard to see the anger beneath her surface, but she was blissfully unaware of it.

Her presenting problem was work. Mary was a sort of secretary-slave to a highly successful real estate broker who obviously used, manipulated, and underpaid her. She baby-sat, ran errands, worked overtime, came in at his convenience, used her considerable intelligence to write his contracts and negotiate some of his deals, and in general jumped through hoops whenever he snapped his fingers. He used praises instead of raises to motivate and control Mary. So hungry was she for approval and for the love of a "father" that she would do almost anything to get it. Mary's emotional involvement with Harry went far beyond the employer–employee norm, although there was nothing overtly sexual in their relationship. Although she was, in her way, in love with Harry, she was unaware of any sexual feelings for him, and he had never acted in any way improperly with her, although he did dole out compliments as part of his exploitation of her.

With all her perkiness, brightness, and Vassar-girl persona, Mary was among the unsophisticated. Were she urban and educated, I would have evaluated her relationship with her boss as more highly pathological than I did. A large chunk of the narcissistic injury inflicted by therapists on patients comes from their ignoring the social and cultural determinants of their patients' behavior. I have had a number of supervisees who, in their fervor to "educate," or should I say convert their patients into their own state of heightened enlightenment, imposed Marxist, or Christian, or Twelve Step, or atheistic, or radical feminist values, evaluations, and agendas on their patients. A social-work student who was doing a field placement in a Hasidic community comes to mind. Although she was supposed to be doing psychotherapeutic counseling of depressed and anxious outpatients, she was horrified by her patients' religious objections to birth control and their many children. To the supervisee, this was a benighted ignorance which she was sure was at the root of her patients' difficulties, and quickly became an advocate of birth control with these Hasidic women. Needless to say, her patients felt criticized and misunderstood, the dynamic and interpersonal sources of their distress underanalyzed, while their birth rate remained stable. I emphasize that the supervisee had the best will in the world, yet was utterly blind to the dismissive nature of her interventions which invalidated an important part of who her patients were.

Another supervisee misread the closeness of the family relations of his first-generation Sicilian immigrant patient as pathological enmeshment. He (and I) would have felt smothered in that family, but the patient didn't. What was mis-seen as a separation-individuation problem turned out to be an acculturation problem in a fairly normal guy. His therapist's empathic failure to understand his cultural situation exacerbated the problem and, in effect, reenacted it in an antitherapeutic way. Once my supervisee stopped being so zealous of "separating" his patient, the therapy, which was on the verge of ending, took off, and the therapist was able to help the patient negotiate the rites of passage into a new society, which was what he had come for help with in the first place.

We all too easily forget how culture-bound we ourselves are and how easily we unconsciously assume that our values are those of health, and those of our patients, those of illness. Engaging from this position of unconscious superiority, we, entirely without wishing to, inflict narcissistic injury on our patients who, instead of finding understanding, find condemnation. My supervisees' commitment to their own ideologies was so strong that they simply didn't see that in their attempts at "consciousness raising" of various sorts that they were indoctrinating, not therapeutizing. These students and supervisees consciously wished to be therapists helping their patients develop their best selves, not ideologues proselytizing, yet their unconscious ideological transference led them to invalidate their patients' experience and values. The resulting therapeutic interactions were injurious to the patients, who felt important aspects of their selves devalued. Mary was a provincial, a traditionalist, and liked being such. This was an aspect of her that was not up for grabs. The question was how to help her be a happier and more fulfilled provincial traditionalist. Consciousness raising in the name of whatever ideology is a valid human activity; it is not therapy.

Life is never simple. Having just said that the therapist injures the patient by imposing his or her values on him, I must say something seemingly contradictory. Just as we can dream too big for our patients (especially if those dreams are our own), we can also injure our patients by dreaming too little for them. What I have in mind is that patients often don't see their own possibilities, potentials, and opportunities, perhaps because nobody, including their parents, envisioned them for them. Thus, the limits of the patient's vision for him- or herself may be the result of ignorance, lack of opportunity, or miseducation. Or it can be the result of fear. "Achievement is forbidden to me; Father will castrate me; Mother not love me; brother or sister will die if I surpass them," with all of its variations.

One of the most popular plays of the Yiddish theater of New York's Second Avenue was the Yiddish *King Lear*. The immigrants really understood that "how sharper than a serpent's tooth it is to have a thankless child" (*King Lear* 1.4.312). These first-generation immigrants feared nothing more than their acculturated children's scorn and rejection, even while they unconsciously feared that they deserved it because they themselves had "abandoned" their parents in the *alte heimat* (the old home). An eye for an eye, and a fear is close to a wish. Mutatis mutandis, this dynamic is enacted in the endless shifts, migrations, and acculturations of "Americans." Immigration across borders and social classes isn't the only blinder that limits the vision of our patients for themselves; psychodynamic as well as cultural forces are at play, but social constraints are powerful.

For the therapist not to see further than the patient is to injure, to cripple by omission, just as surely as conscious or unconscious proselytizing of our viewpoint deforms and devalues. How to achieve the right balance of leading without dominating, of seeing and sharing potential without being dismissive of the patient's conservatism? There is no easy answer. As in every facet of the therapeutic experience, awareness is the key—the best that we can do. If the therapist is aware of the twin dangers of imposition and withholding, the danger of narcissistic injury will be minimized.

During the years when Army's (the U.S. Military Academy) football teams were powerhouses, they had two distinguished running backs who were known as Mr. Inside and Mr. Outside. I often think of them when I'm thinking therapeutic strategy. Is this the time to be Mr. Outside with a particular patient, or is it the time to be Mr. Inside? That is, should I focus on the patient's life outside of therapy, being an ally and commentator, or should I focus on relationship and work primarily in the transference? Patients largely determine whether we work inside or outside, but we have something to say about it too. Technique is a potent determiner of how much we elicit and work in the transference. Greater frequency of sessions and use of the couch intensify transference; the reverse diminishes it. I prefer to work "inside"; it's more alive and more creative, but that is not always possible. Mary was a twice-a-week, face-to-face patient, seemingly not very "psychological minded," and I didn't expect a very intense transference. I was in for a surprise.

Our early work surfaced her anger at Harry. She was afraid of expressing it, fearing retaliation, although it was clear that he was dependent on her and could hardly afford to dismiss her. It was also true that, exploitive an employer as he was, there was a personal bond between them and he was genuinely fond of her. As time went on, the genetic, as opposed to the cultural, determinants of Mary's relationship to Harry became clear. She had been raised the only girl of four children by a small-town businessman father who loved her in a patronizing sort of way, clearly favoring his sons. Although perfunctorily affectionate and attentive, he didn't take Mary very seriously — she was a girl and would get married and have kids. The sexism was so ego- and culturally syntonic that her father would have been genuinely shocked if anyone had suggested that his love and care of his daughter was in any way defective. She grew up as a sort of well-cared-for pet. Father offered to send her to college, but the subliminal message was that college wasn't very important for a girl. Though an excellent student, Mary was not academically oriented, and readily heard the subliminal message. Mother was sort of there, deferring to, although not overtly dominated by, Father. She was dutiful and not particularly warm or loving with her children. Mary was rarely hugged or kissed by her parents. Physical affection was doled out in strictly rationed quantities, so Mary grew up outwardly "well adjusted" in a "well-adjusted" home — a materially comfortable, conformist, church-going, proper, lukewarm rather than cold, "caring" home. Surely "good enough" parenting. So many have worse. One of Mary's difficulties in therapy was precisely the relative "goodness" of her parents and upbringing. She felt guilty and self-pitying — so many were far less fortunate — if she let herself feel her anger at her parents, especially her father, or her deep, helpless longing for his love. Patients who don't believe that they have the right to feel sad, angry, or hurt because they feel that others have less and have been hurt more are common. They are often savage toward themselves, lacerating themselves for their "self-pity." Such condemnation is driven from many directions, but often it is an internalized voice from the past, or maybe a defense against experiencing pain, or it may be a defense of idealized parental imagoes the patient fears to relinquish; usually it is driven by all three. I deal with such resistance by a combination of interpretation and educational interventions, interpreting the source of the prohibition, the avoidance of the pain, and the protection of idealized figures, while educationally saying, "There is a difference between self-pity and having compassion for yourself. You have compassion for others; why not for yourself?"

This approach worked with Mary, and she grew less depressed as she became more angry. Historically, she had acted out her fury and her longing through drug use, heavy drinking, and promiscuous (her word) sex during adolescence. The extent of her rebellion was surprising, given her background and style. While it lasted, it had been intense, exciting, and in some ways satisfying, but it was short-lived. By the time she hit 20, her rebellion had played itself out and she had settled down to her present job, shortly after marrying. As we were still working strictly to the outside, Mary's emotional range broadened. Rage was followed by hurt, deep hurt. For the first time, Mary consciously realized and really felt how little she had been valued by her parents, as superficially kind and caring as they may have been; she was heartbroken, neither acting out nor repressing the humiliation of having been a girl in a family that wasn't "child centered," even with its boys.

In its uncovering work, therapy had inflicted a deep narcissistic wound. Mary was ashamed of not having been loved and of revealing it to me (even though I "knew" it first). Shame was her predominant emotional state now. My comment about being compassionate toward herself allowed her to feel compassionate toward the adolescent she had been. "A 14-year-old kid sleeping with all those guys—not knowing what she was doing, just looking for love, so drunk she couldn't even remember it—it's so sad. Poor kid, nobody cared. She just wanted love, and not one of those guys cared at all. Neither did my father. It was his love I wanted." I couldn't have said it better myself. We spent considerable time working through Mary's hurt, rage, and shame, still with virtually no evidence of "transference." The relationship between us was never mentioned. Obviously, some sort of trust was there, or she wouldn't have been able to do the work she did, yet there was no apparent transferential reenactment. We were still working on the outside.

I did, however, interpret Mary's relationship to her boss as a transferential recapitulation; that is, I told her that she had managed to find a "father" much like her own: superficially kind and caring, yet remote and manipulative, and that she strove for his love just as desperately, and just as unsuccessfully, as she had striven for her father's love. She did all kinds of unnecessary things for Harry to win his love, which was her father's love once removed. Telling patients that they have with uncanny prescience refound the objects of their childhoods is tricky. They tend not to believe us. "How could I know she would turn out like that; it wasn't at all that way in the beginning." The therapist hammers away, massing evidence, yet the resistance continues. The wise therapist backs off, waiting for the interpretation to "take," and the resistance diminishes. Ultimately, the patient does believe us, but feels accused of being some kind of fool, and proceeds to rage against the self. "How could I have been such an asshole, falling in love with a creep just like my father and not even knowing it?" Mary reacted both ways simultaneously, not really believing my interpretation, yet lashing herself for being an "idiot." I suggested that she was angry at me for telling her that Harry was Father, and that she would do anything to be assured of his love. She replied, "I'm not angry at you. I'm ashamed — it's humiliating for me to know that you know I'm such a fool." Finally, on the inside, working within our relationship. But not for long. My subsequent relational comments fell on seemingly deaf ears, so I stopped making them.

The focus of our sessions moved to Mary's marriage. Not surprisingly, it closely paralleled her relationship with her boss. Joe was a "nice" guy who was reliable, hardworking, good-looking, but not particularly emotionally available or affection-ate. Mary was forever looking for signs of his love, but gleaned strikingly slim pickings. Dissatisfied and angry, she felt guilty about feeling that way. I told her that she was afraid to feel, let alone express, her frustration for fear of losing the little love she had. She replied, "Most women would be thrilled with Joe." I returned, "I don't know about most women, but you're not."

Excepting our discussion of adolescent sleeping around, Mary had spoken but little about sex, indicating that her marital relationship was "satisfying." The session following my insistence that she was dissatisfied with her marriage, she opened up with a startling communication. "I was making love with Joe last night, and was about to come, when I started to yell out, 'Oh, Jerry,' and just caught myself in time. I suppose I should have yelled, 'Oh, Dr. Levin,' but that seemed ridiculous. Do you mind that it was Jerry? I'm scared. I don't want Joe to know that I'm in love with you."

Well, so much for working on the outside with a therapeutic alliance with little or no transference. This was transference with a vengeance. (It turned out that vengeance was a well-chosen word.) That session was the opening of the most intense and prolonged erotic transference I've ever dealt with. Session after session, Mary spoke of having multiple orgasms masturbating completely nude in front of a full-length mirror thinking of me. "I've never had sexual pleasure like that. I didn't know I was capable of it." For the first time, she wasn't depressed.

Mary had a wonderful time during the ensuing months. I didn't. I had always found her attractive, and I was not unaroused by her vivid accounts of her sessions before the full-length mirror. She herself was clearly excited by "sharing" her masturbatory activities with me. Initially, I was pleased that she had made some sort of breakthrough and that she was, for the first time, deeply enjoying her sexuality; and naturally I was pleased that she was no longer depressed. I figured I could handle my titillation, and at no time was I seriously concerned that I would act on or out my sexual feelings for Mary. Nevertheless, I was increasingly uncomfortable. Not wanting to spoil the experience for her, not really understanding what was happening, I said nothing for a long time. Along with expressions of overtly sexual feelings for me, Mary expressed wonderment at my compassion, empathy, understanding, and devoted attention to her. She greatly exaggerated both my concern for and interest in her, and my capacity for empathy, understanding, and giving devoted attention. My wife, with whom I have an excellent and satisfying relationship, could have done some instant reality testing with Mary, giving her a far more accurate account of my capacities for those virtues. At times, I thought of telling Mary that, and I have had supervisees do the equivalent with disastrous consequences. Mary needed to go through this stage of idealized, erotic love. Premature interpretation (as I write this, its sexual equivalent occurs to me) would have been narcissistically injurious. It would have been just as much a betrayal of her trust as acting on her advances. Therapists suffer the narcissistic injury of not being loved by their patients (cf. Freud's letter to Lou Andreas-Salomé 1966), and no less the injury of being loved by patients. They know that such love isn't "real" (or is it?); in either case, that love can't be reciprocated, and that is often painful. For all of her open sexuality, there was a childlike innocence and delight in Mary's exhibitionism, and there were other things as well.

I let the transference unfold for several months until it became apparent that it wasn't unfolding at all — we were at an impasse, and each session was a repeat of the previous one. Freud (1914b) said that in the transference, the patient acts instead of remembering; that is, the feelings toward and fantasies about the therapist are an enactment of, rather than a remembrance of, archaic traumatic events, feelings, and relationships. As such, the transference is a resistance — a resistance to affectively reexperiencing the past in its pastness, and working it through.

Following his development of the structural model (1923), Freud (1926) conceptualized resistance as coming from the three agencies of the mind: First, the resistance from the id, deriving from what he alternately envisioned as the "adherence of the libido" and the "conservatism of the instincts" (in short, humans give up nothing gladly). Second, the resistance from the ego, which is threefold: that induced by repression, meaning psychological defenses in general, which protects the ego from the threatening and forbidden; that coming from reluctance to give up the "secondary gains" of the illness; and the transference, which circumvents the remembrance of the "strangulated affect" and "reminiscences" from which the neurotic suffers. In one of his most powerful strokes of genius, Freud saw that the resistance of the transference could be the vehicle of cure, and transference interpretation became the essence of analytic technique. Third, the resistance from the superego—guilt, the feeling the patient has that he doesn't deserve to get well, which is the basis of the "negative therapeutic reaction," the seemingly baffling phenomenon of the patient feeling worse as he gets better. Freud thought that this last resistance, the resistance from the superego, was the most difficult to overcome.

It was clear that the time to interpret the transference had come. In his papers on technique (1912, 1913), Freud says that the analyst should maintain silence as long as the patient is following the basic rule (saying whatever comes to mind) and producing material. Mary was producing nothing new, so analytic technique said interpretation was called for. Although we were doing psychodynamic psychotherapy, not analysis, Freud's advice seemed apropos. So I interpreted.

I might as well have been talking to the moon. At first, I used a "genetic" interpretation, telling Mary that her love for me and sexual attraction and excitement were a repetition of her feelings for her father. I, like him, was unavailable, and her love for me was bound to be just as frustrated as her love for him. I worked the erotic oedipal side of the street, and the tender, yearning, rebuffed side of the street. All to no avail. Mary said, "I don't feel the least frustrated loving you; I've never enjoyed my body the way I do now. My father is too old for me; I don't even know if he can get it up anymore." I thought that I was probably older than her father, and felt hurt by my fantasy that she would reject me if she knew that, but said, "It's the feelings you had for your father when you were 4 or 5, more than those you have for him now, that you feel for me," or something to that effect. She smiled and said, "Nonsense, it's you. You're kind and sexy; I know I can't have your body because of that professional nonsense, but I don't care—I get in front of that mirror anyway. As long as I don't cry out your name when I'm with Joe, everything will be fine." The patient was saying that her love was real, just as real and just as transferential as any other love. Over the ensuing weeks, I varied my expression of the same message to no effect until I gave up, and Mary's delight contributed to my increasing discomfort. Mary's "love" was unrequited, and she didn't mind at all. Something was wrong. This didn't make sense.

I finally started telling her that she really knew very little about me, so that she must be in love with her fantasy of me, not with me, and that fantasy must come from her past. I was reluctant to do that. I didn't want to tell her that her reality wasn't real, although in some sense, I "knew" it wasn't, and I didn't want to needlessly hurt her. (I have no difficulty saying things I know to be hurtful if they will serve some useful purpose [see my comment, "Your father tried to drown you" in Chapter 2].) Freud, in one of his less fortunate similes, said that the analyst must be like the surgeon, ruthlessly excising the pathological to preserve the healthy. Although I rarely think of, or wish to think of, myself as a surgeon, the image sometimes fits the situation, and when it does, I have no difficulty assimilating to it. But here I wasn't sure it would serve any purpose. I felt that this "interpretation" was more to lessen her obsession with me, which was starting to drive me crazy, than for her benefit. I generally tell supervisees to carefully dose or avoid comments like these, as they are generally injurious and ineffective. Although I had doubts, I decided that making myself more comfortable was important and worthwhile, yet I felt vaguely guilty telling Mary that she couldn't be in love with me since she didn't know me. I needn't have worried. She smiled and said, "The only thing I don't know about you is the size of your penis, but I have fantasies." I thought, "You bitch," feeling angry, a countertrans-ferential feeling, in the broad sense, that cast a new light on her behavior. In a countertransferential acting out, I said, "I'm not what you think I am." I realized that I'd been trying to hurt her because I felt teased, and was tempted to try to "fix" my slip. Fortunately, I thought better of it, deciding to let bad enough alone. By then, I was rattled and probably would have made matters worse. Mary left the session delighted; she had gotten a reaction from me.

Of course, the more analytic way of handling Mary's comment

would have been to say, "Tell me more about your fantasy," which presumably would have elicited oedipal and preoedipal fantasies about her father, but I neither had the aplomb to do so, nor had much conviction that approach would have been productive.

With my being now, once again, silent, our sessions continued in much the same way. I dreaded them. I now felt the hostility in the teasing behind the seduction, and was having trouble with it. I wanted to tell her that she was enticing me, knowing that I couldn't respond, and that such hostile teasing must have driven her father away from her, costing her his love. That was probably partly true, but my motivation for saying so would have been mostly retaliatory and I knew it. Besides, I was sure that her hostility was so far from consciousness that even a far more tactful statement of it would have been incomprehensible to her. In thinking about the remoteness, from her consciousness, of what I by now thought of as her sadism, I remembered the quality of innocent wonderment in her first account of her masturbation before the full-length mirror, and suddenly I felt that I understood what was going on. It was Kohut, not Freud, who illuminated these "dynamics of the transference." Mary's behavior was about mirroring: It took place before a mirror—in fact, two mirrors, a literal one, and me. What she wanted from me was not to sleep with her, but to enjoy and reflect her (developmentally) phase-appropriate grandiose exhibitionism, exactly as Kohut described it as a normal developmental stage, albeit in a highly sexualized manner. Most if not all of Mary's sexuality had been a search for such mirroring, approval, and admiration, which she had never received from her beloved and longed-for father. Oedipal yes, but far more saliently, preoedipal. Mary was fixated in some ways to Kohut's stage of the archaic, grandiose, bipolar self, and in an uncannily precise way, had reenacted instead of remembering her desperate attempt to get her father's love and attention, explicitly his mirroring of her then phase-appropriate grandiose exhibitionism. Her innocence had been the joy of a child running naked through

the house. It was the narcissistic, not the erotic, desperation that
was basic. Further, she was using her "femininity," the rejected
part of her, to evoke mirroring. In what was probably a
recapitulation, she had almost elicited rejection from me as she
escalated the attempt to get the response she wanted and needed.
I no longer felt uptight with her.

Kohut (1971, 1977) recommends that the analyst sit still for the
transference and "simply" enjoy it as a parent enjoys a small
child's archaic exhibitionism. This is, so to speak, a nonverbal
transference gratification. But Kohut does not recommend gratifying the transference; rather, he recommends interpreting it.
He is concerned to distinguish himself from his teacher, Franz
Alexander (1943), who advocated a "corrective emotional experience" in therapy; rather, Kohut says he wants to analyze the
transference, but his practice belies his theory, and it is difficult
to know what the Kohutian analyst would do in a given situation.
In this case, I took Kohut's advice to interpret, and started telling
Mary that she wanted me to enjoy her excitement and her
newfound sexuality, and to admire her boldness in her enact-
ments before the mirror. The more I restated my basic thought
that she wanted me to mirror her in language that she could
understand, the less she teased me. She stopped acting and
started to remember—to remember with deep feeling her prolonged, unsuccessful, excruciatingly painful attempts at getting
her father's attention. I now related her current masochistic
relationships with her boss and her husband to those memories
and those feelings. For the first time, she heard that, and started
to be more assertive with both her boss and her husband.

Now I interpreted the communicative side of her erotic
transference. That is, how she induced feelings of frustration in
me, knowing that I knew I could not have her, the "exciting
object," both so I would know how she had felt, and to punish me
for my unresponsiveness to her. Mary was now able to understand this. Only at the very end did I interpret the rage behind
her hostile teasing as narcissistic rage engendered by her father's
and mother's failure to mirror her. Successively, her erotic

transference was understood by us in Kohutian, in oedipal, and in object relational terms, and proved to be a vehicle of insight and mutation.

Mary now, in effect, renegotiated her marriage, getting more from Joe while accepting his limitations. She quit her job and had the first of two children. Shortly after getting pregnant, she terminated. A year later, she called and asked if she could stop in and see me for a few moments. Her request seemed odd, but I agreed. Mary arrived beaming with her baby. She was radiantly happy and expressed gratitude that I had helped make her present state of being possible. I remembered that Freud had equated penis, feces, and baby, and thought that that was his problem, yet in some sense, this woman who felt so castrated had overcome that feeling in becoming a mother. As she left, she said, "A part of me still wishes that I had met you in some other way; it wasn't all what you call transference—you're really very nice and cute too." With that, she picked up her baby, said she was expecting another, and left. I never saw her again.

SAM: A JILTED "INNOCENT" DEVELOPS NARCISSISTIC RAGE

Sam was referred by an EAP. Employee Assistance Programs are far more prevalent these days than they were even a few years ago. They are evaluation, assessment, and short-term treatment facilities within businesses, industries, labor unions, government agencies, and educational facilities. Their basic function is referral and case management. Originally concerned exclusively with alcohol abuse and alcoholism, they now "service," if that is the right word, employees with all sorts of problems. In the old days (the first EAP was at DuPont in the '40s), they were staffed with recovering alcoholics deeply committed to AA who usually lacked professional training. Now most EAP counselors have at least a master's level mental health degree, although the preponderance of them still come from a background of personal

recovery. EAPs deal with two classes of clients: "mandated"—
those with alcohol, drug, or emotional problems that have so
affected their job performance that they must either cooperate
with the EAP counselor's treatment recommendations or be
terminated; and "voluntary" clients—who essentially use the EAP
as a referral source. For many therapists, EAPs are an important
source of patients, and relating to them usually entails "political"
considerations that are incongruent with the therapist's professional self-concept, that incongruity inducing some degree of
tension and narcissistic injury. The quality of EAPs varies from
magnificent service organizations to management busybodies.
Working with them raises issues of confidentiality, treatment
philosophy, and the use of coercion in mandated treatment,
issues the therapist must confront and work through for him- or
herself. Referrals from EAPs for unrequited love are certainly
atypical.

I had ambivalent feelings toward Tony, the EAP counselor,
and I guess he had ambivalent feelings toward me. Tony had
serious doubts about me and my professional activities; I was too
"long-term," too highfalutin, and too intellectual, yet there was
another side of Tony that respected me. I wasn't of much use, but
in some sense, I was a class act. As Tony put it, I was trying to
fix all the chips and cracks in those "damaged plates" (mostly
alcohol and drug users) that he sent me, while all he wanted was
some glue on the pieces where the plate had cracked in two. "Just
stick the pieces together and don't worry about fixing up the
edges; they were chipped before they cracked, and I'm not paying
for restoration. You're a damn museum curator; I need a repair
shop." An interesting metaphor for an aggressively "dees and
dose" anti-intellectual, who characterized himself as a recovering
pecker-checker (an allusion to his activities in his Army medic
days). I seldom received referrals from Tony, but occasionally
would invite him to speak to my analytic or graduate seminars to
expose students to the "real" world of practice. At some level we
wanted each other's approval, and knew that we didn't have it.
Although I enjoyed Tony's rough-guy humor, I also felt devalued

by him. I had business reasons to maintain my relationship with him, but I knew that my involvement continued for other more personal, dynamic reasons; dealing with intangibles, part of me wanted validation from a pecker-checking "realist," and I was angry at myself for wanting it. I was exposing myself to narcissistic injury unnecessarily. Years of teaching and supervising have led me to believe that similar aspirations and conflicts are endemic, albeit usually denied, among dynamic psychotherapists.

I hadn't heard from Tony in a long time when the phone rang, and without introduction he said, "I've got a long-term one for you. He's not a boozer—he's a loony. Want him?" "What's the *DSM-III-R* number for loony?" I replied. "Oh, you know, a nut job, with pussy trouble, big pussy trouble—he wants to check out, so if you want to check him into the flight deck (AA-ese for mental ward, especially one with very sick patients), it's okay with me. Seriously, take good care of him; he's a big-shot TV writer, and his company wouldn't, like, exactly be thrilled with us (Tony worked for an "outhouse" EAP; that is, one that contracts to provide EAP services for a number of corporations, as contrasted with inhouse EAPs, which are far more common and are part of the organizations they service), if *you* lost him." "If *I* lost him; I feel set up." "Oh, come on, Jer. He ain't too suicidal, and he wants to talk—you like that stuff. Why don't you see him? Call me if he needs a locked door—I've authorized all the treatment you want to give him. Sam has your number," and Tony hung up.

Feeling simultaneously manipulated and flattered, I was curious about this case. Tony, highly intelligent in spite of his strenuous efforts to hide it, was an excellent assessor, so I decided to see Sam. Tony did know the *DSM-III-R*, but "suicidal but not too suicidal" was probably more to the point, meaning that he was treatable as an office patient. I hoped to God that Tony had this one right.

Sam proved to be a strikingly handsome man, quietly dressed in a button-down and tweeds that looked as if they aspired to be but were not Brooks. He had the aura of a man who always had women for the asking. He seemed anything but depressed. As soon as he spoke, it was clear why his telecommunication conglomerate didn't want him to "check out." He spoke with precision, yet with resonance; he always seemed to find the right word or phrase, coming up with images, similes, and metaphors that enabled you to visualize that of which he spoke. His use of language was seductive. I looked forward to his sessions for the sheer enjoyment of listening to him talk; it took me a long time to realize that he was far better at evoking places and events than in conveying the lived reality of human experience; he could indeed paint word pictures of people that rang true, being far better at this than most of us, yet they weren't on the same level as his word pictures of towns and landscapes, disasters, corruptions, crimes, and wars. It wasn't that they lacked empathy; it was more that his empathy was "as if"; that is, he spoke of people as if he had empathy for them. Nor did he seem to be lacking in feeling; his range of affect, which turned out to be mostly depressed, was not extensive, but it didn't appear to lack depth. I was envious of his linguistic talent and his verbal facility. Those striking metaphors and vivid images were effortless. They poured forth spontaneously; he was not a hesitant or a calculating speaker.

Well into the treatment, I realized how central and crippling a defense his use of language was, how much it kept him on the surface — a dazzling surface, to be sure — as if he painted emotion brilliantly without feeling it deeply, or better, not feeling important parts of it deeply. I tried to explain that to him, tried to slow him down and break the beautiful flow of his speech, but I got nowhere. Although Sam's style was simple and direct rather than rococo, I was reminded of the late Henry James, who tries so elaborately to convey the precise nuances of feeling while failing to evoke the feeling in the, or at least this, reader. Sam almost died of his talent, which was so ego-syntonic and so much a pillar of his self-esteem that for all his intelligence and all my efforts, he never understood that, magnificently adaptive as it was, it was no less fatally restrictive. My failure to successfully interpret this proved to be paradigmatic of the entire treatment. For the most part, I simply couldn't get through. Frustrated and hurt, I felt like a member of the TV audience for whom he wrote, whose only function was to boost ratings, yet I know that I actually meant a lot to him. It was a puzzlement. Sam proved to be a narcissistic personality disorder, and the feelings of frustration and superfluity I felt were typical of countertransference with narcissists. I knew this, yet felt narcissistically injured anyway. The fact that I could not find a way to use my countertransference (in a broad sense) therapeutically was the most frustrating aspect of the case (see the objectification and retaliation — how I am flattening him out — making him into an esthetic surface, a "case" — just as he did to me). Whenever I tried to break through his defenses, it bombed; he simply didn't understand what I was talking about.

Although his demeanor was not depressed, Sam was eloquent in describing his pain, which was real enough. He was in contact with his pain, but had no inkling of the fury underneath it. He described how, after having been jilted, he was alone on assignment in a hotel room, had had a few drinks (he was a life-style rather than problem drinker), opened the window, loosened his tie, removed his jacket, and stepped onto the sill. He stood there a long time feeling no fear and wanting to jump. For no reason he was conscious of, he didn't. After that, he called Tony, and told him about almost checking out. Asking for help had been galling for him. When I asked him to speculate why he might have stepped down from the window, he thought a long time before saying, "I guess I didn't want to give her the satisfaction, and yeah, maybe my kids were in the back of my mind somewhere." Sam's order of priorities here pretty well reflected and exemplified who he was.

Sam's focus was almost entirely on *her*. "How could she have done it to me? Why did she do it? Why? Why? Why?" Getting Sam to talk about Sam proved extremely difficult. What he wanted was for me to analyze Jennifer, and to tell him why she had jilted him. Somehow, if he could understand why, he could accept it. I empathized with his desire to understand, but my suggestion that it took two to tango fell on deaf ears. Eventually, I succeeded in tapping his joy in narration, his undoubted gift for story-telling. Once he started relating the events leading up to his crisis, he spoke easily and openly about his entire life. Blithely unaware of the problematic nature of his actions, he seemingly lacked the shame that drives much resistance. This openness was punctuated every five or ten sentences with "Why did Jennifer turn on me?", which I pretended to regard as rhetorical. As he told it, Sam's life had been one prolonged narcissistic injury. His tone wasn't self-pitying, but the content somehow was — yet his injuries were real.

Sam had been born into a large immigrant family in Appalachia. Living on the fringe of a medium-sized city, they were dirt poor, the father supplementing subsistence farming on marginal land with mining and factory work. Although rarely actually hungry, Sam had vivid memories of his father having no money to buy the kids an ice-cream cone, of scant Christmas presents, of rusted cars that wouldn't start, and of running out of fuel. Worst of all, Sam was bused to a school where the kids had middle-class parents who could buy them fashionable clothes and petty — sometimes not so petty — luxuries. He was the "hick," the "hunky," the despised and scorned Tobacco Road scum. As luck would have it, the school district was so drawn that most of his "peers" went to a rural school, so he was one of a small number of the bused impoverished. Sam discovered young that he was far smarter than his tormentors, and developed a compensatory secret pride, which was still with him. His pride was real and conscious; not so his deep feelings of shame and inferiority, which were 90 percent unconscious. Sam was routinely severely beaten if he "acted uppity" or disobeyed his demanding, impossible-to-please father. These beatings were not motivated by cruelty or lack of love; they were culturally syntonic, and driven by marginality and desperation. Sam knew this. Nevertheless, he hated his father for having beaten him. Like all children who are beaten, he unconsciously concluded that he was "bad" and felt humiliation at having been beaten, with deleterious effects on his self-esteem. Under his feelings of badness was a strong desire for revenge. His feelings of entitlement flowed from his feeling that the world owed him one for having scorned him and for having given him such a severe father. The mother, constantly pregnant and struggling to eke out a cash crop and take care of a home, gave Sam as much warmth and attention as was possible. Again, Sam knew this and felt simultaneously lucky and cheated.

Therapists underrate the hidden injuries of social class, the narcissistic injuries inherent in class distinctions, racial discrimination, and social snobbery in general. Snobberies at all levels cut deeply and children are particularly vulnerable to them. Sinclair Lewis never recovered from being treated as a provincial at Yale, and other examples are legion. I recall working with a 50-year-old, spectacularly successful professional man who literally took a year to be able to tell me that he hadn't received a bid for a fraternity as an undergraduate, so deep was his shame at this rejection. The wounds from Sam's experience as a farm boy in a suburban school never healed; they weren't scars, they were bleeding lacerations. Sam cringed as he described the bus trip from the school surrounded by trim, well-kept if average homes, into the dilapidated fringe of the urban area where he would be let off on a dirt road, half a mile from his tumbledown farm with its outhouse and bare boards. He remembered his humiliation at his patched clothing and worn shoes.

There was a tragic incident in which one of his brothers accidentally stabbed a friend who consequently died, which cast the family into gloom for years. It was treated as a disgrace, a disgrace for the whole family, so Sam accrued yet more shame, so to speak, by association. Then a highway was put through, and the father had a chance to make big money. He was conned, and made nothing. As with Freud and his father, the degradation of an ideal object, his ambivalently loved yet greatly admired father, narcissistically injured the son.

Before he got out of high school, Sam learned that his good looks, brains, and high grades impressed girls. He gave up on being accepted by the boys who valued cars and athletic prowess, neither of which he had. Sam succeeded in sleeping with several girls, who all regarded him as exotic, exciting to be with, but not someone to be serious about. Sam had probably found the wildest girls in the school and didn't understand that they wanted him for excitement, to rebel, or to hurt somebody else. He wasn't in love with any of them, yet he took their ultimate rejections hard.

One of the few times, except in talking about Jennifer's rejection, that Sam wept was when he told me that his father had taken $100 out of his pocket, handed it to him, and said, "Ain't much, but it's all I can give you," when Sam went off to the state university. The only member of his family to obtain an education or to climb out of poverty, Sam had something like survival guilt for having left the others behind, alongside of contempt for his blue-collar siblings. Secretly, he was both ashamed of them and felt that he was no better than they — just Polack white trash. Sam worked tremendously hard at the university, getting a part-time media job that became full time, so that he worked full time and went to school full time. He was successful from the beginning. At college, his womanizing became compulsive, and just as he was about to graduate, he "knocked up" a town girl. He married her, cheated on her from the honeymoon on, and had three children by her. Seemingly living his variant of the American dream, he soon had the house in the suburbs complete with picket fence, dog, and children. Traveling extensively, he was able to pull off his split life, being by his lights a good Daddy and a providing, supportive, if not genuinely loving husband. His sexual exploits were emotionally meaningless, and he never thought of breaking up his marriage. Then fate rang thrice. A rival was promoted over him, subjecting him to harassment and devaluation at work; his brother was crippled in a farm accident; and he met Jennifer — narcissistic injuries all.

Now he had the worst assignments, his work was criticized and revised; he was haunted by his completely paralyzed brother, somehow feeling responsible and very much in contact with his own mortality; and perhaps worst of all, for the first time in his life, he was in love. Sam knew his wife loved him, and for all his philandering, tried not to hurt her. Aware that he resented her for pressuring him into marriage just as the world was opening for him, he consciously tried not to punish her for it, but now things were different. He wanted to be with Jennifer all the time. Beautiful, educated, a rising media star, she was everything his plain, unsophisticated wife was not. Ellen might be decent and good, but that counted for nothing compared with Jennifer's glamor. A real soap-opera cliché, but Sam thought that he was living something nobody had ever lived before. Delusions of uniqueness are dangerous, grandiosity setting itself up for a fall—the fall came; it couldn't have come at a worse time— hurting at work, struggling to help his family deal with a crippled brother, convinced that he too would die, he really needed Jennifer. When she was promoted to headquarters in New York, Sam used all of his ingenuity to arrange a rendezvous with her. Passion aplenty there was, but it would have been clear to a 2-year-old that she had no commitment to him and didn't want any. With a blindness that amounted to a psychotic denial of reality, Sam couldn't see that. If love is blind, so is justice. A year later, Sam finagled a job in New York. Careerwise it was a good opportunity, but that wasn't what excited him. He badgered Jennifer into agreeing that he would move in with her, left his wife and children, and moved to New York. When he went to Jennifer, she literally slammed the door in his face. From there to the windowsill was a short distance.

What was I going to do with this?—a guy whose character pathology was so ego-syntonic that I might as well have been talking in Sanskrit when I called his attention to it, whose reality testing in relevant areas was nil, and who wanted me to analyze his ex-girlfriend's motives. I decided that the best I could do was to put him in contact with his rage. That might lessen his depression and reduce the suicide risk, which I didn't think was too high. That brings us to *narcissistic rage* and its management. Kohut (1978) distinguishes between aggression and narcissistic rage. If I am being aggressive toward you, I may kill you, but your murder will be instrumental and incidental to my obtaining the object of my aggression—your job, money, food, whatever. I am sure you find the instrumentality of your murder comforting. Of course, ethical restraints may save your life and I may aggress in less direct ways. Not so in the case of narcissistic rage. If you are the object of my narcissistic rage, your murder is of the essence. Narcissistic rage is an unquenchable thirst for vengeance for narcissistic injury; it is the rage of the unmirrored self avenging itself for humiliation and shame. It is the ineluctable concomitant of narcissistic injury. Kohut's preeminent examples are Captain Ahab in *Moby Dick*, and the Nazis' orgy of murder. Murder in the interest of self-aggrandizement can overlap with murder in the service of vengeance. Kohut views narcissistic rage as the most dangerous emotion in man, responsible for all of the horrors perpetuated by man, except those motivated by rapacity. Narcissistic rage turned against the self results in addiction, self-mutilation, other forms of self-destruction, and suicide. Kohut's notion importantly differs from the drive-theory notion that aggression is innate, and that in Freud's stark vision, Thanatos must be externalized lest it destroy us: the choice is between murder and suicide. Kohut's notion has much more in common with Guntrip's (1971) thought that "Hate is love made angry," which makes it no less murderous. More a frustration-aggression hypothesis than a drive notion, Kohut's narcissistic rage, as I understand it, partakes of both—innateness and environmental provocation. In his essay "On Narcissism" (1914a), Freud referred to "His Majesty, the Baby"; when that baby is offended, when his grandiosity is threatened, when acts of lèse majesté are committed, his reaction is "Off with their heads!" The corollary of the notion of narcissistic rage secondary to archaic grandiosity is that anything that reduces archaic or reactive grandiosity replacing it with realistic self-esteem reduces narcissistic rage.

Oral, anal, or narcissistic, Sam had sufficient rage to wipe out a continent. How to work with it? First understand it. Elaborating and modifying Kohut, I see narcissistic rage as arising not only from narcissistic injury but also from narcissistic vulnerability. A portion of narcissistic rage is self-hatred projected outward. At some level, Sam "knew" he was an "asshole" who had had many warning signals along the way and had set himself up for traumatic rejection. That contemporaneous source of self-hatred linked up with the self-hatred residual from being the Polack, the beaten, the scorned, the reviled, the member of a family who killed somebody, and the crippler of his brother by his having "abandoned" the family (of origin). Then, like all addicts, he unconsciously hated himself for his compulsive sexuality; that too was projected outward. Now reinternalized, it was dangerous. So the first task was to put Sam in touch with his rage and help him verbalize it. That much was accomplishable. The achievement of a significant amount of insight was not. In a condition of narcissistic vulnerability, we are totally at the mercy of the environment, the whips and scorns of time do what they will with us. Our self-esteem is totally hostage to the wheel of fortune. So, after helping patients verbalize and express their rage—a rage composed of bottled-up aggression, self-hatred, unexpressed and perhaps unexperienced anger, and reaction to narcissistic injury, the therapeutic task is raising self-esteem, remediating self-deficits through *transmuting internalization*, and reducing narcissistic vulnerability by strengthening the ego. That of course is the goal of all analytic therapy. Transmuting internalization is the Kohutian (1971, 1977) notion that optimal frustration leads to internalization of the self-object function, which the therapist's tolerable failure of empathy did not provide. Winnicott puts it more poetically when he says, "We succeed by failing." What the therapist can do besides giving the patient help in verbalizing and ventilating his or her rage is to help parse it out into self-hatred projected outward, anger turned against the self, His Majesty the Baby stuff—the rage of offended grandiosity, and the rage that comes from having such low self-esteem that any rebuff is narcissistically injurious. Having labels for these components of rage breaks down an overwhelming emotion into more manageable bits and increases the patient's sense of ego mastery, thus increasing self-esteem. The therapist must also be on the lookout for the defensive use of rage, usually to avoid feeling guilt and shame. Others use the intensity of rage as a way of countering feelings of deadness and to feel alive. The eroti-cizing of rage is well known, so rage can also be a sexual equivalent. These dynamics make for "rage-aholics."

As Sam got in contact with and expressed his rage at Jennifer, his depression lessened, and he started taking pleasure in his work again. Coming to New York was a repeat of being bused to the city school. Supporting two households, with a better title than financial compensation, the best he could do was to clothe himself in pseudo–Brooks Brothers. It was the patches again. City women were "too sophisticated" for him. We talked about the connection between his present pain and past pain, especially about the parallels between his quest for his father's love and his quest for Jennifer's, except this time, departing for bigger things, he got slapped in the face instead of being given a hundred dollars. It all helped, yet Sam didn't change much. I tried him in my group. It didn't work. He had no real interest in the men or their problems, and was either intimidated by the women or tried to seduce them. Pointing this out to him accomplished nothing. When the group suggested that Jennifer had rejected him because she figured he would do the same thing to her that he had done to his wife, he looked baffled. Jennifer's having dumped him for a less spectac-ular lower-level co-worker who was reliably there, and who elicited Sam's contempt, leant credibility to the group's hypothe-sis. In a sense, she had chosen Sam's wife instead of him. Sam dropped out of the group shortly thereafter.

In individual sessions, Sam continued to inquire into Jennifer's motives. He just couldn't get out of the victim role, always seeing Jennifer's rejection as unrelated to his own behavior. I managed to help him work through and mourn some of his childhood injuries. He strenuously resisted the mourning, yet substantially benefited from it. The same was true of his rebuffs at work and of his brother's injury. He found less and less to talk about in therapy. Now going from one woman to another, he no longer needed me, so he left therapy less depressed but essentially unchanged. There was no way I could tell Sam so that he could hear it that his problem wasn't unrequited love, but rather the inability to love.

Sam's predominant emotion was shame, repressed, split off, denied. Sam evidenced an eerily absent sense of guilt toward his wife and children. If we had been more successful in making his shame conscious, he would have had a better chance to work it through and have a better therapeutic result. At the risk of adding needlessly to the already voluminous talmudic distinctions between shame and guilt, I offer my understanding of that distinction. Shame involves other people; guilt involves internal objects. When we are feeling ashamed, we are fearful that someone else will see our inadequacies, our humiliations by other people, or our pleasures in the forbidden; guilt is different. The spectator is inside, and what we fear is loss of love of the superego and its savage punishments, to which we submit in order to regain its love. The superego was once our parents, so guilt comes from transgressing the dictates of others. Erik Erikson (1969) makes an important distinction between the *moral* and the *ethical*—the moral being the irrational, driven, compulsive morality of the archaic superego, rigid, relentless and savage. Bolstered by resentment turned against the self, it is a Nietzschean reaction-formation, while the ethical is the rational and reasonable product of empathy. The first is pathological, the second is a necessary renunciation to make social life possible. Freud thought that shame, unlike guilt, was not object relational. Rather, it was a phylogenetic inheritance going back to our relinquishing of anal and fecal sniffing when our species acquired uprightness, and, our shame in still yearning for these pleasures. It becomes object relational only when the olfactory evolves into the moral and we become ashamed of being seen enjoying the phylogenetically more primitive. In short, I feel guilty either because my internalized parents (the moral) tell me I am doing wrong, or because my "capacity for concern" (Winnicott 1965) and renunciation of the egoistic for the sake of the social convinces me that I have done wrong (the ethical), while I feel shame when I feel others will witness my degradation or humiliation, either through instinctual regression or through my mistreatment by others.

Working with patients like Sam is difficult for therapists. Such patients' self-absorption and lack of capacity for insight make us feel futile. Although I felt frustrated, I rarely felt angry with him; for all his scintillating surface, he was pathetic. My basic countertransference feeling was pity. Interestingly enough, I hadn't felt pity for Roberta or for Sally, the horror of their childhoods notwithstanding. Perhaps not being self-pitying, they induced no pity, but more saliently, their capacity for growth elicited admiration more than anything else.

The problems with working with Sams are present in almost all therapies. We analysts and dynamicists pride ourselves on our intellectual acumen, if not on our brilliance, on our ability to interpret mutatively, and on our mastery of difficult theories, yet so much of what we do is simply being there. Listening is often boring. Our most brilliant interpretations glance off, changing nothing; our theories and rigorous training seem little more than cognitive dissonance devices to raise our self-esteem — and fees — and the patients either don't benefit, or seem to cure themselves. Here is enough narcissistic injury to drive anyone out of the business. Yet we stay. Why? Finding out that 90 percent of our most penetrating, profound interpretations are not mutative, while just shutting up is, hurts. It offends our grandiosity, yet that confrontation, if successful, eventuates in professional growth. Realizing how limited, yet vital, our influence is, as Freud did in "Analysis Terminable and Interminable" (1937), we come to terms with our disappointment, our boredom, and hunker down to slug it out in the trenches without much glamor, seldom seeing breakthroughs, yet achieving an inviolate professional self-esteem that knows the importance of our merely being there, and can settle for the 10 percent of our more intellectual activity that is mutative. It is not that therapy doesn't work; it does. It's that most of what we do is to set the stage for self-cures. At some point we realize that setting the stage isn't so bad, and enjoy it all the more the times when we do get to speak some lines in the drama that speed along and influence the resolution of that drama. It is a far more modest role than we initially thought we had. Coming to terms with that involves a relinquishing of grandiosity that can only be accomplished through a mourning process. As in any renunciation, sadness precedes reconciliation.

Treatment of those narcissistically injured by unrequited love is particularly narcissistically injurious for the therapist. The scorned and rejected lover has thoughts only for the beloved, never for us. We provide a sort of chorus of one to comment on the action—the action being the vicissitudes of the lover's infatuation, pursuit, and failure to obtain his or her goal—possession of the idealized object. We are a chorus whose words, unless they echo the lover's lament or provide hope that the beloved will yet be won, are ignored. Our professional activity, the provision of insight and the weaving of a tapestry in which past and present are threaded together, has little value, and we are expected to deliver the goods—the beloved—which of course we cannot do. None of this does much for our professional self-esteem. Listening to the spurned gets boring as we oscillate between empathy and exasperation. Intolerant of our own impatience, which conflicts with our professional ideal self, we judge ourselves aversely and further lower our self-esteem. It is all too easy to proceed to the next step—a combination of projecting our self-dissatisfaction and feeling angry at somebody who is making us feel bad about ourselves, and we become even less enamored with our rejected-lover patient, recapitulating the patient's presenting problem. This new round of "negative" feelings for our patient again conflicts with our ego-ideal, once again causing us pain, pain for which we resent the source. Unless we become aware of what is going on, a vicious cycle results, often ending the treatment.

TOM: DUMPED FOR A ROCK STAR

Thinking about this countertransference dynamic brings to mind a patient much like Sam. Tom was a member of the mega-wealthy. Great-grandfather had made the fortune, but high achievement had continued to characterize the family. Tom had never been a good student and had limped through prodigious schools and colleges, getting through by the skin of his teeth. Since graduation, he had been involved in a series of scatter-brained business schemes in which a variety of con men had been able to part Tom from not insignificant amounts of money. His parents were extremely critical of these activities. By the time I met Tom, he was a classical split between incredible grandiosity derived equally from a developmental arrest and real power in the world, and absolutely abysmal self-esteem consequent upon his failure to live up to family expectations and his barely repressed knowledge that he was a fool, an easy mark for whoever made him feel important. There is an AA slogan to the effect that "only two people, the great 'I am' and 'Poor me,' can get me in trouble," which came to mind in working with Tom, who was not an alcoholic but had all the personality correlatives of alcoholism. Floundering through his twenties, he fell in with a fast, artsy, bohemian crowd where he met an actress (in probably more than one sense of the word) who enjoyed marginal success in off-Broadway theater and who radiated a seemingly magical poise, excitement, glamor, and beauty. One date, and it was all over. Few have been more helplessly in love than Tom, who exempli-fied Plato's insight that love is the child of plenty and poverty — having just enough of that which we lack to know what we are missing, we seek to supplement our lacks by merging with the beloved, who has them in superfluity — or at least so we hope. Tom's actress had the accomplishment, the certainty, and the easy mastery of the world that characterized Tom's ego-ideal. Defying his disapproving parents, which added to her allure, Tom plunged into a torrid and impetuous affair with Zolinda. He had never been so happy. Invidious comparisons of himself with accomplished relatives ceased, and all was joy. Flying on the proverbial wings of lovers, Tom felt the earth become an irrelevancy far below. When his wings failed, he had a long way to fall, and fall he did. His smash into the ground left him bleeding, broken, and barely breathing. The heat that had melted the wax holding his wings was Zolinda's sudden, or what Tom thought was sudden, infatuation with a rock star. She dropped him abruptly. Pleading, pursuing, cajoling, threatening her and her new lover, tears, and rages availed him nothing. Finally, at his parents' insistence, he came for therapy.

"She's a fucking groupie, 34 and a fucking groupie. She's just a piece of meat to him. I love her. He's no Beatle, not even a Jerry Garcia. His voice stinks, and he can't play the guitar. Why the hell does she suck up to him? I'll get her back when he dumps her. A fucking overage groupie. I can't take it. I can't take it when she hangs up on me. I go to all that asshole's concerts, and she runs by me like I'm not there. I can't stand being treated like I don't exist. She loved me; she told me that she loved me. Now she practically sucks him off in public." Six months later, it was still, "She is a fucking groupie. Why? Why? He's a lousy musician— a fucking fad. He'll never last. [As a matter of fact, Zolinda's rock singer was world famous.] She'll crawl back to me." A year later, it was pretty much the same litany. The rock star did eventually drop Zolinda, but instead of groveling back to Tom as his fantasy would have it, she found another.

I came to hate him. "Stop your kvetching already, and get on with your life. You haven't done anything but whine since your first session." Vain, blind, self-important, refusing to believe that anything could be denied to him, he neither worked nor did anything else productive, certainly not work the way I thought therapy patients "should" work. I seemed to have no significance for him whatsoever. I raised his fee and felt better. One day, Tom walked in and said, "I'm in love again. Zolinda's a whore. I don't know why I tortured myself over her. Henrietta's a dancer, with a body like you never saw. I'm so grateful to you. You saved my life; I would never have made it through it if I didn't have these sessions. Thank God my father insisted I get therapy." You could have knocked me over with a feather. I had missed the extraordinary salience I had for him. How transferential Tom's seeming lack of transference actually was became clear only after the fact. As Hegel says, "The owl of Minerva flies only at night."

A SUPERVISEE PANICS

If Tom was an extreme of uninvolvement, frustrating and
narcissistically wounding to work with, Marie was the polar
opposite. Intensely focused on her therapy, she fell hopelessly in
love with her therapist. My supervisee had no idea how to handle
the transference. He constantly mistook love for madness, which,
however closely related, differ. Thornton seemed the ideal
supervisee: conscientious, caring, bright, knowledgeable, and
basically kind. The trouble was that he was overearnest and
overtrained. A psychiatric resident, he had the *DSM-III-R* on
disk in his head and wanted to analyze and interpret everything.
His heart was in the right place; unfortunately his tendency
toward literalness, his stiffness, and his morbid fear of making a
mistake got in his way. There was something excessively narcissistic and self-protecting in his compulsion to "cover his ass," a
self-protection that was discordant with his basic decency and
good will. I wondered how his parents had treated him when he
made a mistake, but he was my supervisee and not my patient.

Few experiences are as narcissistically injurious as bad supervision. Supervisors characteristically make two errors: the first is
a kind of counterresistance, especially prevalent in agency supervision in which the supervisee wants to talk about business
matters, schedules, patient assignments, and agency policy,
avoiding clinical material in which what is supposed to be clinical
supervision becomes administrative supervision, with the supervisor colluding with the resistance, usually because he or she feels
insecure as a clinical supervisor; the injury here is the loss of an
opportunity to learn, carrying the covert message that the
supervisee is incapable of much clinical learning. The second is
far more wounding. It consists in treating the supervisee as a
patient. The supervisee is not. The proper subject of supervision
is the supervisee's work, including his or her countertransference,
and anything that diverts the work from that is a resistance or
counterresistance. To be treated as a neurotic by a supervisor is
humiliating; it carries the message that the supervisee is so

damaged or inadequate that discussions of problems in and with the work would be futile. If that is the case, the proper procedure for the supervisor is to refer the supervisee for treatment—which the supervisee should have been in to start with. "Something from your past is getting in your way here. You should discuss it with your analyst" isn't demeaning. "Your hatred of your father is preventing you from following my suggestion" (supervisor to supervisee) is. It is a form of mind fuck in which role confusion is in the service of power-tripping. Unfortunately, such mind games are rampant in our field. I was fortunate enough to have had wonderful supervision, but I have worked with enough students and have heard all too many stories that would turn hair on end, not to know that the supervisor–supervisee relationship is a luxuriant garden filled with thorns, briars, brambles, and Venus fly traps. Partially a rite of initiation, supervision is sometimes designed to be narcissistically injurious. That is inexcusable. Rigor should not be sadism, and to invite a student or supervisee to make himself vulnerable, only to use that vulnerability as a vehicle for a personal attack disguised as analysis, is unconscionable.

Therefore, I stayed away from interpreting Thornton's "character pathology" and stuck to critiquing his work. Initially, Thornton worked extremely well with Marie. Coming from an impoverished background in a small town in the West, Marie had grown up acutely conscious of her low social status. Unlike Sam, Marie had affluent relatives, which only rubbed salt in her wounds. Her father, a ne'er-do-well, abandoned the family; unable to cope, her mother suffered a nervous breakdown, traumatically witnessed by Marie—searing into her memory a vision of her mother's abrupt, catatonic withdrawal, leaving her to the mercies of her morbidly religious, life-denying, fanatically puritanical, hairbrush-wielding grandmother. Mother recovered, but things were never the same again. A certain security was gone; Mother might revert to her frozen, deathlike state of nonbeing at any moment. She never did, but the threat was omnipresent. Marie was sent away, ostensibly to give her better opportunities with a "rich," probably barely middle-class, relative. Whenever her mother visited, Marie's heart would ache with desire to be taken back home, something she never dared ask for. The anguish of the door closing as Mother departed never left Marie. She didn't return home until she was beginning adolescence. During the years Marie lived with her, the aunt treated her well, except for managing not to see her uncle's not quite overtly abusive sexual inappropriateness, which deepened Marie's feelings of abandonment. Shortly after returning home, she was raped, while alone, by an intruder, an incident which she completely repressed. Afraid to say anything at home lest the fanatically puritanical grandmother put the blame on her and condemn her as a whore, she put it out of her mind so successfully that she couldn't find it. Needless to say, the repressed didn't lack efficacy.

Marie's presenting problem was her daughter's emotional difficulties. It soon became clear that the child's symptomatic distress, evidenced in paranoid ideation of fear of being poisoned, was reactive to a disturbed marriage. With uncanny accuracy, if unfortunate literalness, the child had diagnosed the poisonous relationship of her parents. Thornton had been able to help the child psychopharmacologically. He also correctly diagnosed the significance of the family's dynamics in the child's illness. Referring the child for further psychotherapy, which turned out to be successful, he accrued great value in Marie's eyes. To her, he became godlike. His treatment of Marie now became a couple's therapy. The husband turning out to be unavailable for therapy, Marie eventually became Thornton's individual patient. Marie told Thornton that she had married her husband because he was "stable." She didn't love him and felt guilty about it. Therapy surfaced her rage at her husband, and she shortly left him. The daughter's paranoia resolved. Marie was subject to suicidal depression and murderous rages. She had boundary problems, and easily became her psychotic mother or nonfunctional father. In her rages, she feared killing her daughter. Thornton worked well with all of this. Then Marie began to express her love for Thornton. It evidenced in dreams, in fantasies, and in plain speech. Thornton squirmed, embarrassed and unsure what to do. Marie was able to distinguish between her transference love and her here-and-now warm feelings of gratitude for the real things he'd been able to do for her and her daughter. She saw this much more clearly than did Thornton. By then, the child was doing well, and Marie's rages were rare. Her depressions remained frightening to her, her therapist, and his supervisor. Dr. Thornton couldn't sort out the real from the transferential aspects of her love for him, and was terrified of the "real" aspects of her love. Marie's husband had been a decent, unspectacular, uneducated, emotionally constricted man, which for a man chosen for his stability, was not amazing; while Dr. Thornton was a savior, and an educated man with intellectual and esthetic interests—witness the books, paintings, and tasteful furnishings in his office. Marie, who was highly intelligent, was strongly attracted by these "real" qualities of her therapist. Marie was a diligent reader and esthetically gifted, but the circumstances of her life gave her no access to the kind of man she could have loved. Thornton fitted the bill.

This terrified him, and he used transference interpretation in an increasingly punitive way, to create distance, and to make the situation tolerable for him. Thornton couldn't allow himself to see the real elements in her love for him; that was too hot. She would pour out her yearning for him, and he would tell her that she didn't, she couldn't love him because she didn't really know him, and that she was in love with her fantasy, not with him. That was true as far as it went, but somehow not to the point and certainly not effective in lessening her love, which was his goal. Marie needed to love Thornton, and his inability to allow her to love him was narcissistically injurious, not to mention deleterious to the treatment. He said, "You didn't know your father, just as you don't know me, so you're in love with your fantasy of your father." "My father didn't cure my daughter or help me," replied Marie. "He didn't read books, and he didn't appreciate beauty the way you do." Thornton broke out in a cold sweat. "You see me as the mother you had before her illness who loved you and protected you; that is why you think you love me." Thornton persisted in this vein, elucidating all the ways and all the reasons she didn't love him, until I suggested that he acknowledge that she really did love him, and sit still for her love to pour forth. It wasn't that he was attracted to her then, although he became strongly attracted to her later in the treatment when her love wasn't so desperate and his fear of it not so great. After Thornton changed his tactics and became "less analytical," Marie improved. The narcissistic rage engendered by the narcissistic injury inflicted by Thornton — not only and not primarily by not requiting her love, but much more by denying it and trying to make it go away — lessened, and because this rage had been turned against herself, Marie's depression also lessened.

Freud spoke of the necessity for *therapeutic tact*, the knack of knowing what to say when. The content of Thornton's interpretations of Marie's love was correct, yet it was less than useless because it was delivered unempathically and at the wrong time. In the course of working through that followed Thornton's acknowledgement of Marie's love for him, she herself referred to the transferential meanings of her love for him, and she was able to use these insights mutatively. Freud said that "love is the great teacher," echoing Plato's statement that the pupil learns for love of the teacher. He also said that analysis was the "cure through love." He was right on both counts.

Marie continued to love Thornton as much as ever. The working through and sorting out of the components of her love in no way lessened it, nor did it make the unrequited nature of it less painful for her. Thornton, now much less uptight, was able to empathize with her pain without being patronizing, no easy task. Then the treatment entered its most difficult phase. Marie, with some prodding by Thornton, which I encouraged, remembered being raped. Previously she had reported dreams about the rape but had denied its reality. I encouraged Thornton's rigorous struggle with her resistance to this because I believed that she could not recover without working through the shame and rage associated with it. (I had reasons not relevant in our present discussion for believing that she had really been raped.) Now fully convinced of the reality of having been raped, Marie went through a long period of deep depression, first engaging in self-blame, then feeling horror at having been left alone and having lived in such an emotionally unsafe home that she could not talk about it. Later she felt deep, sustained rage at Mother, Grandmother, and her attacker. Her depression slowly, erratically, lifted. Thornton was magnificently there during all of this; his supervision enabled him to contain his fear that her depression would lead to decompensation or worse and that he would have been to blame for it.

Then Marie reported the following experience. "I was alone, working in the house. I was feeling agitated, afraid, hopeless. As I did my housework, I slowly felt better. I grew calm; my fear left me, and I realized that you were there with me. I wasn't quite sure if you were in the room with me or if you were part of me. I think that it was both. I felt unbelievable joy. The only thing I could compare it to was the joy I felt after the pain and terror of labor, when I held my newborn daughter in my arms. I wept; it was wonderful."

Thornton said to me, "I started to reach for my prescription pad. I feared she was decompensating. You know Marie has always had borderline trends. Her love for me is abnormal; recovering the memory of being raped was beyond her emotional capacity. I fear the worst. Her boundaries are gone and she is hallucinating. The only reason I didn't tell her she was hallucinating and put her on a neuroleptic was that I was afraid of you. I thought you would want me to wait her out. What do you think of neuroleptics against hospitalization?"

I thought, *It's Thornton, not Marie, who is losing it,* but didn't say so. I hadn't realized that he was afraid of me, but I was certainly glad that he was at that moment. After a period of first-rate work, he had panicked at his patient's transference. I told him that his patient had had what was perhaps the central validating experience of her life, and that her love for him, probably rooted in her love for her mother (as he had defensively but correctly intuited), had allowed her to feel loved, valued, worthwhile and protected, and that her experience of him being with her in the house was best seen as a creative validation that was curative and not as pathologically hallucinatory, as it indeed might be regarded. I told him of Shaw's comment in his discussion of Joan of Arc's hallucinations in the preface to his play, *Saint Joan*, in which he says, It isn't a matter of whether or not she heard voices. The question is, what did the voices say. Joan's voices told her how to save France. Marie's vision convinced her that she was lovable and safe. Its connection with birth, with being a mother and having a mother, could be elucidated later. The important thing now was to acknowledge the value of Marie's experience. I told Thornton that if he did so, I was willing to bet him lunch at the Russian Tea Room that he wouldn't have to use his prescription pad. I haven't had the heart to collect my bet, although if residents were better paid, I'd sure enjoy that lunch.

Another supervisee was working with a young man who would have been diagnosed as neurasthenic a century ago. Highly intellectual, he suffered a work inhibition, lassitude, and anxiety. He told my supervisee of an experience that was obviously of transcendent importance to him. While walking alone along the beach in a violent storm, his depression lifted and he felt great exultation; indeed, the words of Schiller's *Ode to Joy* and Beethoven's musical setting of it ran through his head. *"Freude, freude, Tochter aus Elysium*—joy, joy, daughter of heaven." He flung his arms open in welcome reception of the wind and waves. He went out onto a pier to get closer to the sea, feeling the wrath of the breakers about him as the flow of the breaking water swept across his legs. Aware that he might be swept away, possibly even losing his life, he was indifferent. He felt at one with the sea, the storm, all of nature—there was no fear in becoming part of them. To have experienced such a moment was a sense of fulfillment. If life continued, that would be wonderful; if it didn't, that was okay too. For the first time in his life, he felt complete and at peace. He thought, "Death is the price we have for the possibility of having children, renewal is wonderful, and that which I feared is necessary to that renewal." Then the words of Ecclesiastes, "The generation of men come and go, but the earth abideth forever," ran through his mind and he thought, "That should be a depressing thought. It would have been, but it isn't now," and he felt exalted at the thought of the earth abiding forever. "It was okay that the generations come and go; it is necessary, making novelty possible; the earth's abiding is sufficient. That abiding gives me feelings of wonder and awe, commensurate with the glory of having lived and witnessed what I witnessed in that storm." The young man's excitement subsided, and he felt a deep connection with something of value abiding with him and then surrounding him. He felt consummated, calm, and at ease. The young man finished the account of his strange experience in the storm by saying, "It was so odd that I was simultaneously completely immersed in that experience and a spectator of my being completely immersed in it. I was both there and a witness to my being there."

My supervisee, convinced that the patient had had a psychotic experience, saying to me that he felt that he must bring the patient back to reality, told me that he had said, "How many of you are there—one up on the ceiling and one down here on the couch?" The patient was sane enough to terminate. He rightfully felt completely misunderstood and deeply wounded. He had trusted his therapist enough to share an intensely significant experience, exposing his innermost soul in a way to render him completely vulnerable. His trust was betrayed, and his vulnerability used against him as his analyst mocked him. That mocking created a breach that destroyed their relationship. It was a breach that could not be cured.

In the famous correspondence with Romain Rolland, Freud (1960, p. 388) speaks of the "oceanic experience" and of his inability to partake of it. Yet Freud, for all of his tough-mindedness, manages to be both true to himself and respectful of Romain's mystical tendencies. Similarly, when he writes to Ludwig Binswanger (Freud 1960), that although such distin-

guished guests as art, religion, and philosophy may dwell in the
upper stories of the house (of human culture) that Binswanger
visits, he himself lives in the basement, where such guests are not
in evidence. It is clear that Freud takes Binswanger seriously,
even if he can't agree with him. My supervisee didn't take his
patient seriously. His fear of almost panic proportions and
incomprehension prevented him from doing so. Freud discussed
the oceanic experience in terms of regressive re-fusion with the
symbiotic mother. Was the young man's experience such a
re-fusion? Perhaps. Did he undergo a dangerous split? Perhaps.
Did he risk his life in a manic episode? Perhaps. But before
exploring any of these possibilities, his therapist needed to
validate his experience by saying, "Something very significant to
you has happened. We need to understand it as fully as possible
together." The young man's act of innocent faith in sharing his
experience with his therapist was an act of love. It was unrequited.

5

Narcissistic Injury in the Workplace

As has often been pointed out, Freud (1930) defined mental health as "the ability to love and to work," yet wrote voluminously about love but little about work. Freud himself was one of the world's prodigious workers, yet is hardly renowned as one of the world's great lovers. Nevertheless, Freud thought that work offered one of the few possibilities for conflict-free satisfaction. In *Civilization and Its Discontents*, he wrote,

No other technique for the conduct of life attaches the individual so firmly to reality as laying emphasis on working; for his work at least gives him a secure place in a portion of reality, in the human community. The possibility it offers of displacing a large amount of libidinal components, whether narcissistic, aggressive, or even erotic, onto professional work and onto the human relations connected with it lends it a value by no means second to what it enjoys as something indispensable to the preservation and justification of existence in society. Professional activity is a source of special satisfaction if it is a freely-chosen one — if, that is to say, by means of sublimation, it makes possible the use of existing inclinations, or persisting or constitutionally reinforced instinctual impulses. And yet, as a path to happiness, work is not highly praised by men. They do not strive after it as they do after other possibilities of satisfaction. The great majority of people work only under the stress of necessity, and this radical human aversion to work raises most difficult social problems. [p. 80n]

Notice that Freud's comments apply only to professional work, which is not open to all, and that he maintains that even for those fortunate enough to have professional work, most people work only out of necessity. There is some snobbery here — some of Freud's bias toward the "deserving," and some reflection of his own tendencies toward workaholism. Nevertheless, he is basically right, but satisfying work is not available to many people, who suffer deeply from this deprivation, and many, for reasons psychopathological or otherwise, are unable to avail themselves of the satisfactions that work can provide. The preeminent text on the relationship of work and psychopathology was written by Walter Neff. In *Work and Human Behavior* (1968), he traces philosophical, psychological, and psychoanalytic accounts of the function of work in the human psychic economy. In it, he postulates a "semi-autonomous work personality," a conflict-free sphere of ego activity (cf. Hartmann 1958), which sometimes paradoxically allows the severely psychopathological to work. In *Inhibitions, Symptoms and Anxiety* (1926), Freud discusses work inhibitions essentially in terms of unconscious sexual conflict which invades and deliquesces the conflict-free sphere of ego activities. (My formulation; Freud doesn't use Hartmann's notion of ego structure.) Freud says that if the flow of fluid from a pen represents a forbidden discharge of semen, a writing inhibition will result, while if walking unconsciously represents stomping on Mother Earth, an inhibition in locomotion will occur. The inability to work, with its concomitant deprivation of the possibilities for sublimation of instinctual energy, relatedness, and the rise in self-esteem that comes from transforming some piece of reality into the socially useful is one kind of work-related narcissistic injury. Following Freud, we might say that the energies denied expression through a work inhibition ferment, so to speak, and poison us.

ALIENATED WORK

Of course, the loss of the possibility of satisfying work may be due to external rather than internal forces. The massive unemployment of the past few years, as industry after industry "downsized," has inflicted incalculable narcissistic injury. Or the deprivation and injury may be less than total, as when workers are demeaned by management-by-fear rather than fired. We are living through a time of the proletarianization of virtually everybody, an era in which rationalization, bureaucratization, and computerization of the workplace eventuates in the omnipotent control of ever larger segments of the work force by faceless organizations and hierarchies, by businesses and industries, by conglomerates and governments, by outside regulation and all too present managers. At the turn of the century, Max Weber's (1905) pioneering scientific sociology described what he called the rationalization of labor—the conversion of work organized around personal relationships in traditional societies into work arranged by hierarchical organizations with rigidly designated roles and expectations. Weber is here being descriptive rather than judgmental. Weberian rationalization was not an altogether ominous historical development. Such rationalization depersonalizes power relationships and codifies status, task, and relationships in ways that demystify them and make them regular, understood, and normative. For society and its subdivisions, this can be a gain as well as a loss. Weber saw this, but he also saw that seeing oneself as an interchangeable part of a totally defined organization could be alienating and dehumanizing. The result of rationalization and bureaucratization was an increase in efficiency and productivity at the cost of a certain kind of alienation—the worker becomes a commodity and a production tool

instead of, let us say, a craftsman. Weber had no idea how far
this process would go; many modern businesses and govern-
mental organizations have become his worst nightmare realized.
In the worst of these organizations, employees live in Kafkaesque
hierarchies, run on Orwellian principles. The stress and psychopathology concomitant with this change in working conditions
has been underrated. I see patient after patient who has either lost
a job or seen his or her working conditions worsen. The media
and popular press talk a great deal about stress in the workplace,
and President Clinton made "longer hours for less money" an
issue in his campaign; however, thus far, the growing discontent
with growing proletarianization, the loss of autonomy, and the
ability to initiate actions concomitant with more and more
restricted control has not found its spokesperson. A fast-rising
political career awaits the first to articulate and give voice to the
new dehumanization of work. Marx, with his concept of alienated labor, not Freud, seems to be the theorist of most relevance
to understanding these developments. It is interesting that the
philosophical concept of alienation became incorporated into the
language of psychopathology. In the nineteenth century, psycho-
tics were said to be "alienated," and psychiatrists were called
"alienists." In Marx's (1867) original formulation, alienation
referred to a process by which the products of labor were
alienated from, taken away from and turned against, those who
produced them. The notion was that something that should have
been integral to the person, namely, the product of his labor,
which can be seen as an objectification of self, of self made
manifest in that which it creates in a sort of projective identification — that which is projected out, that which is created by
labor — should be in some sense reinternalized so that no alienation occurs. Ideally, we realize ourselves, our potential, and
come into contact with and fruitfully modify reality through
work, and in relating to the products of our labor, learn who we
are by seeing what we produce. When it works, this process is
narcissistically sustaining; when the conditions of work don't
permit this, contemporary forms of alienation, which arise more

from "micro-management" than from economic exploitation (not that there isn't plenty of that), result.

If work provides us with one of the best and most available sources of narcissistic gratification, it can also be the source of the most painful narcissistic injuries. In the course of human history, with its various forms of servitude ranging from conscription to impressment, to serfdom, to slavery, to wage-slavery, to the horrors of early industrialization, to child labor, to sweatshop labor, to the more subtle forms of white-collar servitude, most work has undoubtedly been narcissistically injurious, often to the point of dehumanization or death. The ways the contemporary workplace inflicts injury are more subtle, yet powerful, and from my observation, worsening. Our expectations have risen. More and more people are educated to wish for not merely subsistence or, for that matter, wealth from their work; they want "meaningful work," work that increases their sense of self-esteem and social utility. Paradoxically and perhaps tragically, it is precisely at a time when "meaning" is sought by far more people than before that the opportunities for "meaningful" work are diminishing, and even white-collar and professional workers are becoming cogs in a machine. Rising expectations and lower opportunities to fulfill them do not make for happiness.

As noted in Chapter 2, the theologian and philosopher Paul Tillich (1952) made a crucial distinction between *neurotic anxiety* and *ontological anxiety*. Neurotic anxiety is Freudian anxiety, which comes from unconscious conflict between the forces of the mind, between the "agencies" of the structural model; while ontological anxiety is the anxiety ineluctably concomitant with being human. It is sometimes called existential anxiety. According to Tillich, ontological anxiety takes three forms and comes from three sources: the anxiety consequent upon finitude and mortality; the anxiety of condemnation and guilt; and the anxiety of meaninglessness. The denial of, repression of, or acting out to avoid ontological anxiety feeds, intensifies, and increases neurotic anxiety. Each person must come to terms with ontological anxiety, which is structural — built into our very veins; the failure to do so — all our attempts at avoidance — can never work. From Tillich's point of view, neurosis is a consequence of trying to cheat the human condition. We never can, and if we try, we are paid back in spades.

Tillich's (1952) view of anxiety is a useful supplement, or better, complement, to Freud's conceptualization of anxiety. Clinically it is quite useful, highlighting the saliency of "existential" issues in therapy and in life. Tillich believed that although all human beings in whatever historical circumstances have to deal with all three components of ontological anxiety, different historical epochs brought different aspects of ontological anxiety to the fore. According to Tillich, the predominant anxiety of the ancient world was fear of mortality and finitude; of the medieval world, fear of guilt and condemnation; while the characteristic and most salient anxiety of our own era is fear of meaninglessness. The sociological development of increasingly alienated work I delineated above potentiates this characteristically modern central fear. Lacking transcendent goals and already suffering from the anxiety of meaninglessness, we look to work to find meaning and to give our lives meaning at precisely a time when finding such meaning becomes increasingly unlikely.

Tillich's (1952) concept of ontological anxiety has great saliency in conceptualizing and treating narcissistic injury. Our finitude, mortality, and limitations affront our grandiosity; the self-hatred, guilt, and fear of external condemnation lead us to punish our ego and diminishes our self-love, while the threat of meaninglessness robs our lives of all significance, inflicting perhaps the deepest narcissistic wound. That it is "a tale full of sound and fury signifying nothing" is our worst fear, and we fight it through love, through work, and through belief. When any of these are threatened, we are once again brought face-to-face with the possibility of meaninglessness. When our work is the central source of our sense of making a difference, of our life's value and worth, and that work is threatened either absolutely or in its meaningfulness, the narcissistic injury is profound.

The function of work in our psychic economy has been

understood in myriad ways. Freud, here as in so much, was a pioneer, but Abraham Maslow (1968) with his hierarchy of needs, each of which can be met through work, provides a very useful conceptual scheme. Work successively meets our physiological needs; our safety needs; our need for belongingness and love; our needs for importance, respect, self-esteem, and independence; our need for information; our need for understanding; our need for beauty; and our need for self-actualization. If you could find a job that met all of these needs, you would have it made. That's nice work if you can find it. Most of us can't, and our jobs may do little more than provide the means for meeting our physiological needs. When people try to satisfy the rest of Maslow's hierarchy of needs in their jobs and fail, they suffer narcissistic injury. Sometimes the problem is that they are looking for the right thing in the wrong place, and redirecting them is a relatively simple task. More often, an interplay of the intrapsychic and the sociological, the existential and the economic, makes for a situation of great complexity in which how to help the patient is far from clear.

As Freud said, work connects us to reality and provides a forum for reality testing. It also provides an outlet for our energies; structures our time; connects us to community; provides social and sometimes sexual opportunities; offers the kind of solid basis for self-esteem that can only come from overcoming resistance, both internal and external, to carrying through and completing a task by modifying reality; provides an opportunity for receiving corrective feedback; and in fortunate cases, provides a forum for creativity and self-actualization, sometimes allowing us to approximate our ego-ideals. This is Levin's version of Maslow's hierarchy. In actuality, few jobs do all of this for us, yet we consciously or unconsciously expect them to. When they don't, we suffer narcissistic injury. Work also provides an arena for the playing out of sibling rivalry, oedipal conflict, dominance–submission issues, separation/individuation issues, need-to-control and being-controlled issues, sadomasochistic wishes, and for the attaining of narcissistic gratification and the sufferance of narcissistic injury. The workplace is perforce psychodynamic, and everything from the most universal psychodynamic conflicts to the dynamics of dysfunctional families is instantiated there. Given the fact that most of the world is run by narcissistic personality disorders, the possibilities for pain are at least as prevalent as the possibilities for gratification. All of our patients struggle with these issues, and every case is a case of narcissistic injury in the workplace.

Most work is social, taking place in groups of some sort. In *Group Psychology and the Analysis of the Ego* (1921), Freud cited the army and the church, both working organizations, as his examples of groups and group dynamics. In his analysis, he saw group cohesion arising from identification between members of the group, an identification made possible by the sharing of a common ego-ideal, that ego-ideal being exemplified by the leader. Freud's is essentially a theory of charismatic leadership in which the leader, much like the primal father, is ruthless and egotistic, eliciting obedience from his followers partly through fear; more saliently, through the followers' wishes to bond, to belong, and to submit. The dynamics of the group in which work occurs are basically irrational. The very irrationality confuses and bewilders people who view work as rational and cannot come to terms with the irrationality of their workplaces. Of course, they too contribute their share of irrationality, however ignorant that they are doing so. Bion (1959) distinguishes between *work groups* and *basic assumption groups*. Work groups are task oriented and follow rational procedures leading to clearly defined goals. In theory, the people in your workplace constitute a Bionian work group. Basic assumption groups, on the other hand, are driven by unconscious irrational forces and desires exemplified in such activities as a group allowing couples to pair off and separate themselves from the group because the group has an unconscious collective fantasy that the couple will conceive the Messiah. In reality, work groups, including that constituted by your workplace, are not pure work groups. On the contrary, they importantly and counterproductively function as basic assumption groups, dialectically oscillating between the Bionian forms of collectivity. Insofar as a work group allows itself to become a basic assumption group, it will fail in its conscious goal-directed activities, and in the process, inflict narcissistic wounds on its members.

Beyond this, there is scant psychoanalytic literature on narcissistic conflict in the workplace. Kernberg (1980) is one of the very few to address this issue, doing so in the context of professional staff in the mental hospital. Unfortunately, his efforts, laudably innovative, cast little light on our subject.

In his epigenetic developmental scheme, Erik Erikson (1968) traces a series of discrete challenges each and every human being must meet (or fail to meet) in the journey from birth to death. One's chances for success in dealing with each life task is strongly, but not exclusively, determined by success (or lack of success) in dealing with earlier nodal struggles in development. As Freud had pointed out before him, Erikson believed that no psychic battles are won once and for all, and that regression is an omnipossibility, yet the more solid the psychic achievement, the better building block it becomes, and its deliquescence the less likely. Erikson's epigenetic scheme casts light on the sources of the capacity for work and its psychopathology. It is a conceptualization that is clinically useful. Erikson's perhaps overfamiliar yet clinically underutilized stages are basic trust versus distrust; autonomy versus shame and doubt; initiative versus guilt; industry versus inferiority; identity versus identity confusion; intimacy versus isolation; generativity versus stagnation; and integrity versus despair. It is in the stage of industry versus inferiority, a latency task, in which the capacity to work joyfully and productively is acquired. The smooth acquisition of this capacity predisposes the predominance of trust over mistrust (i.e., successful negotiation of the oral stage of psychosexual development), of autonomy over shame and doubt (i.e., successful negotiation of the anal stage), initiative over guilt (i.e., successful negotiation of the phallic and oedipal stages) — no small requisite backdrop for achievement. Erikson agrees with Hartmann that there must be a sphere of conflict-free ego functioning for work to be free of infiltration by instinctual conflict and to be a source of satisfaction. For Hartmann (1958), this means that an innate potential — the inborn apparatuses of ego autonomy — have not been destructively invaded, while for Erikson, there is less implication of innateness — less of the indwelling, nonconflictual, and more of the notion that areas of ego autonomy are carved out of the realm of the conflictual through struggle. Yet for both of them, mastery is possible. Hendrick (1943) postulated an innate drive for mastery, a notion with which Hartmann seems to agree and Erikson might subscribe to. Hartmann's concept of secondary autonomy, in which areas that were once conflict-ridden are now conflict-free, is a bridge between to Erikson's concept of development around nodal conflict.

Erikson's stages are dichotomous alternatives for development — psychosocial and importantly interpersonal (object relational) rather than psychosexual, as in Freud's more biologically (yet still significantly object relational) developmental scheme, but their correspondence and complementarity are not hard to find. In each Eriksonian stage, there is one alternative (e.g., trust) that is predominant in health, yet the other alternative is always to some degree realized, and that realization is also necessary for emotional balance. To be without mistrust is almost as disabling as to be without trust, yet trust must significantly predominate. The same is true of each of the other stages. The capacity for joyful work is a latency achievement, which Erikson explicitly relates to the culturally determined acquisition of "tools," of the technological skills required for survival and satisfaction in a given cultural situation. We need social support as well as educational opportunity to develop a predominance of industry in the latency stage. However, that acquisition will be impossible or formidably difficult if there is no belief that the world has rewards for me — that effort is worthwhile — that there is sweet milk; if there is no belief that I can master my own impulses and body, and that my anal product will be welcomed and that I will be loved for producing it; if there is no belief that exploration and penetration into the world is welcomed and will be encouraged; and if there is no belief that my competition with others will not end disastrously, but rather that my lust and aggression will be accepted, tamed, and contained. Quite a list of prerequisites, all of which offer multiple opportunities for both narcissistic gratification and narcissistic injury. Emotional injuries in the workplace surface preindustrial, prelatency wounds, which then must be aired, disinfected, and bandaged; that is, narcissistic injury in the workplace always brings to the fore narcissistic injury in earlier developmental stages, which must also be dealt with by the therapist.

Erikson's postlatency stages also have implications for work. Without a reasonably stable sense of identity, an identity that is both confirmed and discomfirmed, validated and challenged, at work, narcissistic injury will occur all too easily. Yet too narrow or rigid a sense of identity—too close identifications with the work role—may undermine the capacity for growth and even flexibility, setting one up for devastation if one's work role is threatened. The capacity for intimacy is less directly related to the capacity for work and vulnerability to injury there, but it too plays a role. One of the most common sources of vulnerability to narcissistic injury at work is the misplaced and ill-advised attempt to be loved and to love in the workplace. If intimacy needs are not satisfactorily met in personal, intimate relationships, desperation for such intimacy sets people up for traumatic rejection in the impersonal milieu of the bureaucratic organization. Mental health professionals, including therapists, are especially prone to seeking to meet intimacy needs in their work. It is a case of looking in the wrong place. Erikson's generativity-versus-stagnation conflict is of the essence of work difficulties. Generativity implies the ability to sublimate our archaic grandiosity and narcissism; to be productively loving of children, cultural products, ideals, aims, goals, and values. It presupposes the capacity for concern (Winnicott 1963) and the capacity to love. Put differently, it assumes the successful working through of the depressive position.

In the depressive position, previously split good and bad self-
and object representations are integrated, and I come to realize
that my aggression against the good object, driven by innate
envy, greed, and hate (derivative all of the death instinct), has, in
part, created the bad object. This brings about what Winnicott
called "primitive guilt." In Klein's version, I work through the
depressive position by making reparation for my greed and envy.
Gratitude (for the good in the good object and its goodness to me)
makes possible such reparation. In Winnicott's version of Klein,
this results in the development of "the capacity for concern"—
empathy. Envy underlies much school and work failure, inhibition, and dysfunction. If my envy of the good breast is too great,
I must destroy it, leaving nothing good for me; even if my hatred
is less than totally destructive, my envy doesn't allow me to
identify with, emulate, learn from, or internalize the good breast
and its successors. Envy, derivative from developmental failures
in the depressive position, disables me from the acquisition of
skills and tools—the cultural good breast—central to the achievement of Eriksonian industry. I cannot acquire that which I hate
and despise. I feel contempt for it and reject it. Additionally, my
envy and greed have turned the good part- or whole object into a
bad part- or whole object, so that it becomes a dangerous
persecutor. I cannot now make it mine because it is too dangerous. When any of these dynamics underlie a work or learning
disability, then there is no hope unless the therapist can make the
underlying envy conscious and help the patient work it through.

In agreement with Freud, Erikson believes that we must love or
grow ill and that the capacity for sublimated love is of the essence
of that encounter with reality in a communal transformation of
that reality that we call work. It gives us continuity, places us in
the succession of generations, and allows us to inherit and
assimilate as well as to contribute to tradition, to have a place in
the ongoing cycle of life. Nonalienated work is generativity
incarnate. Erich Fromm (1964), in his notion of the productive
personality, relates something like Eriksonian generativity to
social conditions that make such generativity possible. The stage

of generativity versus stagnation presents two possibilities for narcissistic injury in the workplace. The first occurs when earlier failures of development and/or intrapsychic conflict make generativity difficult or impossible. That cuts one off from the possibilities of gratification enumerated above, and such stifled lack of fulfillment is narcissistically disastrous. Fixation to Kohut's stage of the archaic grandiose self would be one, especially disabling, psychodynamic correlative of such stagnation. The pathologically narcissistic (in Kohut's sense) lack separate objects, so they cannot be truly generative, as opposed to pseudo-generative. That cuts one off from the possibility of relatedness and intergenerational continuity, necessarily heightening existential anxiety, particularly fear of one's mortality. The potential for transcendence isn't there, and at some unconscious level, the pathologically narcissistic know it. The interpersonal consequences of such regression/fixation may poison the workplace, leading either to dismissal or to misery. Alternatively, the pathologically narcissistic may come to dominate his or her organization, wreaking havoc on subordinates without bringing real satisfaction or narcissistic repair to the damaged leader.

So far, we've been looking at the narcissistic injury that comes from inside (perhaps as a consequence of earlier narcissistic injuries), from the inability, for whatever reasons, to be generative; however, with tragic frequency, we encounter patients who have the capacity for generativity in their work, yet are utterly, atrociously, and dehumanizingly denied the opportunity to express and enact that generativity. We are here talking about the narcissistic injury inflicted by routinized, mechanized, deadening, and alienated work in which the sense of participation in process and transcendence intrinsic to generativity is not possible. This is one of the worst of narcissistic injuries — a form of soul murder many adults suffer in our society, and possibly in all societies. Fortunately for many, generativity is possible outside the workplace.

Erikson's last stage, final integrity, includes affirmation of "the one and only life that has been possible." If work has inflicted substantial and cumulative narcissistic injury, or if narcissistic or other pathology has made work and its pleasures unavailable, then the achievement of such final integrity is well-nigh impossible. The alternative, despair, some degree of which is probably necessary to decathect and let go, will predominate, and the last stage of life will be bitter.

So narcissistic injury in the workplace comes from many sources. The capacity to joyfully and productively work lies at the intersection of the psychodynamic and the sociological, the juncture of the existential and the economic. Putting all that theory together, we may say that narcissistic injury in the workplace comes from narcissistic vulnerability derivative of developmental failures, Freudian, Kleinian, Kohutian, and Eriksonian, and from increasingly prevalent environmental provocation in our productivity-crazed, impersonally routinized and rationalized workplaces.

RUTH ANN: SUBMISSIVE AND SYMPTOMATIC

Ruth Ann was referred by her husband, who had been a patient, because she had developed life-threatening respiratory irregularities that were apparently psychosomatic, or at least stress related. Franz Alexander (1943), who developed the notion of psychosomatic illness, thought that three conditions were necessary for psychosomatic illness: a constitutional predisposition, a childhood trauma, and a current stress. In psychosomatic illness, the current emotional conflict activating the childhood trauma impinges on the constitutional susceptibility to produce organic changes. At first, these are functional, but if the psychological etioants (determinants) persist, organic structural changes result and irreversible damage is done. The physical illness may have psychodynamic roots, but once present, is "real" and must be treated medically as well as psychotherapeutically. Asthma was one of Alexander's examples of a psychosomatic condition, and Ruth Ann's symptoms bore a close resemblance to asthma.

Usually those suffering from psychosomatic illnesses have enormous emotional investment in the physicality of their illnesses,
which makes them extraordinarily difficult to treat psychodynamically. This was not true of Ruth Ann.

She was a perky, lively, energetic, well-turned-out woman in
her late thirties. These qualities, along with her characterological
and personal attractiveness, showed beneath a surface of abject
terror. She had come close to dying and knew it, and was not in
the least unwilling to consider that her palpitations and shortness
of breath might be "psychological" in origin. Her husband was a
pretty nonfunctional guy, so I anticipated that her difficulties
would stem largely from conflicts in her marriage (which were
certainly there, yet not of the essence of her current dangerous
situation), but they did not. Ruth Ann was almost pathetically
eager to be helped. When I asked her if she was under any stress,
she readily answered, "I get upset when my boss sets fires on my
desk." "Sets fires on your desk?" "Yes. He thinks it's funny. He
comes up behind me and sometimes pulls my hair. He doesn't
really hurt me, just sort of tugs at it, and then he reaches over and
crumbles a piece of paper and sets it on fire. He thinks that's
funny. I'm used to it — nothing bad ever happens; the desk doesn't
go up. Yet it frightens me. Oh, by the way, he does that to
everybody, not just me."

It was clear that Ruth Ann thought that something was wrong
with her. After all, the other employees didn't object to fires on
their desks. At the same time, she was on fire with repressed rage.
Her terror was conscious; her desire to retaliate was not. I had
asked her about "stress," because stress is in the papers and on TV
and it isn't in the least narcissistically injurious to acknowledge
that you are "stressed." It is almost fashionable, while the
suggestion that the patient's difficulties come from intrapsychic
conflict or deficit implies, indeed states, that there is something
wrong with them. For the narcissistically vulnerable — and the
self-blamers — such a suggestion early in therapy may either drive
the patient out of therapy or be all too eagerly embraced. Ruth
Ann, who already believed that there was something wrong with

her because she was upset by "a little joke" would have readily
heard that she was deficient when she needed to hear that her boss
was crazy — he was — and that fear of his madness was an entirely
appropriate response. Ruth Ann was in imminent danger, so that
an analytic approach was contraindicated. There was no time to
wait for the transference to unfold, so I approached her treatment
in much the same way I approach the treatment of active
alcoholics and drug addicts. The first task is to halt the active
addiction through confrontation and education. This is more a
counseling than a psychotherapeutic task. You could conceive of
the process as a preliminary cognitive behavioral treatment to be
followed by a psychodynamic one. You must put out the fire
before you rebuild the house. With Ruth Ann, I moved right in
and identified the present, "real" stresses in her work environment
and actively guided her into a more assertive stance. I reality-
tested with her and taught her coping skills. Later, we worked on
her underlying dynamics, the unconscious recapitulation, the
fantasized consequences of counteraggression, and overcoming
the genetic roots of her dilemma. I have found that early (not
before rapport has been established), active, educational, didactic, cognitive behavioral interventions do not substantially interfere with working more dynamically later on. They do, of course,
change the transference, yet the unconscious being what it is, a
full transferential relationship remains entirely possible. Freud's
(1910) paper on "Wild Analysis" comes to mind. In it, a young
woman goes to a "wild" analyst, after developing anxiety attacks
in widowhood. The wild analyst, assuming that her anxiety was
repressed libido gone sour, told her that she must either remarry,
take a lover, or satisfy herself. Freud's mordant comment was
that if the patient could do any of these, she would not need the
analyst. In dealing with a patient who, like Ruth Ann, must do
something — stop drugging, be more assertive — immediately, the
trick is to not ask the patient to do what is impossible for
psychodynamic reasons, while teaching the patient how to do
things he or she has hitherto not known how to do. The wild
analyst had no relationship with his patient, and nothing is

possible without relationship. Incidentally, the wild analyst undoubtedly inflicted a grave narcissistic injury on his patient, who had to have heard his comments as insulting or worse.

Ruth Ann was a paradox: college educated, sophisticated, knowledgeable, smart as hell, yet intimidated and terrified to a point where her health was being undermined by an obviously crazy and sadistic superior, and having no awareness of what was happening to her. She had been raised a strict Catholic by a disabled father who omnipotently controlled her, and she had enough superego to rehabilitate the population of a penitentiary if she were to distribute it to the inmates. Rigid, perfectionistic, driven, and a workaholic, she had married a pot-smoking rock devotee who took her to hear the Grateful Dead, a welcome relief from listening to religious cantatas with her now widowed mother. Her husband worked odd jobs, intermittently and reluctantly functioned as a househusband, and listened to rock while smoking pot. A tinkerer and a collector of junk, he was an amusing companion when he wasn't too stoned. Overage to be a Deadie, he was increasingly depressed, simultaneously proud of, overwhelmed by, and resentful of his highly "successful" wife. It was as if each were half a person: husband playful, irreverent, rebellious, hell-raising, childish and at his best, childlike, not in the least work oriented, regressed not exactly in the service of the ego, capable of esthetic and sensual pleasure, and both amusing and amused; wife serious, reverent, conformist, contained, "adult," a workaholic and unable to regress in the service of the ego, wanting to be capable of sensual and esthetic pleasure, and neither amusing nor amused. When it worked it was Yin and Yang; when it didn't, which was when he smoked too much pot, it was hell. It was as if id had married superego, ego being nowhere to be seen. They had no children, which sort of worked. He preferred to be the child, and most of the time, she was content to have him as her child. However, not entirely; a part of Ruth Ann wanted a baby and felt deprived.

Her marriage was an act of creative genius by her unconscious. Horace, her husband, enacted all that was unexpressed and unrealized in Ruth Ann, allowing her to be uninhibited, "wild," rebellious, "countercultural," uncontrolled, and less than perfect. What better way to have what she could not be and simultaneously say, as she had so long and so unconsciously wanted to say, "Fuck you!" to her father. All this was not very far from her consciousness, but she had not only said "Fuck you!" to Father; she had married him. Horace, like Father, didn't work, barely functioned, stayed at home, and was waited on by Ruth Ann. This was not close to consciousness. Father's and Horace's surfaces were too different. Yet Father sometimes drank too much, just as Horace sometimes smoked too much. When I interpreted, "Horace does it for you, enacts a part of you that you cannot," she readily understood, but when I interpreted that Horace was much like Father, and that she had repeated in adulthood her relationship with her father in order to gain mastery by converting a passive experience into an active one, she was a long time baffled. (Both of these interpretations came far into therapy.) It was, however, a repetition with a vital difference. Ruth Ann was not dominated and controlled by Horace, at least not in the same kind of way as her father had controlled and dominated her. So her repetition allowed her to actually master the trauma of her relationship with her father by repeating it without the domination. The compulsion to repeat is driven by, among other things, the hope that this time it will turn out differently. It rarely does, but for Ruth Ann, it did. On another level, she had to avoid a "strong," or even functional man, because of her fear of being dominated by him. Her marriage also allowed her to be her father, dominating and controlling, or at least trying to dominate and control, Horace, albeit at the cost of supporting him. It was a marriage that also allowed her to avoid the demands of a healthy, interdependent peer relationship with all that would mean in terms of demands for intimacy. Truly a marriage made in heaven, or was it purgatory? There was a level at which Ruth Ann resented supporting Horace and yearned for a more "suitable" mate, but as long as his pot smoking was under "control," she was content. It was a good deal. All of those psychodynamic gratifications, plus a modicum of here-and-now adult companionship (they had mutual interests around music, sailing, and travel). Horace was "fun" and had intelligence, wit, and a sense of humor. An only child, she could be the "star," and Horace, like Father, would admire her achievements, which he ambivalently did. When his love of grass got the better of him and he was so stoned that he fell into the refrigerator, Ruth Ann demanded he enter therapy. He did, dealt with his pot smoking and not much else, and things continued on a now even keel, as long as things went well for Ruth Ann at work.

I dwell on her marriage and the trade-off in it because part of the "contract" was that she would renounce family and adult mutuality in exchange for career success, with its resulting admiration, mirroring, opportunity to realize her ego-ideal, and to gain the love of her superego (Father). When that ceased to be forthcoming, the whole stack of cards collapsed. She was certainly not narcissistic in the ordinary-language sense or in the *DSM-III-R* sense of the word. Nevertheless, Ruth Ann was a Kohutian narcissist, one whose psychic equilibrium depended on continuing narcissistic gratification at work. Ruth Ann was a "Santa Claus narcissist" who gave a good deal to elicit the admiration she needed to survive. When the manager whose protégée she had been retired and Lawrence was brought in, she was made his deputy in a major promotion. Life was better than ever. Horace's relationship with pot was minimal, and at work she shone as never before. Then Lawrence's irrationality started manifesting itself. If Ruth Ann was a Santa-Claus, Kohutian narcissist who did not let her psychopathology interfere with her excellent management skills, Lawrence was a barely compensated Kernbergian "malignant narcissist" with more than a touch of sadomasochistic character disorder.

The "contract," probably at some unconscious level with God, had been violated, the homeostasis thrown into disorder, and the overcomplicated trade-off vitiated. The result was a very rapid decompensation, which manifested itself not in a "breakdown," but in physical illness. Given her rigidity, upsetting the apple cart — seeing the "system" go galley-west — damn near killed her. Her marriage was not acceptable if the instinctual and narcissistic gratification derived from work was not forthcoming, and her whole life became a meaningless failure. Suicide was ruled out by her Catholic conscience, as was murder, although she assuredly wished to commit one, but dying of heart disease or respiratory failure was both ego-syntonic and superego-syntonic. Death would avoid the pain of realizing how poor a compromise she had forged, and such realization would force her to recognize that she was neither perfect nor capable of making perfect decisions. That threatened more narcissistic injury than she could sustain. Her dying of psychosomatic disease would also punish Lawrence, and in her unconscious, her father, for what he was doing to her. (In reality, he would have mourned but little for her.) Lawrence was, like father, into omnipotent control. He was far more sadistic, but Father too could be cruel. She had married the dysfunctional side of Father; now she worked for the tyrannical side of him. It just wasn't possible. Something had to give. Tyrannical as he was, Father had loved and admired her for her consistent academic achievements; the issue of getting less than an A never came up — Lawrence didn't in the least admire or love her. He did know how good she was at her work and used her, but that was something else. Her narcissistic rage knew no limits and was entirely internalized, turned against herself. No wonder that she almost died.

So much for the psychodynamic side of things. What about the reality side? As events eventually confirmed (Lawrence was eventually dismissed for abuses including but not restricted to sexual harassment of numerous employees), her boss was a tyrant who terrified the entire staff. Not only was he completely unreasonable and constantly demanding the impossible, he was suspicious to the point of paranoia, flew into rages, screamed at and demeaned Ruth Ann in front of others, and did "weird" things that were supposed to be funny. He laughed when employees jumped up from their burning desks. Yet he was an extremely shrewd businessman, negotiating major contracts with great skill and saving the university whose purchasing department he headed money while getting top-notch goods and services. In short, he produced, and management didn't care about his "eccentricities." A series of complaints to the personnel department were ignored until an employee threatened a sexual harassment suit. It turned out that Lawrence was after every secretary in the department, although he never approached Ruth Ann; rather, he had his jollies by reducing her to tears.

Why didn't Ruth Ann take some action in her own behalf? Partly because her whole life hinged on the validation she got at work; without it, her life was a "failure," and indeed, its continuance would not be possible, partly because to do so would entail admitting to herself and others how shamefully she had allowed herself to be treated. She couldn't do that. Partly she thought that there was nothing she could do. Being sane entails knowing how to be sane, and Ruth Ann could see no action she could take to better the situation. With her rigidity, she couldn't envision another vocational role. She had attended the university, and had always worked for it. Her very real talent had been recognized and rewarded from the beginning. Her career there was her "life." She knew that nobody in the office of the vice president for business affairs cared in the least how Lawrence ran the department, as long as the "bottom line" was smooth, reliable, minimal-cost goods and services for the university. Amazingly, it was. Besides, universities tolerate "eccentricity," and Lawrence was a campus "character." Ruth Ann was truly trapped. She was humiliated, shamed, and enraged, yet could do nothing, not even allow herself to feel those feelings. She could neither leave nor change things where she was. It never occurred to her that like most bullies, Lawrence would desist if confronted, and her father transference made that impossible in any case. Nor did it occur to her that she had far more clout "up-front" than the low-level employees Lawrence "hit on." Instead, she started winding up in emergency rooms on oxygen. Fortunately, Horace turned the tables on her and insisted, as she had with him, that she get psychotherapy.

Ruth Ann proved to be an "ideal" patient. Always the perfect student, she learned rapidly. So terrified was she of Lawrence, of her own rage, and of dying (however much she desired it as a way out) that she almost instantly responded to empathy and to openly expressed commiseration (not my usual style). After listening to her for a few sessions, I told her that she was working for a crazy, sadistic SOB, and that her rage at him would kill her if she did not start expressing it, at least to me. With little resistance, she did, and her tears — tears of liquid rage — soon dried. I told her that she was driving herself to collapse to get Lawrence's approval, which would never be forthcoming, and that she was deeply ashamed at being yelled at and insulted in front of her subordinates. Before long, we were rehearsing confrontations with her ogre boss. She role-played well. I used a lot of humor, and played for relationship, talking about her interests. It worked. She stood up to Lawrence and told him she refused to be treated in demeaning ways. He retreated to his office, ignored her except for very businesslike exchanges, and let her run the department. I then went after her perfectionism and lack of self-care directly and persistently. When, a year later, after Lawrence's dismissal, she became a spectacularly successful department head, I was not surprised. The only thing I interpreted during the first 3 months of therapy was her father transference to Lawrence; the rest was cognitive behavioral stuff and rehearsals.

Therapy rarely goes so well. Within months, she was no longer being abused at work or having physical symptoms. Only then did we settle down to dynamic work, which over the course of years, surfaced the fragility and emotional and genetic determinants of Ruth Ann's ingenious compromise. She has decided to stay with it, but now knowing what she is doing and why, she is much less narcissistically vulnerable. The more interpretive side of our work reduced Ruth Ann's shame; understanding why she had allowed herself to be treated so badly helped her not feel ashamed that she had allowed herself to be treated so. She still wonders why she has settled for "so little" in her personal life and worries that there is something wrong with her for doing so, but she is happy and doesn't believe that at this stage of her life, being who she is, she will wind up with anything better. As she puts it, "Who would put up with me with all of my quirks, and besides, Horace is so much fun when we get along." Who am I to say differently? I predict Ruth Ann will wind up vice president for business affairs at the university.

PETER: PASSED OVER

Standing straight as a ramrod, Peter almost broke my hand shaking it. He didn't exactly sit down; rather, he neatly folded his knees and lowered his still perfectly straight back into the chair. Staring straight at me, he said, "This is bullshit. I have commanded many men, and I didn't need to be a patient in order to do it. What you do is pretentious bullshit. I studied philosophy in college and I know that the concept of the unconscious is logically fallacious." He slammed his fist into his palm. I felt afraid. "They fucking passed me over. Twenty years and they fucking passed me over. It isn't possible. Like everyone at the Academy, I thought I would make general, but you get more realistic. But I never thought I'd go out anything less than a chicken colonel. Passed over for light colonel; it can't be! It is! Five years ago I retired. I went back to school and got an MBA. I have a new career. Not great, but not bad. Who cares? It isn't the Corps. I still can't get over it, so I'm in your fucking office."

This time he slammed the chair so hard the room shook. I didn't want this case. "I love the Corps. I was a kid from a fucked-up home when I went in. After serving as an enlisted man, I was appointed to the Academy. I am very smart; I have a master's degree in engineering. I did very well. Serving gave me pride. It made a *mensch* out of me. Yeah, I'm Jewish. There aren't many General Cohens in the Marine Corps. I was going to be the first. There was an Admiral Levy; he bought Monticello in the first half of the nineteenth century, so why not General Cohen now? I never encountered prejudice in the Corps. Always respected. Outstanding fitness reports. I don't understand. Why passed over for light colonel?

"I had doubts about Vietnam, but I kept them to myself. It was a horrible war. There wasn't much I didn't see. My business is, or was, war, so I could hardly object. I didn't. Yet I was still passed over. If I had gone Navy instead of Marine, I'd be up there. I loved the Corps. You can never leave it. I haven't. I look at my uniform every day. I wear my hair regulation. I loved everything about being a Marine, yet they rejected me. Have you read Dostoyevsky? Yeah, I'm a fucking Jewish intellectual — that has nothing to do with it. I was a Marine's Marine. There are plenty of intellectuals in the Corps — an asshole, arrogant shrink like you looks down on guys like me. I know you were protesting while I was getting my ass shot at, watching my men being killed. I read Dostoyevsky between shellings. You probably read him smoking pot with some chicks in an East Village pad (he wasn't too far off on that). You remember *Notes from the Underground*? 'I am a sick man, I am a spiteful man, a mean man. I am an unattractive man. I believe my liver is diseased.' 'I feel something is wrong with my liver' is exactly the way I feel. It makes no sense. A Marine, a successful businessman identifying with the underground man, a beaten-down clerk in a Russian slum, in a novel written by an anti-Semite. But I am sick, just like Dostoyevsky's clerk. And I'm getting spiteful and mean. I am sick with despair and I'm starting to have physical problems too, and I'm one mean sonofabitch. My liver is fine; it's my knees — I can't jog, and that's important to me. I'm proud of my religion; my kids went to temple, otherwise I would have beat the hell out of them. Always made a point of my Jewishness in the Corps. You get respected that way. Doctor, the truth is I despise you and your profession. But I can't stand it. All I think about is my being passed over, so I'm here. I have rages. I don't see anything wrong with them; my wife does. She maintains that I have posttraumatic stress disorder and wants me to go to the V.A. No way. Tell them I should have been a general? I rage when my wife acts like a cunt. Why shouldn't I? I love her when she isn't being a ball-buster. You can't give me a star, so why am I here?"

Some therapies begin auspiciously. This one didn't. Peter's character pathology was all over the place, but so what? What could I do with it? Indeed, I couldn't give him a star and that is what he wanted. My life had indeed been lived differently and my values were diametrically opposed to his. I did protest the war and would not have fought in it. Should I refer him, in fairness to both of us? I seriously considered it, yet did not. He was pathetic. I felt sorry for him and was afraid that he would sense it. I've treated many people who, like Peter, devoted their lives to an organization or institution and were kicked in the teeth. For some the narcissistic injury went so deep that they could not integrate it, and either reorganized at a lower developmental and emotional level, or died. A part of them had died and they too had to die, partially and symbolically or actually. I thought that Peter might succumb to a heart attack or a stroke. I was genuinely afraid of his rage and didn't want to get hurt. I usually respect such feelings and do not work with people from whom I sense physical danger, but his intelligence, honesty, and extremity led me to attempt to work with him. My efforts succeeded only minimally. He was heartbroken, and however courageously he had tried to recoup, the wound would not heal.

I came to respect him and even like him. His life-style had an integrity I would have been reluctant to acknowledge if I had not met him. His values and their realization were diametrically opposed to mine, and I would have continued to be contemptuous of them if I had not known him. The Major's courage was beyond question, and I came to admire it. When he described himself as a professional killer, I had some difficulty even allowing for rhetorical exaggeration, yet I learned a great deal from him. I came to realize that I had just as much primitive aggression, albeit differently channeled, and that my contempt for the virtues of the warrior had more than a little envy in it. I was simply not as courageous, at least physically, as he, nor had I given myself to a cause or an institution—something outside of myself—with the same abandon or level of commitment as he. I was surprised at the range and intensity of feelings that working with him elicited. I realized that what I felt was something akin to envy. There was also a certain voyeuristic pleasure in seeing him enact, or to be more exact, hearing him enact the joys and sorrows of a warrior. He activated a part of me I hadn't known existed, and however incapable of enacting it myself, I enjoyed participating in his reenactment of it. This is not to say that there didn't remain a certain ironic distance from and something of a judgmental attitude toward him. All of that was okay and could even facilitate the treatment as long as I remained conscious of it and didn't act it out.

Feelings of envy toward patients are far more common amongst therapists than is usually acknowledged. We envy our patients their wealth, fame, "freedom," beauty, youth, work, loves, and feeling states, including murderous rage, fatal passion, consuming greed, and pathological ecstasies. The worst case of countertransferential envy I have had to deal with came in working with a best-selling novelist. Supervisees are extremely reluctant to and resistant of acknowledging envy of their patients. The reason, I think, is that envy is narcissistically wounding. It entails acknowledging a deficit state—we are lacking what the other has. Further, we are deeply ashamed of being envious, especially if we are therapists envious of our patients. Envy is one of the affects most likely to be denied. Finally, envy entails rage—rage at the good breast, rage at the rich Jews, rage at the instinctually gratified blacks. As can be seen by my social examples of rage consequent upon envy, envy sometimes involves a primary projection in which an unacceptable aspect of self is projected onto the object, which is then envied for its possession of the projected trait or affect. Winnicott goes so far as to say that God is a projection of our "goodness," which we project to protect it from our "badness." The rage engendered by envy is dangerous; it has been responsible for some of the worst horrors in history as well as countless tragedies in personal life.

From Iago to Hitler, rage secondary to envy has killed. Therapists are not immune to it. Unacknowledged, it is acted out by objectifying, demeaning, distancing, and punishing their patients. They do not murder their patients (mostly), but they do inflict narcissistic injury, committing a kind of soul murder. The Major's previous therapist (surprisingly, he had had several) had told him, "You're a kike from the slums; that's why you didn't get promoted." I'm sure there was some truth in this, but that is beside the point. The conscious motivation of the therapist (who was Jewish) was to break down denial, to puncture defensive arrogance and grandiosity, and to loosen the Major's idealization of his love object, but his unconscious motivation was surely to hurt. Motivation aside, his "intervention" was a narcissistic injury to the already bleeding Major. I fantasized that he too was envious of the Major's "honor," although this may not be so. His injurious comment could have been driven by many countertransferential feelings. We are prone to punish patients we envy not only for what we envy them, but even more for "making" us feel envy and the shame and rage that accompany it. We are not supposed to be envious (at least of our patients), and we hate them when we are because the feelings they engender puncture, violate, and vitiate our ego ideal.

Closely related to therapeutic envy is the therapist's role as voyeur. There is something intrinsically voyeuristic in what therapists do; we are spectators of our patients' lives. There is pleasure in that, and good therapists are good voyeurs, but there is also narcissistic injury in being voyeuristic. It is observing, not living; it is as if we went to the movies instead of having lives. Our voyeuristic pleasures are not exclusively sexual; with our having heard fifteen stories of patients' going down on their horses, the titillation fades and boredom becomes more of a risk. Although it is undeniably true that voyeuristic pleasure was originally sexual and that later voyeuristic satisfactions are derivatives of that first view of the primal scene, it is our — at least my — enjoyment in the careers and adventures of our patients that titillate, shame, and induce envy. I haven't been a cop, a career officer, a housewife, a lawyer, a cabinetmaker, an artist, a contractor, an actor, or a fisherman, but I have lived all those lives vicariously through my work. It is an odd feeling. Sometimes I feel like a child listening to the grownups talk, which I relate to one of my most fondly remembered childhood experiences, of being allowed to stay up with the grownups when company came and talked about their professional and business activities in the "grownup" world. Sometimes I was sent to bed but surreptitiously listened from the stairwell, giving that which I heard a forbidden allure, enhancing my pleasure. When I do therapy, I unconsciously go back to that stairwell and the feelings I felt there. Other therapists do too. The pleasure is there, but so is the hurt. The therapist's feeling is that he is the child listening and observing, while the grownups are out there doing things and "living." I am sure that at a more unconscious level the therapist is feeling the pain of being excluded from the primal scene. Therein lies the narcissistic injury in our voyeuristic activity, compounded by the shame we feel for experiencing our vicarious pleasures. The most common countertransferential acting out of conscious or unconscious narcissistic injury secondary to voyeurism is becoming too active. Now we are no longer spectators; we begin to live the patient's life, usually with highly deleterious consequences. The cure for this is increased empathy so that we feel with, rather than observe from outside and feel excluded and alienated. If we repress our eroticized vicarious pleasure in the patient's life, we become bored. Our work becomes dead, a drudgery, and the very maneuvers we use to avoid the narcissistic injury of voyeurism inflicts yet worse ones.

Boredom wasn't a problem working with the Major. I found him fascinating. I tried to understand why he couldn't let go of his past. Perhaps he was right—once a Marine, always a Marine— yet I knew that this was a rationalization. His tie to the Corps was more than a core identification; more had been lost than an identity—devastating as that was, something else was going on. The theoretical construct I found most helpful in understanding him was Kohut's (1971, 1977) notion of the self-object. The

Corps was the Major's self-object, and the disruption of that self-object bond threatened him with regressive fragmentation, hence the stringent necessity of his holding on to it, literally for dear life. I could neither prematurely suggest that his self-object was less than ideal, nor (as his previous therapist had done) prematurely suggest that he had set himself up, thereby contributing to his being passed over. Neither were sustainable, yet. What was needed was for him to establish a self-object transference to me. His initial attack notwithstanding, this happened — not without resistance — more quickly than I would have predicted. Pain drives people into therapy, and his pain was exquisite. Once our transference was solid, we could work through his loss of an identity, a script, a role, a relationship, a love object, a self-object, and an opportunity to live up to an ego-ideal, for his loss was all of these. That's a lot to mourn for, and that mourning was prolonged, resisted, and excruciating. You can't give up something without something to replace it, and a therapeutic transference bond isn't a life (although transference bonds are), but sometimes it will do.

Seeing Peter's relationship to the Marines as simultaneously a mirroring and idealizing transference changed my attitude toward him, if not my overt behavior, and my increased empathy (in Kohut's sense of accurate understanding) for his clinging to a no longer serviceable identity was enabling, enabling of the establishment of a mirror and much later idealizing transference toward me. The genetic meanings of his career choice surfaced, the most salient being the structuralization — channeling and containing — of archaic rage, long antedating his entrance into the Marines, and his reexperiencing of the service as an austere yet nurturing mother and a replacement for a father who had never been there for him. Although he had seen horrible things in 'Nam, he told me that he enjoyed killing Gooks, until he came to believe that that was unjustified. He never articulated that, but spent the rest of his tour flying rescue helicopters. His ambivalence toward the war undoubtedly hurt his career. Psychodynamically those killings represented the death of siblings, ambivalently loved and hated rivals. His survivor guilt alone dictated that he assume that he did not deserve to make colonel. The ways in which he made sure that was the case, as well as the fact that he did so, were far from consciousness and were only discussed at the end of therapy. There was also an oedipal level to his rage and his needs to be punished for it. To rise too high above his ne'er-do-well father aroused too much anxiety. Promotion also represented separation. All that was on the psychodynamic — the self-undermining — side.

On the reality side, he had indeed encountered anti-Semitism from his recruit days, through the Academy, into his officer days. He had in fact been treated, at times, unfairly and even brutally by his beloved. One reason that he clung so tenaciously to his identity as an officer was that his identity was actually extremely complex, and many of its components were incompatible with his core identity. Fixation to Kohut's stage of the archaic nuclear self made working any of this through impossible. It was only after, through transmuting internalization, he began to develop what Kohut calls a mature self-structure that we were able to deal with these issues. The most painful for him was the deidealization of his mother self-object, and the Corps was that. No mourning could take place without this disillusionment. Only that would allow him to experience his rage at the treacherous and betraying self-object. This occurred only tentatively and intermittently; there was too much of real value in his ideal for him to relinquish it. This limited his therapeutic gains.

Peter left therapy functioning better, both in his business career and in his family life, and he was certainly less depressed, but he was never to be the same man again. Some losses cannot be assimilated, and the Major would spend the rest of his life yearning for his lost love, missing her, intermittently feeling rage at her, and craving all that she had represented. That yearning was less painful, more tolerable and livable as a result of therapy, but it was not to be surmounted. Freud said of loss, "We will accept no substitute."

MIKE: AUTOMATED INTO DEPRESSION

"Doc, I can't concentrate on anything. I'm afraid to leave my yard. I'm afraid to drive. I can't read anymore. I don't sleep. I haven't gone to work in weeks. I was demoted. Demoted for the second time. I'm no good, Doc. Not the man I was. Maybe I can open some little business. But I can't even do that. I had to bring my little daughter with me today; I couldn't come by myself."

Mike, looking disheveled and disconsolate, sat weeping. Needless to say, Mike was in a severe clinical depression that needed psychopharmacological treatment, which he received. What interests us here is the relationship between narcissistic injury on his job and his depression. Mike was a middle manager in a major corporation. A man of modest but adequate native endowment, he worked his way up through the ranks through hard work and good interpersonal skills. As long as things were informal, as long as the "corporate culture" was based on personal relations and task-oriented working together, Mike had functioned well as a leader. He was probably working at the limits of his capacity, but he did what he did adequately and effectively. Then he was caught in a paradoxical and contradictory shift in "management style." There was a reorganization, and what had been a Bionian basic task group of middle-management peers regressed into a basic assumption group in which raw aggression, paranoid projection, and sadomasochistic power games became the modus vivendi. Although Mike had seen his share of the world playing football in high school and doing well in the service, he was rattled and shaken by the outbreak of primitive emotion and irrationality triggered by insecurity in his company. He didn't quite know how to survive in that storm-tossed sea but probably would have survived if another wave of change hadn't drowned him. Just as craziness became the norm, "rationalization" became the order of the day, rationalization in terms of computerization and micromanagement. Now everything was quantified, controlled, observed. Big Brother had arrived. Mike kept his job but lost his autonomy. He was no longer a manager in anything but name. Every decision was now made from on high, and he had but to execute them. Reduced to a nodal point in an information system, Mike decompensated.

Mike had enjoyed his work. It had been eroticized. Without such eroticization, work becomes drudgery at best, slavery at worst. When Freud was assembling his list of publications to be sent to the Ministry of Education to qualify for a promotion to associate professor, he wrote to his friend, Wilhelm Fliess, saying he was now assembling his "Catalogue," an allusion to Leporello's Catalogue Song — "A thousand and one in Spain," and so on — listing Don Giovanni's conquests in Mozart's opera. The eroticization of work could hardly be more clear. Mike didn't know from the Catalogue Song, but he did experience joy in his work until the printouts, data entries, and microcontrols invaded the domain of the erotic. Along with the introduction of these "labor-saving devices" came a greatly increased workload and longer hours. Being "management," Mike received no overtime, and was expected to stay as long as needed. His workday, never short, grew to 12, even 14 hours. A "family man," whose tie to his children was of transcendent value to him, he found himself missing out on their growing up, not getting to their sports events, concerts, and parent–teachers' days. Being a person who dealt with separation not at all well, and who had recently lost his parents, his sense of deprivation was as acute as his pain was deep. He started to panic. Never having worked for anyone else, he felt trapped. It was true that Mike's lack of higher education and limited ability to deal with technological innovation contributed to his difficulties; however, having treated other managers in the same industry, I knew that the "stresses" he complained of were real. From a happy if limited guy with a reasonably stable and healthy level of self-esteem, he became a narcissistically wounded white-collar sweatshop drone. He then drove the nails into his own coffin by blaming himself. "I should be able to handle the job . . . I'm a weakling . . . I'm not a man . . ." and the like were cognitions that brought Mike to collapse.

Initially, treatment consisted in validating his perception of the impossibility of his work situation. The first trick was to turn his anger away from him. Not being very psychologically minded, he worked better cognitively-behaviorally than dynamically. Eventually, I helped him mourn the loss of his parents and gain insight into the pathological aspects of his clinging to his family as a substitute for his lost parents. As his separation anxiety lessened, his functioning improved. He came to accept that he could not handle his old job as it was now restructured, and that there was no reason why he had to. Mike returned to work in a different capacity. Six months later, he was back in treatment in the same shape. He had returned to the manager's job to "prove" that he could handle it. We are still working through his second "breakdown."

The psychotherapeutic point I want to make about Mike is that a therapist who went for the psychodynamic determinants of his breakdown, which were certainly there and real enough, rather than validating how veridical Mike's perception of his reality situation was, would have inflicted severe narcissistic injury on him. That would only have confirmed his self-loathing as "weak," and "not a man." Only after consensual validation was mourning and readjustment possible. I have seen overzealous supervisees unwittingly "blame the victim" in similar situations. Lest you think that such corporate events are restricted to undereducated managers, I currently have a strikingly similar case in which a brilliant, highly educated manager is being destroyed in a "reorganization." The patient isn't paranoid, and even if he were, "paranoids have enemies, too."

Perhaps the deepest kind of narcissistic wound derivative of work experiences lies in denial of the opportunity to work. Just as we must "love or grow ill," we must work or grow ill. Self-actualization is impossible apart from it. It is only through the transformation of reality through productivity that we can know who, and indeed become who, we are. It is only through work that our creativity can become manifest, so that anything that deprives us of that potentiality is narcissistically injurious. That is why there is so much death and illness immediately following involuntary, and not always involuntary, retirement.

In work, as in any major life area, one can be stifled from without or stifled from within. Sally, who was introduced in the chapter on ACOAs, was stifled from without. Work can be totally unfulfilling, meaningless, compulsive drudgery from either of these directions. Pascal (1966) long ago wrote of "busyness," as an existential distraction; workaholism uses work as such a way of not feeling and not relating. Perhaps even more tragic are those who long, with aching heart, for meaningful work and cannot find it. Sally was among them. Sally experienced her family's denial of a higher education as even more narcissistically injurious than her father's incest. Although too troubled and distraught to do anything about it for the first 5 years of therapy, Sally eventually returned to school. I have worked with many patients similarly stifled with whom the central therapeutic task was the clearing of internal obstacles to learning, as well as helping them deal with external barriers — reality constraints — that hinder them from pursuing their educations. For Sally, the alluring yet inaccessible goal was entry into the local community college. When I first met Sally, she was holding onto, as if for dear life, Thoreau's *Walden*, and a book by Norman Vincent Peale. The first represented freedom; the second, hope. In her carrying those books, there was something of (unconscious) defensive arrogance that served to separate her from her peers, which shored up her then necessary, fragile, schizoid defenses, as there was denial of who she "was," sociologically and economically, yet there was so much more than defense there — aspiration, self-transcendence, a goal, a way out, and just maybe the possibility for raising self-esteem.

My associations took me to a different time and place, to the illiterate Jewish immigrants of New York's lower East Side, at the beginning of this century, who had conspicuously displayed fountain pens and glasses in their jacket pockets to give the impression that they could read and write. That too was a defensive equivocation in the services of raising self-esteem, which simultaneously incarnated ideals and values, goals and ambitions, those hallmarks of Kohut's "mature self." Here we are most certainly deep in the territory of narcissistic injury and its opposite, narcissistic gratification. This association led to another, to Abraham Cahan's great novel of pathological narcissism, *The Rise of David Levinsky* (1917), in which the protagonist dreams of attending City College:

> My plan of campaign was to keep working until I had saved up six hundred dollars, by which time I was to be eligible for admission to the college of the City of New York. . . .
>
> The image of the modest college building was constantly before me. More than once I went a considerable distance out of my way to pass the corner of Lexington Avenue and Twenty-Third Street, where that edifice stood. I would pause and gaze at its red, ivy-clad walls, mysterious high windows, humble spires; I would stand watching the students on the campus and around the great doors, and go my way, with a heart full of reverence, envy, and hope, and with a heart full of quiet ecstasy.
>
> It was not merely a place in which I was to fit myself for the battle of life, nor merely one in which I was going to acquire knowledge. It was a symbol of spiritual promotion as well. University-bred people were the real nobility of the world. A college diploma was a certificate of moral was well as intellectual aristocracy.
>
> My old religion had gradually fallen to pieces, and if its place was taken by something else, if there was something that appealed to the better man in me, to what was purest in my thoughts and most scared of my emotions, that something was the red, church-like structure on the southwest corner of Lexington Avenue and Twenty-Third Street.
>
> It was the synagogue of my new life. Nor is this merely a figure of speech: the building really appealed to me as a temple, as a House of Sanctity, as we call the ancient Temple of Jerusalem. [p. 168]

Sally felt much the same way about the Community College. It too was not merely the avenue to vocational meaningfulness, although it was very importantly that; it was a place in which the forbidden and denied could be realized. Unlike David, who never got to City College, making a million dollars instead, Sally did go to community college.

Thinking about David Levinsky, I also thought of a poignantly expressed account of narcissistic injury secondary to educational deprivation in the same milieu. It is reported by Irving Howe, in *World of Our Fathers* (1976).

> Sometimes I think my life came to an end even before it began. I sit here talking to you this evening, a man of fifty-eight, with the feeling that there is little for me to look forward to. But that feeling doesn't make me sad. I have learned to accept it as I have learned to accept other things.
>
> While I was growing up in Russia, I developed a tremendous hunger for learning. . . . I went for some years to the *heder* and got from it what I could, but all my religious education did was to teach me how little it could give me. I wanted to drink from strange wells. . . .
>
> I began to take an interest in books. Some were by Yiddish authors, some were Yiddish translations of Russian classics. Since I had also gone a little to the Russian school, I began to swallow — I mean, really swallow — Russian books. I read everything I could get my hands on. Turgenyev was my favorite, perhaps because there is such a sweetness to his voice. And then Tolstoy and Dostoyevsky. I read, of course, Sholem Aleichem, who made the ugliest things in life seem beautiful, and Peretz, who, in his own way, taught me not to lose respect for myself.
>
> How can I describe to you, you who live with mountains of books, the hunger that I and my friends felt? The excitement we shared when we discussed Dostoyevsky? The pleasure we took in going to a shabby little book store in our town? For us it was books and only books. We had nothing else. . . .
>
> By the time I came to America, I had to pull my nose out of the books to get a job. . . . What disturbed me most about my early years on the East Side . . . was not so much the physical suffering, but the feeling that I was lost, in a desert. My fellow workers weren't always friendly. Cutters, you know, aren't the most

refined people in the world, so I learned to be quiet. I did my share of work, no one had to prop me up, what went on in my mind was my own business.

I would go home in the evenings . . . and read translations of Gerhardt Hauptmann and Charles Dickens and your Edgar Allen Poe. I went to night school, and picked up a little English so I could read the easier books, but it never seemed enough. I was like a hungry man who gets fed, but either the food isn't right or it doesn't agree with him, or maybe it's not what they call nowadays a balanced diet. . . .

I got married, my wife was a sympathetic person with a mind of her own. Life became easier, I went into a business and while I never got rich — I wasn't a pusher — things were comfortable after a while. . . .

Still, if life became easier in some ways, it also became harder in other ways. I had to chase after the dollar and take care of my family. Each passing day I felt a little more tried. As a result, I couldn't read as much as I had in my earlier years. . . .

What else can I tell you? My children went their own way. I am proud of them, but there are things we can't talk about. Still, I have no complaints. My circumstances were what they were. My family has been a whole world to me. I still take pleasure in a page of Sholem Aleichem, and to me Bazarov and Raskolnikov are like friends from my youth. *But to think of them is to be reminded that there was a door which, for me, was never opened.* [p. 247, emphasis added]

Fortunately, the doors are starting to open for Sally. The barriers to her remediating her educational deficits, which are prerequisite to remediating her vocational agony, were multiple. Working through her incest issues and stopping her amphetamine abuse were a necessary prolegomena (see Chapter 3) to helping her enter the temple of Community College. Nor could this work be done before she had mourned her mother and made substantial progress in resolving her separation issues.

As this work waned (it could never be completely resolved, no emotional gains are once and for all), her despair over her current life came to occupy more and more of our time together. Session after session, Sally lamented the now precious minutes, hours, and days of her life slipping by without growth, development, or expressivity in the deadly boredom of filling out forms, processing papers, and typing memos unimportant even to those who dictated them. Sally's job at first represented economic survival, and she was so engaged in therapeutically reliving the past that such mindless work served her purpose and inflicted no narcissistic injury. The healthier she became, the less tolerable her job became. Now she spoke of it as a prison sentence — a life sentence of dull drudgery. She was imprisoned in the "pink ghetto." Seeing herself as different and superior, she exacerbated her misery by alienating herself from whatever human solidarity was available to her. I knew that her superciliousness was partly driven by fear. Underneath lay low self-esteem and fear of rejection. Given her extreme sensitivity, I was reluctant to confront her on this issue, and did not do so until I had communicated my very real empathy for her feelings that her life would drain away at this petty pace until she died or retired.

In a similar situation, a supervisee said, "You think you're better than other people," without laying a relational foundation for it. His patient's trust in him was damaged, not because the content of the intervention was "wrong" — indeed it needed to be said — but because it was said unempathically, that is, without an understanding of why the patient acted and felt the way he did. A needless narcissistic injury had been inflicted.

Sally experienced her sense that it was "too late" with bitterness, and savaged herself for "the years I have wasted." Sally's self-blame, although being dynamically complex, was consciously focused on her years of amphetamine abuse. "If only I hadn't been such an asshole, ad infinitum." Such reactions are universal in "recovering" persons, and the Twelve Step programs wisely focus their members' attention on action in the present. This, however, does not allow for mourning, and mourning there must be. Therefore, Sally and I spent much time mourning her lost years; that is, in acknowledging the reality of time lost, time which was not to be regained, and feeling sorrow for that loss.

The hoped for outcome of this process is self-compassion as opposed to self-pity.

As the mourning work continued, its effectiveness also diminished as Sally seemed "stuck" in a hateful present. I became weary of listening to "I'll be there till I die." Any suggestion that that wasn't necessarily so was met with angry withdrawal at "not being understood." I found myself being drawn into and sharing her sense of futility. Call it projective identification, if you wish; whatever it was, it hurt. I felt futile too. My work was as meaningless as hers. I rebelled and started to feel angry. I thought of the Cornell Psychiatry Department's Chairman, Bob Michaels, saying, "I tell my patients that I'm a fantasy doctor, not a reality doctor." I wanted to scream at her, "I can't solve your reality problems." Somehow she had managed to pressure me into thinking that I was supposed to. The real problem was that I really wanted to, and knew that I couldn't (at least not then). It was that old narcissistic injury to the therapist again, the injury that flows from being induced, albeit with our cooperation, at least acquiescence, to believe that our professional activity is valueless. Blaming her for "making" me feel that way, I felt that my anger was entirely "reasonable." Then I had a dream about Jacques Lacan. "Why Jacques Lacan?" I asked. I find him unreadable and pseudo-profound, admiring neither the man nor the theory. Not coming up with anything, I filed that one away. During a consciously irritating session with Sally the following evening, my dream about Lacan popped into my mind. The thought, "the 'short session,' that's what that dream was about" constituted a minor Eureka experience. Somewhere Lacan speaks of the short session, of walking out on the patient who isn't going anywhere, and the disguised wish in my dream was my desire to give Sally a short session. That told me that the time for confrontation had come. I had long been aware that my 6 frustrating years in the chronic ward of a state hospital (on staff) gave me a strong identification with Sally's vocational despair. It formed the basis of my empathy for her. Since our situations were as much different as alike, I was leery of overidentifying lest I be falsely optimistic about her odds of substantially improving her situation, as I had mine, but I decided that the empathy coming out of my identification with her gave me the connectedness necessary to confront, so to speak, from within. Dan Buie tells the story of his borderline patient who came upon him, sitting with his toddler daughter on his lap on a park bench, and who felt such rage and jealousy that she said, "I'm going to kill your daughter." Buie says that worse than his terror and rage was his sense of impotency, until he connected with a memory of his parents giving his younger brother a stuffed animal that he had wanted but had not received because "he was too old for that," and feeling such rage and jealousy that he had shredded the bear and burned it. Only after making this empathic connection could Buie find a way of dealing with his patient's murderous jealousy. When we make such empathic connections with our patients, we can say hurtful things without inflicting narcissistic injury because our patients "know" that we are confronting them from within the same existential position, not from above or outside it.

I now had that empathic connection, and my Lacan dream told me that my patience was at an end, so I moved and became more confrontational, successively confronting Sally's defensive isolation, haughtiness, contempt for her co-workers, and refusal to take the steps necessary to better her situation. Each confrontation was more than a pointing to a behavior; it included the reasons, genetic, dynamic, and existential, for those behaviors. I acknowledged and confirmed the "reality" of her differences in intelligence, interests, goals, and background from her fellow workers in the course of those confrontations. Surprisingly, Sally took it all in, and we were out of our impasse. This is not to say that she didn't continue to feel pain about the meaninglessness of her work, yet her misery decreased as she formed a series of relationships of varying intimacy with her co-workers.

The next step was to lend her my vision of possibility without falsely reading the possibilities of my life into hers. This essentially consisted in analyzing her fears of entering the temple of

Higher Education, fears based on separation anxiety and terror of entering the forbidden and unknown, unconscious wishes to "kill" her father by besting him educationally, fear of oedipal and negative oedipal victories, and fear of superego punishment for doing good for herself when she deserved only bad. This dynamic work was interleaved with "vocational counseling," exploring what in light of her interests, skills, talents and restrictions, limitations and opportunities she could realistically accomplish. She is currently and successfully studying mathematics with a view toward some sort of computer work. Her employers pay most of her tuition, and anticipate that they will be able to use her newly acquired skills. But the ache of waste is still there, and at times the seemingly endless, exhausting grind of work and school becomes too much for her and suicidal thoughts reemerge. At those times, she is, in Oscar Hammerstein's immortal words, "Tired of living and scar'd of dying." For Sally the door did open, but late and not as wide as she would have wished.

LARRY: A CASE OF WORK INHIBITION

Although not without its psychodynamic determinants, the narcissistic injury inflicted by Sally's work was essentially the fruit of deprivation and lack of opportunity; not so Larry's. His presenting problem was a work inhibition that tortured him, throwing him into paralyzing depression. It was circular: depressed because he was not productive; not productive because he was depressed. Larry held an important technical job in a research facility; he had no trouble with the engineering aspects of his work, having such deep understanding of the complex interactions of the systems upon which he worked that he alone had a synoptic vision of the dynamics of the system he had created. His forte was conceptual, almost philosophical, analysis and synthesis of what was in effect an integrated, interactive information system vital to the safety of those who worked at the research facility. His work also required managerial and interpersonal skills in order to obtain cooperation from the researchers and their compliance with the safety system he had created. Larry, being a "reasonable" man who communicated well, as long as emotional intimacy was not involved, and who was not interested in dominating or controlling others, that is, was not a power-tripper, carried out his managerial and persuasive functions with skill and efficacy.

What, then, was his work inhibition? "I can't write reports; they pile up on my desk. Everything piles up on my desk. It can take me days to find a paper clip. It's irrational. Here I am, a senior engineer, and I can't organize an in-and-out basket. But it's when I look at a blank screen (Larry wrote at a word processor, being totally inhibited on paper because that was too "hard copy," i.e., too definite a commitment), cold sweat goes down my back and I become paralyzed, sometimes for weeks or even months. I'm a turd, a real turd, a turd in a lake of pure water."

The reports Larry could not write were not meaningless paperwork nor bureaucratic boilerplate (although he had his share of that, which constituted the mountain of paper on his desk). The smooth functioning of the research facility, even people's safety and very lives, depended on them. They were also the vehicle by which his technological creativity could be shared and made available to his peers around the world. It wasn't that the addition of a technical writer to the staff would have solved the problem; articulating his thoughts was intrinsic to the task he was well paid to do. I wondered how this man, who clearly couldn't do the job, held such a high-level position. The world is pretty much run by narcissistic personality disorders, but they can usually "perform." Of his suffering I had no doubt. His work paralysis was pure agony, and the narcissistic wound his incapacity inflicted was wide open and hemorrhaging. Was it a skill deficit? Did he simply not have it? People do get promoted above their capacity, with disastrous consequences for themselves and their organizations, but this was not Larry's case. When I later got to read some of his reports, his technical writing turned out to be masterly. The problem wasn't that he couldn't do it, but that he couldn't do it without suffering the agonies of the damned. His long delays had serious consequences, and even if his job wasn't in jeopardy, he clearly had many people furious with him. Perhaps that was the payoff.

Larry had grown up one of a large family of an impoverished rural clergyman of liberal persuasion who preached and practiced the "social gospel," and an eternally busy, "socially committed" mother. I always envisioned Larry's father as a sort of village Norman Thomas, whom I had once interviewed. Father was a highly respected leader who could not write his sermons. Every Saturday, the house ground to a halt as panic set in. Somehow Father had something to say by Sunday morning. As you may have guessed, Father's desk was piled high with disorder. Since other family members had similar problems, Larry argued that he had the "blocking gene." He had been on antidepressants, which did nothing to ease his writing block, although when he was on them he felt somewhat less miserable about it. Larry had had considerable therapy before coming to see me. He hadn't found it to be helpful. On the contrary, it had added to his sense of humiliation. When he was a college student, his mother had been summoned by his therapist, without his knowledge and for reasons that were never clear to him. Apparently his student health therapist had wanted to hospitalize him. I found his haziness about this incident frustrating; it was never cleared up. Later he had had to drop out of a highly prestigious graduate school because he couldn't pass a course in advanced differential equations. Talk about narcissistic wounds. Numbed by his failure to enter the top level of research scientists, Larry spent several years profoundly depressed. "Bogging down" had also plagued him as an undergraduate, but his native brightness had gotten him through, albeit with sufficient emotional distress to alarm his therapist. Without recovering from his graduate school debacle, he finally found a job related to his present work, which used his technological creativity without demanding a doctorate. The ensuing 20 years were a strange mixture of success and progres-

sive promotion, interlarded with depressive paralysis. Aspects of
his work never came easily, and he hated himself; I mean, really
hated himself, for his periods of dysfunctionality. Larry married
and had a family, barely managing the intimacy demands of
family life, which threatened his schizoid defenses. He found his
marriage emotionally tepid and sexually unsatisfying, expressing
fears that his wife didn't love him, which were partially a
projection of his fears of not being capable of love. His parenting, like his work, limped by. He certainly tried, yet failed to
"connect" with all but one of his children. Although there were
satisfactions, there was a sad and unfulfilled quality about him.
Not that his demeanor was sad. On the contrary, this tall, thin,
good-looking man dressed in button-down denim shirt and jeans
had a casual jauntiness about him, manifesting a sly sense of
humor, usually but not always defensively, and a certain crisp-
ness of mind. From under — and not always so under — that
attractive surface, his predominant affect, shame, was seldom
absent. When I think of Larry, my first association is to his
shame.

Although it was hard for Larry to engage in the therapeutic
process, much as it was hard for him to engage in life, he tried,
and over the first months of therapy, related one shame experience after another. In some cases, they were experiences in which
he had felt shame when they occurred; in others, it was more that
he was ashamed of having done, or more usually, not having
done something, and in all cases, he experienced deep shame in
the retelling. He spoke of losing his virginity to a cow; of once not
having performed his chore, on a blistering hot day, of watering
the livestock that his parents kept, and of having a neighbor come
in saying, "How could you do that? Those animals were suffering"; of having his mother catch him half undressed with his high
school girlfriend; of having left a girl stranded because he was too
socially awkward to carry through his date; and of having asked
a girl he hardly knew to talk to his mother on the phone. There
were many others. In all these situations, he felt the guilty fool,
whether it was not doing the chores or acting gauche with girls.

He was ashamed, ashamed of having done it and ashamed of telling me. The unwatered stock was the paradigm for his work life; whenever he couldn't write a report, the thought of being castigated in front of his family for cruel irresponsibility flashed through his mind, and he literally turned red with shame. The stock were still unwatered, and the scolding, condemning, humiliating neighbor had many heirs and successors. In short, a long list of humiliations, humiliatingly retold. Hardly an experience to make therapy alluring, but for Larry, all that was a piece of cake compared to "getting stuck," of not knowing what to say, of having nothing come to mind. "It's just like staring at a blank piece of paper or a blank computer screen with nothing coming, nothing at all. I sit here and nothing comes. I feel like a turd. When I was in therapy before, that would go on for weeks, sometimes months, and he (the therapist) never said a word. I went back week after week, and nothing happened. It was awful. It never got better; it just made me feel like an asshole."

Larry's previous therapist, who later became famous, had at the time been "classical." He wasn't going to deviate from "proper technique," even if it killed his patient. The narcissistic injury inflicted by the therapist's silence was enormous. His treatment only confirmed and recapitulated Larry's inadequacy, deepening his depression without giving him any insight. Larry had been in two further therapies with similar results. One of those therapists told him that his silence meant that he was having a homosexual transference, which merely bewildered and frightened Larry. I am not sure of the accuracy of this interpretation, which probably derived from a comment of Freud's that when the patient is silent, he or she is having sexual thoughts about the therapist, and which might well have been true at some "deep" level, but I am sure that it totally lacked utility. Worse, it was wounding. Homosexuality was bad enough, but the idea that he was "resisting," that is, was a "bad" patient, was just the sort of thing Larry was all too ready to buy into. Once again, his inadequacy was confirmed. Further, he felt totally misunderstood; whatever his unconscious dynamics, what he experienced was hopeless frustration at not being able to express himself to the therapist, feelings which went unrecognized.

Larry's parents had been frantically busy, "socially committed" idealists who loved from a distance. He complained of their lack of guidance, counsel, encouragement, discipline, or involvement. Late in treatment, I talked about our relationship and his denial of its importance to him, and pointed out that he was afraid to love me because such a love could and probably would be as unrequited as his childhood love had been — he dared not risk such disappointment. The earlier therapist's "technique" had recapitulated the parents' distance and detachment, not transferentially, but really. It made him worse. He remembered his traumatic disappointment when his mother was indifferent to his thrilled presentation of the evidence of his having defecated in his potty.

Naturally, we spun out the implications of his disappointed love for his own parenting and husbanding, as well as its transferential recapitulation in his fear-driven distancing from me. We also elicited how his fear of eroticizing his work froze his thoughts, how his conflicts about exhibitionism paralyzed him, how his failure to mourn his traumatic disappointments led to his avoidance of that possibility by "not producing," how his work paralysis was an identification with his father — if he couldn't love his father, then he could be his father — how he needed to punish himself for his unconscious oedipal wish to vanquish his father by surpassing him, and how his getting stuck was a "Fuck you!" to his parents, to the critical neighbor, and to the world. None of this interpretation was particularly mutative. Larry's attitude was essentially, "Interesting, but so what?" Freud used the simile of the boat tied to the dock by many cables; only when the last cable is severed will the boat sail. This boat wasn't sailing. Were there yet more cables holding it to the dock? Undoubtedly, but somehow they were irrelevant, or at least underrelevant. Interpretation was narcissistically injurious to Larry; it seemed only to increase his shame. Indeed, interpretation is frequently narcissistically injurious. The mere idea that someone knows us better than we know ourselves lowers our self-esteem, even if there may be reassurance in it. But the quality of Larry's reaction to interpretation was different from that of most patients.

In spite of this, he ultimately improved. What did the trick was not interpretation, transferential or genetic; it was relationship. I took my cue from his experience with his previous therapist and realized that letting him stare into the blank screen of his mind was antitherapeutic. Instead, I actively and vigorously intervened when Larry got stuck. I engaged him in an alliance in which we worked together to unstick him. As soon as he didn't feel alone, his "resistance" disappeared, and he could "work." Only then would we uncover thoughts about me, or far more usually, his conscious awareness that he was too ashamed of being stuck once more at work to bring it up. We struggled together to learn how he could solve whatever his current problem was. I didn't solve any problems for him, let alone make "reality" choices for him, but I did provide him with a forum in which he could problem-solve with my active participation. Larry learned to work by "working" with me in therapy. The spin-off of being helped to get started in sessions was his becoming unstuck on work projects. As our alliance progressed, I returned to my various interpretations. Now they were mutative. I don't know that I would hire Larry for a project with a strict deadline, but he has sufficiently improved to have been given a major promotion and to have achieved an international reputation in his specialty. The work of internalization is not over, and Larry needs continuing treatment to maintain his gains.

6

Loss

Psychodynamic psychotherapy is centrally, not peripherally, or contingently, or tangentially, or accidentally, about coming to terms with loss. John Locke said that "time is perpetual perishing," so each moment of life entails loss. Mourning is of the essence of the therapeutic process and we therapists are, as I tell my supervisees and students, professional mourners. The narcissistic injury of loss is most frequently that of object loss—loss of those we love; however, it need not be. We, and our patients, mourn the loss of the parents of our childhood, of earlier stages of our own lives, of values, of beliefs, of ideals, of opportunities, of health, of bodily intactness, of youth, and of life itself. So every case is a case of coming to terms with loss. All of the case material hitherto discussed importantly concerned mourning. There is a sadness about transition, even when that transition is to a happier state. Something has ended. A part of us is no more; a segment of life is gone forever. Nevertheless, it is death that inflicts the ultimate loss. Each and every loss is an anticipation of death, and death, in some sense, represents and summarizes all other losses. Yet it is different from them. Death leaves us with no hope of recovery of the lost object. I have worked with the religious, who believe in the immortality of the soul, and with the agnostics and atheists, who do not; none of them expect to have the relationship they had with those they have lost, however much they believe that they shall have some sort of "contact" with those they have lost. The unique thing about death is its finality. As Lear so searingly says as he looks at Cordelia's body, ". . . No, no, no life!/Why should a dog, a horse, a rat, have life,/ and thou no breath at all? Thou'lt come no more,/Never, never, never, never, never!" Edmund Wilson and Vladimir Nabokov argued whether or not those five noes constitute a line of trochaic pentameter. I don't know about that, but I do know that I frequently think, "Never, never, never, never, never!" when I think of the losses in my own life or when I am with patients who are mourning. Narcissistic injury ineluctably follows object loss. To amend Donne, "Each man's death diminishes me," if I love him. William James (1890), in his chapter on the self in *Principles of Psychology*, says that everything that I care about is part of me, and when those we love die, part of our very selves is gone. Loss entails a "shrinking" of our selves. Shrinking is a term the dying Freud applied to himself. That rings true; people *are* diminished when they suffer certain kinds of losses. Aging is experienced as loss, and the narcissistic injury of aging is more than many can negotiate; they succumb to late-onset alcoholism, depression, and/or psychosomatic disease. Many die before they need have.

MOURNING

The inevitability of death reminds us of our ultimate powerlessness. What could be more offensive to the narcissistically regressed, to those who are developmentally in Kohut's stage of the archaic nuclear grandiose self, than the realization that "As flies to wanton boys are we to the gods./ They kill us for their sport." We are and feel just as helpless, just as powerless when we watch those we love die as when we contemplate our own deaths, and as we watch them decline, our sense of helplessness is, in some ways, the most intolerable part of our loss. It takes us back to our infantile helplessness with all the feelings and defenses—rage, pain, shame, fear, anxiety, denial, hallucinatory wish fulfillment, manic defense, and projection for protection—that went with that helplessness. The early Freud said that just as there is no negation in the unconscious, there is no concept of death there. For him, fear of death is always fear of castration. I sense some denial here. In *Freud: Living and Dying*, Max Schur (1972) traces Freud's changing attitudes toward death. Here I would like to highlight only some of Freud's thoughts on the topic. In "Mourning and Melancholia," Freud (1915b) compares a "normal" phenomenon, mourning, with a pathological one, melancholia (depression), and finds them to have parallel structures. In each case, "an object relation regresses to an identification" (p. 251) and the lost object is internalized. Then "the shadow of the object falls on the ego" (p. 249). It is only after the first stage of mourning, identification and internalization, is complete that it becomes possible to decathect, to withdraw one's libidinal investment in the lost object. According to Freud (1915b), each single one of the memories and hopes which bind the libido to the object is brought up and hypercathected, and the detachment of the libido from it accomplished. The mourner must recall with intense feeling and deep emotion every significant bond with the lost one. It is as if the mourner were tied to the lost object (a person, a goal, an ideal, a life stage, or a part of self) by a bundle of rubber bands, each representing an emotional tie to the object; by recalling a given emotional tie with sufficient intensity, the mourner stretches that rubber band until it snaps, and when each of the emotional ties has been reexperienced with this degree of intensity and the last rubber band has been snapped, the mourner can recollect his or her emotional investment in the lost object and become free to reinvest it in a new object. In short, the mourner is then capable of loving again. Freud called this process "mourning work," and indeed, it is work.

Freud was talking about mourning for lost objects experienced as truly separate; however, this is only part of the process. Patients must also mourn the loss of the self-objects of childhood, the grandiose self and the idealized parental imago. In a sense, the whole process of working through a self-object transference is a mourning process; it is a mourning for the loss of these ideal objects. In a successful therapy, the ideal objects are replaced by real objects, objects that are in turn internalized, and the patient's emotional investment in them slowly relinquished. Only then are patients free to reinvest their love in the world and in those they find worthy of that love.

Miller (1974) believes that the dynamics of masochism, depression, and self-destructive behavior importantly involves refusal to, or inability to, mourn. In practical terms, helping patients mourn is like taking them through a mental photograph album and allowing the feelings elicited by each photograph to emerge. Time and time again, the therapist must say, "Tell me more about Uncle Joe and the time he took you fishing." This intervention aims not at finding out more about the fishing trip, but at eliciting the patient's feelings about the now departed Uncle Joe. Like so much of therapy, mourning work is, as my piano teacher used to say, "one more time with feeling."

In melancholia as opposed to mourning, the introjected object, which is hated for its abandonment, is cathected with aggression, Thanatos if you will, and hatred of the lost object becomes self-hatred. Freud believed that many suicides were attempts to "kill" the detested internal object. In treating mourning, it is the libidinal ties that are hypercathected and severed; in pathological mourning, it is the aggressive ties that are hypercathected yet not broken. Yet in every case of mourning, there is hatred of the lost object for abandonment, so that both the love and the hate must be reexperienced before the mourner is free to love (and to hate) again. Perhaps there is also a difference between the identification with the lost object in healthy mourning, and the introjection of the lost object in pathological mourning and melancholia. Freud is far from clear on this, probably because the distinction between healthy mourning and melancholia is a matter of degree, the two processes having so much in common. This is congruent with all of Freud's theorizing, which establishes the continuity of illness and health. At any rate, Freud is right in viewing the mourning work as a two-stage process. Somehow the lost object must be brought into the center of the experiential field of the mourner (in pathological mourning, that part of the work is often resisted), whether that centering is understood as the centering of attention, as a focusing on an external object, as an identification, or as an introjection. We must hold the lost object directly before us, or within us, before we can reexperience our love and hate for it and let it go. As Freud points out, the lost object is indeed lost. He or she is not present in reality, so that in some sense, the mourning work must be performed on an internal object. The distinction, insofar as there is one, on a continuum between melancholia and mourning, lies in the degree to which the lost one becomes me — self — the extent to which the shadow of the object falls on the ego. Does it cover it completely, so that the distinction between self and object is lost, or is the eclipse partial, leaving a part of self that has not become object?

Edith Jacobson (1964) saw psychotic depression as resulting from the regressive fusion of self- and object representations. It would seem that at some point, a reexternalization of the introjected lost object is necessary in order to separate from it. Then my aggression against it, my hatred of it, is externalized and is no longer turned inward on the introjected lost object. Therein lies the bridge between the two most mutative tasks in therapy, *the mourning work* and *getting the aggression out front*. Relationship with the therapist makes these events possible, provides the security to go through the pain and take the risks requisite to those achievements, but they themselves are not relationship phenomena, do not derive from transference or transference interpretation, although these may enable the mourning and externalization of aggression. Freud said that the mourner must take back his or her libido, and that is true, but the mourner must also take back his or her aggression from its

investment in the lost object so that too is accessible for investment, investment in the modification of reality that we call work,
achievement, and development. The mourner's aggressive cathexis — or just plain hatred, if you aren't a drive maven — of the
lost object, unlike the mourner's libidinal investment, is usually
not conscious so that much interpretation work may have to
precede the mourning, let alone externalization of aggression.
Guilt drives resistance to recognizing one's hatred of the lost
object. The superego plays a curious role here, punishing the
mourner for hating the lost object by preventing the mourning
work from proceeding, keeping the mourner in a state of
melancholia. Some of the shadow of the object is still on the ego
at this stage of mourning; this is severe punishment indeed, and
as Freud points out, may become capital punishment. It is as if
the superego spitefully says, "Okay, since you hate the lost one,
I'll keep you hating it; too bad the lost one is now you." The
punishment fits the crime. People also have magical fears of
retaliation by the lost object, which contribute to the resistance to
being conscious of the hatred toward it.

Throughout his life, Freud struggled with the great conun-
drums of life: sex and death. As a young man, his focus was on
sex; as he aged, on death. His aging was reflected in his
theorizing, his metapsychology. Always the psychologist par
excellence of conflict, his metapsychology was always dualistic in
the sense that two opposing life forces, which he called *Treiben*,
perhaps best translated as instinctual drives, pushed against one
another and against the environment in their quest for expression. Freud was a dualist in another sense: the early Freud was an
epiphenomenological monist; that is, one who thinks that ordinary physical and chemical events are the only *ontos on*, sources of
being, including thought and feeling; that is, the mental is
derivative of the physical. But finding that the science of his time
was not able to reduce the mental to the physical-chemical, he
derived a psychoanalytic psychology, or metapsychology as he
called it, that was independent of the physical world. Thus,
psychoanalysis became a hermeneutic science that decodes sym-

bols and explores meanings. Yet Freud never really gave up on the hope that the mental could be reduced to the physical-chemical, and the resulting tension runs throughout psychoanalytic theorizing (Freud's, at least), lending it a certain ambiguity and confusion. Freud's instinct theory, in which he defines an instinct as being on the border of the physical and the mental, with the instinct being biological while its "derivatives" are mental, is a sort of bridge between the physical-chemical and the mental as well as ambiguously monistic and dualistic.

Returning to the dualism of the instincts, the early and middle Freud postulated two sets of instinctual drives: the ego (self-preservative) instincts and the libidinal (sexual) instincts. Each has "component instincts"; for example, the sadomasochistic or exhibitionistic-voyeuristic components of libido, and each pushes for discharge and expression. Freud saw them as both existing in parallel, and interacting and intertwining, so that they sometimes worked in tandem and sometimes were in conflict. In fact, he said that the sexual instincts were *anaclitic*, leaning up against, the ego instincts, making the self-preservative instincts primordial. Since the sexual instincts are in the interest of preservation of the species, while the ego instincts are in the interest of the preservation of the individual, there is an intrinsic conflict, a duality between the basic life instincts. Each of us simultaneously fulfills the self and acts in the interest of the species (this sounds suspiciously teleological for Freud), and as Freud says, "We are paid with our toll of pleasure" in fulfilling our procreative function. Yet, if the instincts are in conflict, they are also intertwined, or to use Freud's word, fused. Failure of fusion is pathological for him. Always seeking to integrate the dynamically opposed, the monist in Freud is always at war with the dualist in him. His theories embody this conflict. Illustrative of fusion of the ego and sexual instincts, Freud says, "Love and hunger meet at a woman's breast." Therein lies one of the most universal narcissistic wounds of the analysand. The fee. As one of Winnicott's patients said, "A good session is like a good feed," and at some level, conscious or unconscious, therapy is an oral experi-

ence. It is a being fed by a symbolic mother. Therein lies the rub:
"Who pays for mother's milk?" The patient, feeling loved, seeks
love and is charged for it. No matter how "adult" and "contrac-
tual" the patient, that hurts, and like all narcissistic wounds,
engenders narcissistic rage. Naturally the more regressed, the
"sicker" the patient, the deeper the wound and the stronger the
rage, but it is always there.

Freud revised his instinct theory in his 1920 monograph, *Beyond
the Pleasure Principle*. In it, the ego instincts, which always had a
component of aggression (as did libido, judging from Freud's
simile for the connection between "ego libido" and "object libido"
of the amoeba sending out its pseudopodia to "cathect" an object,
thereby engulfing and assimilating it), now become Thanatos,
the death instinct, and the eternal war of competing and con-
flicting instincts becomes the struggle between Eros and Thanatos, Love and Death. In this formulation, the desire to die
resides within us, and indeed within all organic life, which seeks
and desires a return to the quietus of the inorganic. The wish to
die is intrinsic, and if it is not externalized as aggression toward
the environment, destroys us. So to speak, the choice is between
suicide and murder. Freud cites the evidence ranging from his
infant grandson's desire to endlessly repeat a game with a piece of
string, to the negative therapeutic reaction, to self-destructive
acts and behaviors including addiction, moral masochism, self-
mutilation, and suicide. The repetition, the endless turning about
one point, the "eternal return" of the repetition compulsion, is a
simulacrum of the quietus of death. In each case, there is stasis.
Further, the indescribable horrors of World War I, in which
Europe destroyed itself, separated Freud's first instinct theory
from his second. Human behavior, clinical and historical, simply
could not be accounted for by a theory that humans were
motivated solely by a "pleasure principle" or by self-preservative
and reproductive drives. Now Freud, identifying himself with the
pre-Socratic philosopher Empedocles who wrote of the eternal
war between Eros and Strife, sets forth one of the great tragic
visions of human life in which cosmically and intrapsychically

Eros and Thanatos, the anabolic and the catabolic, the forces of unity and the forces of disintegration, anti-entropy and entropy, love and hate, combat each other until the end of time.

Mourning ourselves and perhaps others now becomes a different task. Death is no longer something that happens to us or to others; rather, it comes from within, from the ineluctable succumbing of Eros. Now we see a new and different meaning of Freud's injunction that we must love or grow ill. It also provides us with another link between mourning and directing our aggression outward. Whatever the ontological status of Thanatos, or its utility as an explanatory principle (most analysts have rejected the death instinct, opting instead for a dual-instinct theory in which the instincts are libido and aggression), one of its psychodynamic meanings for Freud has to be turning the passive into the active. All of his life, Freud hated poverty and helplessness above all else, and there is no more ultimate experience of helplessness than dying. By moving death within, Freud made it his choice, and he does so at a time not far removed from the diagnosis of his cancer, already anticipated in the lesion in Irma's mouth in the specimen dream of psychoanalysis, the Dream of Irma's Injection, dreamt twenty years earlier. But internalization of death is strange—although I, like all of the organic, desire to return to the inorganic, that desire is id stuff—an impersonal drive of nature rather than ego–self stuff. If the goal of psychoanalytic therapy is "Where id (it) was, ego (I) shall be," then Thanatos must also be deinstinctualized and personalized, made part of my conscious self—my ego. I think that this sometimes happens at the end of life, when people embrace their death as something they now desire, experiencing their death as neither coming from the outside nor driven by a blind force within them. "Men must endure/Their going hence, even as their coming hither/Ripeness is all" becomes something more than and different from endurance. Of course, but few die with the kind of serene choosing to go hence that "ripeness is all" implies.

Immediately before the Great War, Freud wrote "On Narcissism" (1914a), which provides a bridge between his first instinct

theory and his second. "On Narcissism" gropes toward the
structural model, but far more saliently, sees that energy unex-
pended poisons and narcissistically injures. Narcissism, here
meaning pathological narcissism, also provides a bridge between
libido-Eros and Thanatos. As noted in Chapter 1, the word
narcissism comes from the Greek root *Narke*, meaning to deaden,
which is also the etymological source of the English word *narcotic*.
Both narcissism (pathological) and narcotics deaden, and indeed
in the legend, Narcissus' self-love kills him. We must love
(objects) or die. So libido and Thanatos were related in complex
ways and not only inversely all along. This casts light on the
love–death obsession of the Romantic poets. As we might phrase
it, narcissistic object choice — falling in love with ourselves once
removed — is fatal: nothing less than true object love will do. That
sheds some more light on mourning. Narcissistic as mourning
must necessarily be, its resolution requires the restoration of the
power to love — yet the ability to love again depends on successful
mourning, a tricky dialectical process at best.

Mourning in the presence of and in relationship with the
therapist is a halfway station toward object love. Mourning is a
dreadfully lonely experience, both because of its intrinsic egoistic
nature and because other people flee from the mourner. Mourn-
ing-in-the-presence-of is the beginning of a libidinal relationship
with. As someone has said, "Being alone, alone is the worst of the
human condition, while being alone together is as well as we can
do." Mourning in the presence of the therapist is a being-alone
together.

REACHING THE DEPRESSIVE POSITION

Most analysts reject the death instinct; Melanie Klein does not,
and her work too offers some insights into mourning. Klein was
an analysand of Karl Abraham, from whom Freud gleaned some
of the theoretical underpinnings of "Mourning and Melancholia,"
so that there is a direct link between Freud's and Klein's respective

notions of mourning. Klein places Thanatos within the infant who must externalize it, at first in fantasy, and later through aggression against the object. In the fantasy, the death instinct is projected onto the object — or rather, part-object, the breast — creating the "bad breast." Once it is projected, the death instinct plays no further role in Kleinian theory, which then becomes an object relations theory. The bad breast, repository of the dangerous death instinct, is now itself a dangerous persecutor. Inevitable environmental frustration facilitates splitting the part-object breast into the good object and bad object. The bad breast that is the recipient of the projected death instinct is the breast that frustrates; the good breast is the recipient of the projection of inner goodness — libido, or Eros, if you prefer, which is projected to protect it from inner badness, the innate death instinct. It is the breast that feeds. This casts a new light on Freud's observation that love and hunger meet at a woman's breast. Which breast? The good breast or the bad breast? If the lost object is to be a whole object, then it must be a successor of the part-object, of the good-bad breast, and this is only possible if splitting has been relinquished and integration has occurred. Before these developmental achievements, mourning is not possible. This suggests that much clinical developmental work is prerequisite to mourning work. In the Kleinian scenario, the bad breast, now a dangerous environmental persecutor, is reintrojected to gain control over it, which puts the badness and danger once more inside, albeit now as a bad (part-) object rather than as an innate destructive force. The bad internal object is now reprojected, a dynamic that can be extended indefinitely in the Kleinian object relational ping pong game. This already murky picture is further complicated by the existence of an alternate source of the badness, another evolutionary pathway eventuating in the bad breast. I not only project my death instinct; I aggress with it, and now my aggression toward, hatred of, and envy of the good breast (which ironically is good in part because I have projected my goodness onto it) turns it into the bad breast. According to Klein, I want to bite, rip to pieces, piss on, shit on the good breast. All this happens in what she calls the *paranoid-schizoid position*. Then I come to see that I have created, by these alternative pathways, the bad breast, and also "realize" (all of these realizations being preverbal and unconscious) that the good breast and the bad breast are one. There is little room here for the environmental determinants of the badness of the bad breast, and we are as far away from a frustration–aggression hypothesis as possible. Only now can I *mourn* the destructive consequences of my primitive aggression, and here we have the genetic root of the capacity to mourn. In that mourning process, I make reparation for my envy, greed, and hatred. I can only do so because of my *gratitude* for the good breast, and it is gratitude that makes overcoming envy possible. This is interesting in light of the current practice of *celebrating* a requiem mass in which gratitude for the life of the deceased and celebration of his or her life takes precedence over sorrow and grief. Other religions have moved in the same direction in their death rites. Klein would have understood this. There is certainly denial here, yet there is clearly something else. Integrating the good and bad breasts (and good and bad self), moving from part-objects to whole object, from splitting to an ambivalence in which love overshadows hate, in which Eros is in ascendance over Thanatos, is the task carried out by working through the *depressive position*. Mourning through reparation enabled by gratitude both consolidates the depressive position and makes further mourning possible. Put differently, those who have not reached the depressive position lack the capacity to mourn. As is well known, the stronger the ambivalence toward the lost object, the harder it is to mourn. This makes sense from the point of view of the Kleinian developmental scheme. Further, the notion of the internal bad object also makes sense. We started with bad internal objects so that regressive reintrojection during the stress of the libidinal deprivation of object loss occurs with ease; the pathway is already greased. For Klein also, the shadow of the object falls on the ego. Further, regressive splitting, which impedes mourning the lost object, also easily occurs.

So Klein casts light on the origins of the capacity to mourn and on the developmental arrests that impede mourning. Tangentially, but interestingly, Klein's emphasis on the innate aggression against the good breast, the desire to bite it and tear it to pieces, casts light on the Jewish dietary laws — the laws of *kashrut*, which proscribe the eating of milk and meat together. Is this a reaction formation against the desire to bite the good breast? If the milk is separated from the meat, the breast cannot be bitten, and the desire to do so frustrated. Freud said that where a prohibition is stressed, the desire must be great, and that seems to fit this situation. Enough of historical fantasy.

Freud's thoughts about death and mourning were not consistent. Walking in the Alps with the poet Rainer Maria Rilke just before the outbreak of the Great War, the poet lamented and found intolerable that all the beauty they were witness to would vanish, and lamented the transience of all things. Freud replied to him, in one of his most beautiful essays, "On Transience" (1916),

> No! It is impossible that all this loveliness of Nature and Art, of the world of our sensations and of the world outside, will really fade away into nothing . . . Somehow or other this loveliness must be able to persist and to escape all the powers of destruction.
>
> But this demand for immortality is a product of our wishes too unmistakable to lay claim to reality: what is painful may nonetheless be true. I could not see my way to dispute the transience of all things, nor could I insist on an exception in favor of what is beautiful and perfect. But I did dispute the pessimistic poet's view that the transience of what is beautiful involves any loss in its worth.
>
> On the contrary, an increase! *Transience value is scarcity value in time.* [My emphasis] Limitation and the possibility of an enjoyment raises the value of the enjoyment . . . A flower that blossoms only for a single night does not seem to us on that account less lovely. Nor can I understand any better why the beauty and perfection of a work of art or an intellectual achievement should lose its worth because of its temporal limitations. The time may indeed come when the pictures and statues which we

admire today will crumble to dust, or a race of men may follow us who no longer understand the works of our poets and thinkers, or a geological epoch may even arrive when all animate life upon earth ceases; but since the value of all this beauty and perfection is determined only by its significance for our own emotional lives, it has no need to survive us, and is therefore independent of absolute duration. [p. 305]

In *Thoughts for the Times on War and Death* (1915b), written during the fighting, Freud said:

[War] destroyed not only the beauty of the countryside through which it passed and the works of art which it met on its path but also shattered our pride in the achievements of our civilization, our admiration for many philosophers and artists in our hope of a final triumph over the differences between nations and races. It tarnished the lofty impartiality of our science, it revealed our instincts in all their nakedness and let loose the evil spirits within us which we thought had been tamed forever by centuries of continuous education by the noblest minds. . . .

But have those . . . possessions, which we have now lost, really ceased to have any worth for us because they have proved so perishable and so unresistant? To many of us this seemed to be so, but once more wrongly, in my view. I believe that those who think thus . . . are simply in a state of mourning for what is lost. Mourning, as we know, however painful it may be, comes to a spontaneous end. When it has renounced everything that has been lost, then . . . our libido is once more free (insofar as we are still young and active) to replace the lost objects by fresh ones equally or still more precious. It is to be hoped that the same will be true of the losses caused by this war. When once the mourning is over, it will be found that our high opinion of the riches of civilization has lost nothing from our discovery of their fragility. We shall build up again all that the war has destroyed, and perhaps on firmer ground and more lastingly than before. [p. 307]

There is a nobility about both these passages, an acceptance and serenity, realistic, courageous, and beautiful.

In 1920, Freud came to know grief not theoretically but personally. His beloved daughter Sophie died suddenly in the flu epidemic and his *Beyond the Pleasure Principle* may be in part a working through of his loss, just as *Interpretation of Dreams* was his working through of his father's death. He had written to Fliess at the time of his father's death that loss of a father was "the most poignant loss of a man's life." Perhaps, but the death of a child differs from the death of a parent. He wrote to Oskar Pfister, the Swiss pastor who promoted an alliance of psychoanalysis and liberal religion:

> That afternoon, we received news that our sweet Sophie in Hamburg had been snatched away by influenzal pneumonia, snatched away in the midst of glowing health, from a full and active life as a competent mother and loving wife, all in four or five days, as though she had never existed. Though we had worried about her for a couple of days, we had nevertheless been hopeful; it is so difficult to judge from a distance. And this distance must remain distance; we were not able to travel at once, as we intended, after the first alarming news; there was no train, not even for an emergency. The undisguised brutality of our time is weighing heavily upon us. Tomorrow she is to be cremated, our poor Sunday child!. . .
>
> Sophie leaves two sons, one six, the other thirteen months, and an inconsolable husband who will have to pay dearly for the happiness of these seven years. The happiness existed exclusively within them; outwardly there was war, conscription, wounds, the depletion of their resources, but they had remained courageous and gay.
>
> I work as much as I can, and am thankful for the diversion. The loss of a child seems to be a serious, narcissistic injury; what is known as mourning will probably follow only later. [1960, pp. 327–328]

To Sándor Ferenczi, he wrote,

> Please don't worry about me. Apart from feeling rather more tired, I am the same. Death, painful as it is, does not affect my

attitude towards life. For years I was prepared for the loss of our sons; now it is our daughter; as a confirmed unbeliever I have no one to accuse and realize there is no place where I can lodge a complaint. 'The unvaried, still returning hour of duty' and 'the dear, lovely habit of living' will do their bit towards letting everything go on as before. *Deep down I sense a bitter, irreparable narcissistic injury.* [My emphasis] My wife and Annerl are profoundly affected in a more human way. [1960, p. 328]

"In Mourning and Melancholia," written during the war before Sophie's loss, Freud (1915a) had stressed, as he did in the passages on transience above, the working through of the mourning process so that the libidinal investment in the lost object is withdrawn and we are free to love again. Experience made him more realistic. In 1929, after having lost Sophie, he wrote a letter of consolation to his old friend the Swiss existential analyst Ludwig Binswanger, in which he says,

> My daughter who died would have been thirty-six years old today. . . .
> *Although we know that after such a loss, the acute state of mourning will subside, we also know that we shall remain inconsolable and will never find a substitute. No matter what may fill the gap, even if it is filled completely, it nevertheless remains something else.* [My emphasis] And actually this is as it should be. It is the only way of perpetuating that love which we do not want to relinquish. [1960, p. 386]

In the same year, Freud wrote to the widow of his Hungarian friend and financial supporter, Anton von Freund, consoling her for the loss of her mother. He wrote,

> I have purposely allowed your first period of mourning to pass before sending you a few words of sympathy. I feel that someone who has suffered a great loss is entitled to be left in peace. In fact, I think this period of silence ought to be extended for a long time if the fear of appearing unsympathetic did not compel one to communicate. As it is, anything one can say must sound to the

bereaved like so many empty words. The 'work of mourning' is an intimate process which cannot stand any interference.

My thoughts go back to another occasion [her husband's death] of painful mourning which Fate brought to you—but to me, too; and I cannot get over it that so much sorrow has been inflicted on you, undeserved as usual in such cases and out of all proportion to the strength with which nature has endowed you. *Where are we to look for justice? No one inquires after our wishes, our merits, or our claims.* [My emphasis] But if the wishes of your friends had any power, your life would have taken a happier course. [1960, pp. 373–374]

Ernest Becker (1973) and the existential analysts like Yalom (1989) put great emphasis on patients confronting their own mortality, claiming that only by overcoming our denial of death (cf. Freud's view that there is no concept of death in the unconscious) is it possible to live fully. Tillich makes much the same point in his discussion of ontological and neurotic anxiety. I am currently working with a patient who has cancer and seems to have faced and come to terms with her own mortality. She reports, and I have every reason to believe her, that this has freed her from the neurotic inhibitions of a lifetime, and I have known others who have reported similar experiences. My patient, Carol, worked through her confrontation with her mortality in pretty much the way that Kübler-Ross (1969) described. Her initial response was denial, very much reinforced and supported by her husband (this was a couple therapy), followed by bargaining—If I undergo an especially rigorous treatment, I will live, I will live until my daughter graduates college, and similar "contracts" with God—which in turn broke down in a further stage of the relinquishing of denial, which is never total. Once she realized that her various bargains would not keep her alive, she became deeply depressed. After a long period of depression, her rage emerged, a rage I had probed for. According to Kübler-Ross, rage precedes depression in the mourning experience; I find that depression precedes rage, although there is a dialectical relation-ship between them. Only after her experiencing her rage did Carol come to acceptance.

TECHNOLOGY AND IMMORTALITY

As Becker pointed out, denial of death is not only personal, it is cultural. One of the manifestations of our cultural denial of death is the deification of technology. There is something manifestly irrational about our relationship to technology. At times, we mindlessly plunder and despoil the environment with an almost psychotic denial of the deleterious concomitants of a given technological process; at other times we angrily turn away from technology, as if in bitter disillusionment with a failed God. Human greed being seemingly boundless, economic motives certainly account for much of the blind rapacity of man's desecration of the ecosphere. Powerful interests control and withhold information necessary for rational decision-making, spending millions on self-serving propaganda and manipulation of public opinion. Nevertheless, there is such an irrational quality to our use of technology, with its resultant biological, chemical, and radiological pollutions and toxicities, that some additional motive must underlie the "surplus" irrationality of our relationship to technology. The dynamic underlying our attitudes and behaviors toward technology is an unconscious, magical belief in the power of technology to confer immortality. It is a belief that science will allow us to escape the inevitable, to cheat death. This unconscious, magical belief system prevents us from acknowledging the inherent limitations of science. If technology is to be able to avert the ultimate disaster, death, then its power must be limitless, and any admission of its limitations becomes faith-shattering and anxiety-provoking. Thus, our hope that technology will confer immortality entails faith in the omniscience of science and the omnipotence of technology. Since neither is the case, our thinking is based on illusion.

Paradoxically, our very inability to acknowledge the limitations of our knowledge, lest we arouse anxiety by threatening our immortality, prevents us from rationally responding to real danger and increases our chances of premature death from unwanted "side effects" of technology.

Science as the highest manifestation of the reality principle;

that is, as the disinterested pursuit of "truth," has never had wide appeal. However, science as ideology, "Better Things for Better Living through Chemistry," with its promise of never-ending plenty, is congruent with American optimism and has been widely subscribed to. We project our repressed infantile feelings of omnipotence onto technology, and we react as if to a deep narcissistic wound when our projected omnipotence is threatened. Our reaction is either denial of technological limitations, or indiscriminate rejection of the legitimate claims of science. The current religious revival is a consequence, in part, of disappointment in science and technology. Disillusionment with the new god results in return to the old god. The worship of science and technology, with its attendant irrationalities, is ironically a late nineteenth- and twentieth-century phenomenon, a period in which science has become acutely aware of its own limitations. The distinguishing characteristic of contemporary science is its self-consciousness, embodied in a set of "you can't have your cake and eat it too" laws.

Each of these laws postulates an inverse relationship between the exactitude with which we can know reciprocal aspects of certain phenomena. The more we know about X, the less we can know about Y is the case in very important instances in which we would like to have complete knowledge about both X and Y. The most famous of these laws is Heisenberg's principle, which states that we cannot simultaneously determine the location and momentum of an electron. Similarly, Gödel showed that the consistency and completeness of a mathematical system cannot both be demonstrated. Shannon demonstrated a parallel indeterminacy in information theory by proving that there is an inverse relationship between information and randomness, such that the more information you convey, the more "noise" there will be.

Thus, our practice, which proceeds as if we were omniscient, is totally at variance with the ethos of modern science, and we persist in this conduct in spite of our extensive experience of unpredicted, unanticipated, unintended, unwanted, disastrous consequences of our technology.

However, if the next technological intervention may confer

immortality, then our infinite gullibility, our utter lack of critical perspective in matters technological, becomes intelligible. The unconscious projection of primitive feelings of narcissistic omnipotence is indeed a powerful force. Somewhere in the '70s, the reality of air and water pollution, widespread environmental radiation, damaged food chains, dissemination of carcinogenic chemicals, and the grossly manifest deterioration of the quality of life as a spinoff of high technology became so blatant that some of that reality penetrated our rigid, near psychotic denial of the fallibility of technology. This break in the illusion of technological omnipotence caused great anxiety. It was reacted to in diametrically opposite ways: on the one hand, there were rational, realistic attempts to deal with the above problems; on the other hand, there was a resurgence of older absolutisms accompanied by a rejection of science altogether. In the words of one contemporary bumper sticker, "God said it, I believe it, and that settles it." The repudiation of evolutionary theory, which had inflicted a deep narcissistic wound and which had little connection with the bread-and-butter benefits of science, became a rallying cry of the new irrationality. Our anxiety-tinged doubts about the beneficence and power of technology were given confirmation of another kind by America's experience in Vietnam. Our defeat was a deeply traumatic narcissistic blow. All our technological sophistication could not defeat a technologically primitive foe. The quintessence of our irrational belief in the efficacy of quantification, that sine qua non of modern scientific technique, was the body count in Vietnam. It failed to win the war.

At the same time, the humanistic tradition, with its flawed yet heroic attempt to uphold the values of reasonableness, skepticism, broadness of perspective, critical thinking, and objectivity, was dying. The study of philosophy in the universities ceased to have any relation to the love of wisdom and became another specialty, a pseudo-science obsessed with technique. Liberal studies were largely replaced by the study of computer technology. The more the potential programmers were programmed, the emptier they felt. It is no accident that the trivialization of philosophy was contemporaneous with the religious revival. The questing young that philosophy lost by default were quickly absorbed by the newly fashionable religiosity.

As our subliminal hope that technology would allow us to evade death became less and less tenable, the general level of anxiety rose. Humanity cannot bear facing the reality of its situation; a brief moment between two nothingnesses, lived on a blood-drenched earth, spinning through boundless and empty space. People cannot live without hope. As a powerful, unconscious belief system faltered, it was replaced by another, and we purchased hope at the price of tolerance and rationality. We were left with a choice between the slavish worship of numbers without relevance on computer printouts and the equally slavish worship of creeds without compassion in sacred texts. Truly, this is a schizophrenic prescription for disaster. Our culture seems hell-bent on reducing our options to a choice between scientism or dogmatism, and we see this reflected in the patients we see. Their attempts to deal with loss and their own mortality bring to the fore their irrationalities and those of our culture.

Earlier I stated that mourning work was not transference work. That is not altogether true. In one sense, the therapist merely provides a safe place, a holding environment, in which to mourn, yet in many cases the mourning work is importantly mediated by the transference. Sally's (the ACOA patient) mourning of her mother was enabled by her separation experiences with me in which her abandonment rage became manifest (see Chapter 3). Each of her separations from me were losses representative of the loss of her mother and provided occasions for mourning work. This is generally true, and every separation of patient and therapist is an opportunity for mourning. Termination is even more so. Every termination phase is a mourning process—a mourning for the anticipated loss of a highly valued, perhaps even lifesaving relationship, and simultaneously a mourning for all of the patient's earlier losses. Each succeeding loss activates and recapitulates our earlier losses. So the transference and termination become highly complex. Their many layers include all of the object losses in the patient's life, so that the therapist is simultaneously or successively the actual parents, the imagoes of the parents of childhood, dead siblings, dead friends, perhaps lost mates or lovers, and even lost children. It is important, if the patient is to receive optimal benefit from treatment, that each of these meanings of termination be made conscious. There is often strong resistance to this, sometimes manifest in denial of the importance of the therapeutic relationship and the significance of its loss in the patient's life. Other patients cannot stand the pain of the mourning work and terminate abruptly to avoid it. Timely interpretations of this phenomenon may prevent it. Fear of the pain of loss prevents some patients from staying with or developing relationships. Hopefully we do not fear loss so much that we lose whatever opportunities for relatedness life may offer us.

All of the feelings in termination are not sad. As in the end of any relationship, there may be joy as well as sorrow; an acknowledgement of the release the patient feels is just as important as is the patient's experiencing of sadness over separation. Patients often repress or suppress their joyful feelings at termination for fear of hurting us. Termination is also a loss for the therapist, and we too suffer narcissistic injury when our patients leave us. I have felt tears welling up in my eyes during a final session, just as I have felt relief when therapeutic relationships ended.

Since every case is a case about the narcissistic injury of loss, each of the cases discussed in this book has been about enabling mourning. Accordingly, the case material to follow is relatively brief.

FRED: AFRAID TO LOVE AGAIN

One of my most successful cases was the brief therapy of a 79-year-old man whose presenting problem was that he was "tormented with carnal desire." As with so many patients, the problem didn't seem to do with loss, yet he was suffering from a failure to mourn. One can't mourn behind an addiction, a depression, or an acting-out defense. Addiction, chemical or behavioral, deadens the feelings so that mourning work is impossible, however maudlinly the still-addicted patient may bewail his or her loss. Depression similarly is in lieu of mourning — its pathological equivalent, while acting out diverts and takes one away from the pain of separation. Any symptom or characterological defense can serve as a defense against mourning, and that function of the symptom or characterological trait may render it resistant to treatment. Better to be anxious, phobic, or compulsive than feel the pain of loss. Therefore, it behooves us to probe for hidden object loss and its accompanying repressed narcissistic injury with all patients. Fred readily talked about his widowhood, but failed to mention his daughter's death. He was a sprightly, short, thin, white-haired, casually but well-dressed man who looked and acted younger than his years. I would have taken him for a healthy 65. His advanced years had twice exposed him to narcissistic injury from mental health professionals. Telling his physician that he felt tense and unhappy, he was referred to a psychiatrist who spoke to him for 5 minutes, wrote a prescription, and dismissed him. Fred *wanted* to talk; his age in no way disqualified him as a psychotherapy patient, yet the psychiatrist, whom I knew to practice psychotherapy, had brushed him off. Persisting, he had gone to a counselor who had told him, "There is something pathological about your preoccupation with sex, and it's time to put that behind you and to concentrate on your grandchildren." The counselor's comments had hurt far more than the brush-off from the psychiatrist; they so stuck in his mind that he quoted them, probably word for word, the counselor's language being so different in word and style from Fred's that there was no mistaking who said what. He had had no psychotherapeutic experience before the age of 78. Fortunately, one of Fred's daughters was in treatment, and her therapist referred him to me.

Fred was a strict Catholic, and his participation in the life of the church was important to him. He was also a worldly man whose beliefs, although deeply felt, were not fanatical. He had been happily married to the same woman for 54 years until she had died 5 years before. As in any long-term relationship, their level of intimacy would vary, and they had had their share of conflicts, yet his memories of her were of mutual love, successful parenting, and shared interests and values. He did not idealize her, and the relationship did not appear to have been unhealthily symbiotic; both had a life of their own as well as a life in common. He seemed to have adjusted well to widowhood, had good relations with his children and grandchildren, traveled, took pleasure in things, and didn't appear depressed. He did come across as struggling to contain considerable tension. I wondered what medication the psychiatrist had prescribed, Fred having crumpled the prescription on his way out of the office. He stated, "Doctor, when I walk down the street, I look at all the women. I want them. Especially the good-looking ones in their early sixties. But to tell the truth, I am turned on by the younger ones too. I'm tormented by carnal desire and feel awful about it. I feel disloyal — to my wife. If a young girl walked by bare-assed, I probably wouldn't get it up, but I want to try. What should I do?"

The phrase "carnal desire" jumped out; that wasn't Fred's idiom. Did he get that from a sermon? He sounded like a case of the Catholic crazies — neurosis secondary to sexual guilt — but that didn't turn out to be the case. I also wondered if he was still mourning his wife. In the first 2 months of therapy, we talked almost exclusively about his marriage. He clearly missed his wife, yet he was not unhappy in his widowhood, nor had he been sexually inhibited. Something didn't add. Then out of the blue, Fred said, "I was happy to retire. I was just a technician without much education, but that didn't matter for a long time. I was in the defense industry and I got to run a department. I did it well. Then they upgraded the educational requirements and the 'real engineers' took over. After that, I was treated like shit. I just held on until I could retire. It was a good thing I did; my daughter got sick right around then, and I was able to spend time with her while she was dying." He had never mentioned that he had lost a daughter. The memory of one narcissistic injury had led to another. His displacement from a position of authority at work had wounded him deeply. Twenty-five years later, it still rankled. When I suggested that he must be very angry at the "young punks" who had pushed him aside, he quickly began to express his rage. He had never done so, and it was still there after all those years, but it was his failure to come to terms with the loss of his daughter that was the real problem. We spent 3 months talking about her death from cancer and how it had affected Fred and his wife. He was surprised that he still felt such sorrow and pain. Eventually, I told him that his guilt about having a girlfriend was survivor guilt, that he didn't feel that he, the father, who in the natural course of things should have predeceased his daughter, should have sexual pleasure while his child had no pleasure at all. Although Fred did feel some disloyalty toward his wife, that wasn't really the problem. He had displaced his survivor guilt vis-à-vis the daughter onto the wife in order to avoid the pain of mourning for her. He did that mourning in therapy and became free "to love again." Shortly after starting to date a 50-year-old, Fred terminated. I never interpreted that the sexual relationship with a younger woman that he sought contained incestuous wishes toward his daughter.

AARON: A CASE OF FAILURE TO MOURN

Aaron was a mid-thirties schoolteacher with a ponytail. He wore boots, jeans, and a woodsman's shirt. He presented himself as aggressively countercultural. Highly intellectual, he punctuated his speech with quotes from the poets and allusions to Marx. Intelligent as well as intellectual, he just missed being pretentious, his sense of humor being his saving grace. He came to therapy because he was experiencing anxiety attacks. "Doctor, I was living in the bathtub in my pad. I had been living there for about 3 weeks, ever since I started feeling this unbelievable anxiety. It's like my whole body is on fire. My head pounds. My vision distorts. That was the worst part of it. I walk down the street and the curbs raise and lower, and sometimes the whole street goes askew, as if I had a new prescription for astigmatism and hadn't adjusted to it. My heart pounds and I can't get my breath. Sometimes I'm afraid that I'm having a heart attack, other times a stroke. It was after I was sitting in philosophy class (he was a professional student, at the moment a nonmatriculated, would-be doctoral candidate) as the professor was lecturing on perception, and the walls and floor started slanting. Then I heard this *ping, ping, ping*. I couldn't figure out what was causing the pinging. The visual distortions got worse and the pinging got louder. Then I looked down and saw gobbets of sweat rolling off my fingertips and hitting the floor — that was the pinging. It was then that I started worrying that gravity would fail and I would fall off the earth. I ran out of class and ran-walked 10 miles back to my pad. I didn't want to be in the subway when gravity failed, and besides, my heart pounds like mad when I go down there. It feels like I will be pulled in front of a train. When I got home, I took some blankets and a pillow and moved into the bathtub. I stayed there. My roommates didn't like it, and it was embarrassing for all of us when they used the toilet, but I wouldn't — couldn't — leave.

"I had been anxious ever since I was teaching at the Grave School. That's on Corpse Road out in the boonies. [These turned out to be slips for the Grove School on Copse Road.] I couldn't stand it there so I came back to town. Earlier I had tried to teach in a little college in New Hampshire. I think I was a pretty good instructor, but when they didn't rehire me for the next semester, I flipped out. I was so phobic that I couldn't take the bus back to New York, so I cooked up a scheme to canoe down the Connecticut River to Long Island Sound and follow the coast to Manhattan. When I confided my plans to another prof, he sort of shanghaied me into his car and drove me to the City. I stayed in the fetal position in the backseat all the way and didn't say a word. When we got here, I invited him into my pad, but he sped off and I've never heard from him again. When I got inside, there was some jagged glass from a broken window that started saying, 'Aaron, come here and put your wrists on me.' I couldn't hack that, so I went and taught at the Grave School.

"Finally, my roommates insisted that I leave the bathtub, so I went down to the street. I thought I was going to die. I had the most horrible chest pain and thought of the end of 'Dover Beach': 'And we are here as on a darkling plain/Swept with confused alarum of struggle and flight,/Where ignorant armies clash by night.' Then I started to fall and grabbed onto a passerby to ask for help. The poor bastard thought I was crazy. [Was he?] So I sort of stumbled into a hospital emergency room. The resident did the knee taps and all that jazz, and said I was having an anxiety attack and should get some therapy. I thought, 'Fuck you!' and had a few drinks and smoked a joint. I felt fine. I wasn't worried about gravity failing anymore. I'm a logical guy, so I figured out that if a few shots and a joint could take my anxiety away, I wasn't having a heart attack, so I came to you. Have you read van Gebsattel?"

Hardly sounds like a case in which the central issue is object loss and unresolved mourning, does it? It was. Aaron, like Freud, couldn't come to terms with his father's death; unlike Freud, he had absolutely no idea that his father's death 15 years earlier had any bearing on his condition. Always overreaching himself, Aaron had had a long list of academic and job failures, narcissistic wounds all, and had engaged in a series of pathetic compensatory maneuvers, none of which shored up his crumpled self-esteem for long, or decreased his self-hatred. Existentialism, Marxism, despairing poetry, and political revolt absorbed his energies and gave him a means to externalize his rage, probably staving off suicide, which was frequently in his thoughts. His gravitational concerns and the broken window having spoken to him suggested serious pathology, but for all of his pressured speech and sometimes bizarre behavior, he impressed as sane, albeit terrified. He refused a referral for psychotropic medication for panic and possible delusional ideation. To have insisted would have been to have inflicted a needless narcissistic injury. He was already sure that he was crazy, and if I confirmed it, as my insisting on medication would have, that would have only further reduced his self-esteem and in all likelihood, driven him out of therapy. When his anxiety became intolerable, he drank and smoked pot. He felt that he could control their effect on him, but not the effect of medication. I interpreted that *this* was delusional, but since he didn't appear to have a chemical dependency problem, I didn't make an issue out of it.

As it turned out, he was looking for a lifeline and grasped onto me for dear life. The transference was intense and complex, but this is not the place to discuss it. The point I want to make about Aaron is that all roads led to his father. This surprised him; he was acutely conscious of his anger toward his mother and of his feeling smothered by her; and as treatment went along, he became aware that part of him wished to symbiose with Mother and that his anger at her was in part a defense against his wish for a regressive fusion. His feelings of not being able to breathe were certainly related to his wish/fear of Mother's smothering. But he saw no problems in his relationship to his father, nor in his feelings about his father's death. He did allow that his father, a commuter, had not been around much, and that although Aaron felt loved by him, his father had been emotionally distant, using humor (as did Aaron) as a distancing device. Aaron also allowed that his father had failed to protect him from the women's (he had three older sisters) envelopment. His intense bond to me was, whatever else it might be, that male solidarity he had lacked in childhood. Aaron's criticisms of Father were intellectualized and not deeply felt, yet dream after dream and association after association dealt with Father.

Six months into therapy, I said the obvious (to me): "Your father died of a heart attack, and your symptoms are the symptoms of a heart attack. When you feel that you are dying, you are identifying with him. If you can't have him, you can be him. And you're punishing yourself for your rage at him for throwing you into the lioness's den, rage that you unconsciously believe killed him." The floodgates opened. A period of intense mourning followed. Notice that I didn't interpret, at that time, the oedipal side of Aaron's rage at his father and his fear/wish to possess the mother; to have done so would have made him feel that he was even worse than he already felt he was, and would not have led to any useful insight. About a year later, we did discuss the more oedipal aspects of Aaron's relationship to his parents. He mourned nontransferentially in my presence and not in relationship to me, and he mourned transferentially in relationship to me. The most moving of the nontransferential mourning was the session in which Aaron lay semifetally on the couch and wept like a 3-year-old, sobbing over and over again, "I miss my Daddy. I want my Daddy." Given his defensive arrogance and intellectualization, that was amazing. If his sorrow was shared, his rage was expressed transferentially. The breakthrough there was when Aaron called me shortly after a session and, using every word in the book, berated me for ignoring him and distancing myself from him when I had looked down at my desk as he was leaving. Those, of course, were the feelings he had felt toward his ironically humorous, distant father. Shortly after the "I want my Daddy" and rage sessions, Aaron had a dream in which his mother said "We lost him," which she had said when she called Aaron at graduate school to tell him of his father's death. He then told me that he had refused to say *Kaddish* for his father, wanting no part of that superstitious nonsense, but that he had now decided that he had to, "in order to exorcise a demon." He told me that he had spoken to a rabbi to "get a fix on the ritual," and that he would say the *Kaddish* for eleven months as ritually prescribed for the death of a parent. "I think it will be good for me to follow the ways of the tribe for once, to relinquish some of my sense of uniqueness. I guess you would say I was relinquishing some of my narcissism." Aaron didn't exactly join the tribe, since he said the *Kaddish* alone, not as a member of a *minyan* (a religious quorum), as is customary; that way, he could belong and not belong at the same time, which, given his character structure, was an adaptive compromise. Aaron assumed that I, like all analysts, was an atheist, and he was deeply afraid of my mocking his saying of the *Kaddish*. For that reason, I didn't comment on his compromise.

At about the end of his year of ritual mourning, Aaron had a dream about looking down from a mountain toward a college town in the Rockies where he had gone to graduate school. When his father had had his first heart attack, there had been family talk of Aaron's staying home and running the family business, but his father had told him to go back to school. A second heart attack had killed the father while Aaron was studying there. He flunked out the following year. I interpreted, "You dreamt that dream now because you have finished mourning for your father and are now able to use the permission he gave you to finish your graduate studies." Aaron wept. Mourning and getting the aggression out front went together in his case. He has since finished graduate school, and is teaching in the university.

CLARENCE: THE DEATH OF CHILDREN

Clarence was a very different case; he knew all too clearly that he was in my office to mourn. "It happened again," was the message on my answering machine. A year before, I had seen Clarence for about 6 months following his young adult son's death in a car accident. He had been hit by a drunken driver and had himself been drinking. Clarence was angry at him. He had long been a "difficult child." Clarence also felt enormously guilty toward him. He was a recovering alcoholic who had been a highly functional, conspicuously successful businessman who had supported his family in high style, notwithstanding his getting smashed each and every night. To the extent that his drinking allowed, he was an attentive, caring father, but I sensed that the kids weren't where it was at for Clarence. In college, he had had strong homosexual feelings, occasionally enacted; after his marriage, he had made a pact with himself that he would drink, but not sleep with men. For the most part, he lived up to that pact for 20 years.

His business life was also a compromise. He hated business, his interests being esthetic and intellectual, but felt that he had to make big money for the kids—and to justify his drinking. His mother had died of cirrhosis; he was alcoholic and knew it. One day he simply decided to stop drinking. Joining AA, he met and fell in love with a man. He left his family and "came out," selling his business at the same time. He now had an entirely new life as a gay piano teacher living in the City. For the first time, he was happy. There was an enormous sadness to Clarence's earlier renunciation. He had lived in a loveless marriage and had done work he hated because he thought that was "the right thing to do."

Now tragedy struck, and Clarence was certain that his homosexuality had "killed" his son. Throughout therapy, Clarence had spoken about his son's death in a calm, matter-of-fact way, only occasionally expressing emotion. Several times, he wept controlled tears. He said that he couldn't stand getting any more upset than that, and I respected his stated limitation. I said very little during his therapy. I didn't seem to much matter to him, as long as I listened without pushing him. I didn't think that he should terminate, but he gave me no choice. I considered our work minimally useful. Now, following his chilling call, he returned. A second son had been murdered in a sordid love triangle. I was afraid to take Clarence back; what had happened to him was simply too awful. I didn't want to deal with that much pain. Yet, I didn't feel that I could decently turn him away. I was amazed when he told me that our first therapy had saved his life, and that our relationship had been one of the most important of his life. That was gratifying, but it also increased my apprehension of working with him again. I didn't want to be so important to him. The second therapy proceeded exactly like the first. I felt torn between letting him continue to talk with minimal feelings about his losses, his hatred of his father, his compassion for and annoyance with his ex-wife, and his current relationship, and probing for the rage, hurt, pain, and guilt that surely were there. Not that he didn't want to talk about these feelings; he did, but with very little emotion. He told me that he had gone to

"Compassionate Friends," a self-help group for those who have lost adult children, but that the sorrow and pain of the group members were more than he could bear and that it made him feel worse.

My predominant feeling in working with Clarence was helplessness. This was one patient I couldn't empathically identify with. I could find nothing in my experience congruent with his. I disliked myself for feeling so distant from him. Not only was I having trouble understanding him, I didn't want to know from such pain—it might be contagious. Then I happened to see a ballet version of Gustave Mahler's *Kindertotenlieder* (children's death songs), and I am not sure how, but that experience stirred up feelings in me that allowed me to empathize more deeply with Clarence, probably by reducing my fear. After that, I said and did nothing different, but Clarence must have sensed that I was no longer pulling away from him, or contributing my counterresistance piece to his already powerful resistance. Our work became more affective. Clarence again terminated against my advice after less than a year. Had he done as much mourning work as was useful or possible? Possibly. Perhaps I had projected expectations of depth of grief onto him that he didn't feel for the children he had been dutiful toward but not close to. A striking behavioral change had been a deepening of his ties to his remaining two children. Perhaps there are some narcissistic wounds that are so profound that they are best sealed off. Clarence, who allowed that he would never be the same again, seemed to have been able to do so. Some mourning, some diversion, and some repression was the best we could do. So far, it has been serviceable.

Sometimes patients can't mourn because of unconscious denial. Jennifer "knew" perfectly well that her mother was dead, yet didn't know it at all; she had had a horrendous childhood and had engaged in years of extremely dangerous acting-out behavior, getting herself "team banged," drug addicted, and badly beaten. All of that was behind her when I worked with her. Her mother had died violently 3 years before. A disturbed, charismatic woman, she had a powerful hold on Jennifer. We worked on her

love–hate relationship with her mother, including her overwhelming feelings of abandonment, for years without making
much of a dent in them. Then she came in and reported,
"Yesterday I went to the cemetery to visit my mother's grave. I
kept looking at it expecting her to speak. Then I screamed,
'Mother, move the grass. Mother, move the fucking grass.'
Mother didn't move the fucking grass. I got hysterical, and just
kept screaming, 'Move the fucking grass!' but she wouldn't.
Suddenly, I thought, 'Jesus Christ, she's dead. She can't move the
grass because she is dead.' Then I started crying and haven't been
able to stop since." After that, Jennifer was able to mourn. From
that episode, one might conclude that Jennifer is psychotic, or
that her denial was psychotic; she isn't in the least. There was a
narcissistic injury in my work with her on her mother's death
because I didn't understand that the mother wasn't dead at all,
and that I was talking past Jennifer. The entire quality of her
therapy changed after her epiphany in the cemetery.

Patients use not only denial of loss or other narcissistic injury,
but also rationalization, minimalization, and justification, as well
as denial of the shame and humiliation concomitant with the loss
or narcissistic injury. When I think of rationalization in the
service of denial of the shame of narcissistic injury, an example
of a much less serious injury comes to mind. Randy had been
trying to seduce a woman he had been dating off and on for quite
a while. He reported, "Last night, I finally got her into bed. I was
going down on her and was really excited by it when she pissed in
my face. I mean really drowned me. But it didn't bother me. I
didn't take it personally. I thought, 'She's Black [Randy is white],
so this must be a political statement.'" Subsequent therapy
uncovered that Randy was deeply ashamed of having been
urinated upon.

HILDA PREVAILS

The patient was 92 years old. I found her capacity to withstand
object loss awesome. She was the oldest of six children, five of

whom she had raised following her parents' deaths. One by one,
her siblings had predeceased her. It was as if she had buried all of
her children. Her niece had referred her, following the death of
the niece's father, who was the last of Hilda's siblings. Although
sorrowful, I would not say that she was depressed. She lived alone
in an apartment building with many elderly residents. Unfortunately, few of her generation were left as the "junior gerries"
replaced her now dead friends and neighbors. Although beginning to weaken and having some difficulties in her walking, she
was basically healthy. Although skeptical of therapy, which was
alien to her experience, she was willing to come and talk. "My
niece wants me to come, and I'll do whatever I'm told. I want to
cooperate. I want to live." As she told her life story, it became
clear that she was far from a passive follower, but at this juncture
in her life, her isolation frightened her, and she uncharacteristi-
cally followed others' suggestions. My role was that of a listener.
I occasionally reflected a feeling or asked a question, but mostly
I was there. Sometimes she fell asleep, and I did not interfere.
She would wake and continue as if there had been no interrup-
tion. She told of her mother's death after having borne six
children in rapid succession, and of her promotion to "little
mother." She was harshly critical of her father as a dreamer, a
charmer, who gambled and failed in one business after another.
"I hate cards; it wasn't that he lost much, but it was all we had. I
guess playing with the men was the only pleasure he had; it gave
him companionship." Her empathy was characteristic; it wasn't a
pulling of her punches; her anger remained, yet her compassion
and understanding existed parallel to it, or better, within it. That
ability to feel without excusing or idealizing proved to be the trait
that allowed her to surmount all of that object loss. She was
capable of sustaining an ambivalence in which love predominated. She spoke of her sense of having outlived everyone. "When
I read the community paper, I don't know anybody anymore. It's
a different generation."

At other times, she expressed feelings of irreality. She had lived
so long and seen so much that it had all thinned for her. Like

Prospero, she had discovered that "We are such stuff/As dreams are made on." The way she put it was, "Life is just a dream," a phrase that recurred in our sessions. Yet with her sense of the phantasmagorical nature of life, she was a realist. She had a gift for seeing and describing people three-dimensionally. I was surprised at how much anger there was in Hilda, but no bitterness. Her anger, in some way I didn't understand, in no way diminished her capacity for love, expressed in her deeply caring relationships with her niece and grandnieces and grandnephews. Hilda had suffered many narcissistic wounds in life. A mother's early death; her father's death from a ruptured appendix when she was in her teens; and the coming of a hard, demanding grandmother to live with her and her siblings after the death of the father. The only time I saw her exhibit shame was when she confided that she had not graduated from high school. "My father wanted me to go back and finish, but I didn't. I have always been sorry. I don't tell people that. Let them think what they want." Seventy-six years later, the shame of dropping out of high school remained. I wondered if the father had really urged her to go back, but she came across as such a realist that it was probably true. The other great shame of her life was not having married. She had lived more than 70 years with another single sister, and her relatives did not expect her to survive that sister's death. She was forthright about the sibling rivalry between them.

Hilda had worked for 29 years in a department store that folded one year short of her qualifying for a pension. "That wasn't right. For a long time, I felt bitter about that. Then one day I saw Mr. Harris, the store owner, on a bus, and he was just another old person like me. It wasn't right. I was cheated, but I didn't hate him anymore." I realized that Hilda was an egalitarian. She was neither awed by the great nor felt superior to the lowly. She told me of her relations with the homeless who lived on the streets of her neighborhood. Hilda was narrow and parochial in many ways and shared the prejudices of her time and place, but there was no hatred in her actual relations with people and her prejudices seemed to play no role. She was impressive, but I still didn't comprehend how she went on as she buried one "child" after another. She told me, "I have pictures of all my sisters and brothers on the TV. I talk to them every day. Not a day goes by when I don't cry. My doctor says I'll always be mourning and I suppose I will." That was the trick; just as she let herself feel her anger, she let herself feel, on a continuous basis, her sorrow and bereavement. Because she was able to mourn, she was able to go on living. She had a capacity to enjoy life. "I can't see trees or flowers from my windows, but my niece has beautiful grounds. I look forward to the changing seasons and seeing each flower bud when I visit." We talked over the course of several years until she developed cancer and died. I learned a great deal from Hilda. I think that she was able to sustain all of that narcissistic injury, all of that loss, because she possessed what the Shaker hymn calls "the gift to be simple," which allowed her to enjoy "little things" such as the changing of the seasons; because of her capacity for empathy and love; because she neither repressed, suppressed, nor denied her feelings including the so-called "negative ones"; and perhaps preeminently because of her capacity for and willingness to mourn. I imagine that I was her "good" father in the transference, although she could be critical of me, and that my presence in her life served as an anchor allowing her to feel more deeply. As we went through her mental "photograph album," she seemed to do exactly that.

At the end of his Nobel acceptance speech, Faulkner said that "Man will not only endure but prevail"; in what was undoubtedly an idealizing countertransference, I felt that Hilda had prevailed.

Freud was another realist. As he aged, he spoke more and more of *Ananke*, as the Greeks termed and deified Necessity. A strict determinist, Freud felt that what is, must be, and that the best we can do is to accept that which must be. Like the philosopher Spinoza before him, Freud thought that "freedom is the acceptance of necessity." So in the end, it is insight, an affective insight, into the nature of things and the nature of ourselves that frees us and allows us to integrate loss. This is not to say that the narcissistic injury doesn't remain, yet it is transformed. That transformation modifies but does not remove our affective response to loss, including loss of ourselves. The aging Freud wrote Lou Andreas-Salomé,

> First of all, thank your dear old man [her husband] for the kind lines he wrote to me, a stranger. May he keep going as long as he himself wants to!
>
> *As for me, I no longer want to, oddly enough. A crust of indifference is slowly creeping around me; a fact I state without complaining. It is a natural development, a way of beginning to grow inorganic. The 'detachment of old age', I think it is called. It must be connected with a decisive turn in the relationship of the two instincts postulated by me. The change taking place is perhaps not very noticeable; everything is as interesting as it was before, neither are the ingredients very different; but some kind of resonance is lacking; unmusical as I am, I imagine the difference to be something like using the pedal or not.* [My emphasis] The never-ceasing tangible pressure of a vast number of unpleasant sensations must have accelerated this otherwise perhaps premature condition, this tendency to experience everything *sub specie aeternitatis*. [1966, p. 154]

After he had gone into exile in England, Freud's study was reconstructed in his London home. A visitor remarked, "O, Professor Freud. It is all here." Freud's response expressed the ultimate narcissistic injury, the loss of self. "*Ja, aber Ich bin nicht hier.*" "Yes, but I am not here."

7

"*Tsouris*" Isn't in the *DSM-III-R*

"*Verstehst du tsouris, Doktor?* Too much *tsouris*, that's what's wrong with me. I have more *tsouris* than I can handle." Yes, I understand *tsouris* — troubles, agonies, hurts, woes, griefs, injuries, pains. All of our patients have too much *tsouris*, and we do what we can to make *tsouris* tolerable by listening, by interpreting, by being with, by following the fundamental rule of medicine, "To inflict no harm," and we partly succeed. We also partly fail, and that is an affront to our narcissism. We too must come to terms with necessity and recognize, like the Freud of "Analysis Terminable and Interminable" (1937), that analysis and psychotherapy can only do so much.

The possibility of *tsouris* is omnipresent. In each life stage, we are subject to injury — Erikson offers us one developmental roadmap; here is another, along with the possibilities for *tsouris* with its concomitant narcissistic injury each age brings.

All the world's a stage [already a narcissistic injury; our lives aren't even real, but mere play acting],/And all the men and women

291

merely players: They have their exits and their entrances;/And
one man in his time plays many parts [another narcissistic injury;
we don't even have continuity of self],/His acts being seven ages.
At first the infant,/Mewling and puking in the nurse's arms [birth
trauma, lack of mirroring, feeding disturbances, the paranoid-
schizoid position, primitive anxiety and guilt, persecution by the
bad breast, risk of abandonment and abuse.] /And then the
whining schoolboy, with his satchel,/And shining morning face,
creeping like snail/Unwillingly to school [the pain of the depressive position; oedipal defeat or, worse, victory; risk of failure;
rebuff by school fellows; educational deprivation; sexual and
physical abuse]. And then the lover,/Sighing like furnace with
woeful ballad/Made to his mistress's eyebrow [unrequited love].
Then a soldier,/Full of strange oaths, and bearded like the
pard,/Jealous in honor, sudden and quick in quarrel,/Seeking the
bubble reputation/Even in the cannon's mouth [premature death,
mutilation, loss of peers, dishonor, failure to win promotion or
recognition]. And then the justice,/In fair round belly with good
capon lined,/With eyes severe, and beard of formal cut,/Full of
wise saws and modern instances;/And so he plays his part
[stagnation, fall from power, stifled ambitions, loss of parents,
first intimation of mortality]. The sixth age shifts/Into the lean
and slipper'd pantaloon,/With spectacles on nose and pouch on
side,/His youthful hose, well saved, a world too wide/For his
shrunk shank; and his big manly voice,/Turning again towards
childish treble, pipes/And whistles in his sound [loss of friends,
loss of mate, loss of position, fading looks, growing infirmity,
undeniable evidence that our sense of omnipotence is an illusion].
Last scene of all,/That ends the strange eventful history,/Is second
childishness, and mere oblivion/Sans teeth, sans eyes, sans taste,
sans everything [loss of self, death]. [*As You Like It* 2.7]

In Shakespeare's, as opposed to Erikson's, developmental
scheme, there is no epigenetic growth, no unfolding of earlier
stages into later ones. There is merely succession toward oblivion.

In face of all this, can we achieve Erikson's acceptance of "the
one and only life that was possible"? I don't know, but since we
can't stop time's flow or ward off life's blows, the best we can do

is to live as fully and intensely as possible each moment, and to mourn our losses and injuries. Ideally, that is what happens in every therapy session, and this rehearsal of intensity, immediacy, and mourning becomes a prologue to a similarly lived life. "Though we cannot make our sun/Stand still, yet we will make him run."

References

Adler, A. (1927). *The Practice and Theory of Individual Psychology*. New York: Harcourt, Brace & World.

Alexander, F. (1943). Fundamental concepts of psychosomatic research. *Psychosomatic Medicine* 5:311–329.

Becker, E. (1973). *The Denial of Death*. New York: The Free Press.

Binswanger, L. (1944). The case of Ellen West. In *Existence*, ed. E. Angel, R. May, and H. Ellenberger, trans. W. M. Mendel and J. Lyons, pp. 237–364. New York: Simon and Schuster, 1958.

Bion, W. R. (1959). *Experience in Groups*. New York: Basic Books.

Bradshaw, J. (1988). *Healing the Shame that Binds You*. Deerfield Beach, FL: Health Communications.

Cahan, A. (1917). *The Rise of David Levinsky*. New York: Harper & Row, 1960.

Cooley, C. (1902). *Human Nature and the Social Order*. New York: Scribner.

Descartes, R. (1637/1951). *Discourse on Method*. Trans. L. J. Lafleur. New York: Library of the Liberal Arts.

―――― (1642/1951). *Meditations on First Philosophy*. Trans L. J. Lafleur. New York: Library of the Liberal Arts.

Eissler, K. R. (1958). Remarks on some variations in psychoanalytic technique. *International Journal of Psycho-Analysis* 39:222–229.

Erikson, E. (1950). *Childhood and Society*. 2nd ed. New York: W. W. Norton, 1963.

―――― (1968). *Identity, Youth, and Crisis*. New York: W. W. Norton.

295

_____ (1969). *Gandhi's Truth: The Origins of Militant Nonviolence*. New York: W. W. Norton.

Freud, S. (1900). The interpretation of dreams. *Standard Edition* 4/5.

_____ (1905a). Dora: a case of hysteria. *Standard Edition* 7:7–124.

_____ (1905b). Three essays on sexuality. *Standard Edition* 7:135–243.

_____ (1910). Observations on "wild" psychoanalysis. *Standard Edition* 11:219–230.

_____ (1912). Recommendations for physicians on the psychoanalytic method of treatment. *Standard Edition* 12:109–120.

_____ (1913). Further recommendations on the technique of psychoanalysis: on beginning the treatment. *Standard Edition* 12:121–144.

_____ (1914a). On narcissism: an introduction. *Standard Edition* 14:67–104.

_____ (1914b). Further recommendations on the technique of psychoanalysis: remembering, repeating, and working through. *Standard Edition* 12:145–156.

_____ (1915a). Mourning and melancholia. *Standard Edition* 14:237–258.

_____ (1915b). Thoughts for the times on war and death. *Standard Edition* 14:273–302.

_____ (1916). On transience. *Standard Edition* 14:303–308.

_____ (1920). Beyond the pleasure principle. *Standard Edition* 18:7–66.

_____ (1921). Group psychology and the analysis of the ego. *Standard Edition* 18:69–144.

_____ (1923). The ego and the id. *Standard Edition* 19:12–68.

_____ (1926). Inhibitions, symptoms and anxiety. *Standard Edition* 20:87–178.

_____ (1930). Civilization and its discontents. *Standard Edition* 21:64–148.

_____ (1933). New introductory lectures on psychoanalysis. *Standard Edition* 22:7–184.

_____ (1937). Analysis terminable and interminable. *Standard Edition* 23:209–254.

_____ (1940). Splitting of the ego in the process of defense. *Standard Edition* 23:275–278.

_____ (1960). *Letters of Sigmund Freud*. Selected and edited by Ernest Freud. Trans. T. Stern and J. Stern. New York: Basic Books.

Freud, S., and Andreas-Salomé, L. (1966). *Sigmund Freud and Lou Andreas-Salomé Letters*. Trans. W. Robson-Scott and E. Robson-Scott. New York: W. W. Norton.

Freud, S., and Breuer, J. (1895). Studies on hysteria. *Standard Edition* 2:1–306.

Fromm, E. (1964). *The Heart of Man*. New York: Harper & Row.

Glover, E. (1956). *On the Early Development of the Mind*. New York: International Universities Press.

Groddeck, G. (1930). *The Book of the Id*. New York: Nervous and Mental Disease Press, 1923.

Guntrip, H. (1971). *Psychoanalytic Theory, Therapy, and the Self*. New York: Basic Books.

Hartmann, H. (1958). *Ego Psychology and the Problem of Adaptation*. New York: International Universities Press.

———— (1964). *Essays in Ego Psychology*. New York: International Universities Press.

Havens, L. (1986). *Making Contact: Uses of Language in Psychotherapy*. Cambridge, MA: Harvard University Press.

Hegel, G. W. F. (1807). *The Phenomenology of Mind*. Trans. J. A. Baillie. New York: Harper & Row, 1967.

Hendrick, I. (1943). Work and the pleasure principle. *Psychoanalytic Quarterly* 12:311–339.

Howe, I. (1976). *World of Our Fathers*. New York: Simon and Schuster.

Hume, D. (1738). *A Treatise of Human Nature*. New York: E. P. Dutton.

Jacobson, E. (1964). *The Self and the Object World*. New York: International Universities Press.

James, W. (1890). *The Principles of Psychology*. Cambridge, MA: Harvard University Press, 1983.

Jung, C. G. (1945). The relations between the ego and the unconscious. In *The Basic Writings of C. G. Jung*, ed. V. deLaszlo, trans. R. F. C. Hull, pp. 105–182. New York: Random House, 1959.

———— (1961). *Memories, Dreams, and Reflections*. Trans. R. Winston and C. Winston. New York:Vintage.

Kant, I. (1781). *Critique of Pure Reason*. Trans. J. M. D. Meiklejohn. Buffalo, NY: Prometheus, 1990.

Kernberg, O. (1975). *Borderline Conditions and Pathological Narcissism*. New York: Jason Aronson.

———— (1980). Organizational regression. In *Internal World, External Reality*, pp. 235–252. New York: Jason Aronson.

Khan, M. (1974). The concept of cumulative trauma. In *The Privacy of the Self*, pp. 42–58. New York: International Universities Press.

Kierkegaard, S. (1843). *Fear and Trembling*. Trans. W. Lowrie. Princeton, NJ: Princeton University Press, 1941.

———— (1849). *The Concept of Dread*. Trans. W. Lowrie. Princeton, NJ: Princeton University Press, 1944.

Klein, M. (1946). Notes on some schizoid mechanisms. In *Envy and Gratitude and Other Works, 1946–1963*, pp. 1–24. New York: Delacorte, 1975.

———— (1955). On identification. In *Envy and Gratitude and Other Works, 1946–1963*, pp. 141–175. New York: Delacorte, 1975.

———— (1975). *Envy and Gratitude and Other Works, 1946–1963*. New York: Delacorte, 1975.

Kohut, H. (1971). *The Analysis of the Self: A Systematic Approach to the Psychoanalytic Treatment of Narcissistic Personality Disorders*. New York: International Universities Press.

———— (1977). *The Restoration of the Self*. New York: International Universities Press.

———— (1978). Thoughts on narcissism and narcissistic rage. In *The Search for the Self*, pp. 615–658. New York: International Universities Press.

Kübler-Ross, E. (1969). *On Death and Dying*. New York: Collier/Macmillan.

Levin, J. (1987). *Treatment of Alcoholism and Other Addictions: A Self-Psychology Approach.* Northvale, NJ: Jason Aronson.

—— (1990). *Alcoholism: A Bio-Psycho-Social Approach.* Washington, DC: Hemisphere/Taylor & Francis.

—— (1991). *Recovery from Alcoholism: Beyond Your Wildest Dreams.* Northvale, NJ: Jason Aronson.

—— (1992). *Theories of the Self.* Washington, DC: Taylor & Francis.

Locke, J. (1690). *Essay on Human Understanding.* Vols. 1 and 2. New York: Dover, 1959.

Mahler, W., Pine, F., and Bergman, A. (1975). *The Psychological Birth of the Human Infant: Symbiosis and Individuation.* New York: Basic Books.

Marx, K. (1867). *Capital: A Critique of Political Economy.* Vol. 1. Trans. B. Fawkes. New York: Vintage, 1977.

Maslow, A. (1968). *Toward a Psychology of Being.* 2nd ed. New York: Van Nostrand Reinhold.

Meade, G. H. (1934). *Mind, Self, and Society From the Standpoint of Social Behaviorist.* Chicago, IL: Chicago University Press.

Miller, A. (1981). *The Drama of the Gifted Child.* New York: Basic Books.

Miller, C. (1974). Depression as a consequence of the failure to mourn. Paper presented at the American Association for the Advancement of Psychoanalysis on October 8 at the Karen Horney Clinic, New York, N.Y.

Neff, W. (1968). *Work and Human Behavior.* New York: Atherton.

Ogden, T. (1979). On projective identification. *International Journal of Psycho-Analysis* 60:357–373.

—— (1990). *The Matrix of the Mind.* Northvale, NJ: Jason Aronson.

Pascal, B. (1966). *Pensées.* Trans. A. J. Krailsheiner. London: Penguin.

Pine, F. (1985). *Developmental Theory and Clinical Process.* New Haven, CT: Yale University Press.

Plato (1961a). Phaedrus. In *Plato: The Collected Dialogues*, ed. E. Hamilton and H. Cairns, trans. R. Hackforth, pp. 475–525. Princeton, NJ: Princeton University Press.

—— (1961b). Symposium. In *Plato: The Collected Dialogues*, ed. E. Hamilton and H. Cairns, trans. M. Joyce, pp. 526–575. Princeton, NJ: Princeton University Press.

Saint Augustine (1961). *Confession.* Trans. E. P. Pusey. New York: Collier.

Schur, M. (1972). *Freud: Living and Dying.* New York: International Universities Press.

Spinoza, B. (1677). Ethics demonstrated in geometrical order. In *The Chief Works of Benedict De Spinoza*, trans. R. H. M. Elwes, vol. 2, pp. 4–272. New York: Dover.

Spitz, R. (1965). *The First Year of Life.* New York: International Universities Press.

Stern, D. (1985). *The Interpersonal World of the Infant.* New York: Basic Books.

Tiebout, H. M. (1949). The act of surrender in the therapeutic process. *Quarterly Journal of Studies on Alcohol* 10:48–58.

Tillich, P. (1952). *The Courage to Be*. New Haven, CT: Yale University Press.

Weber, M. (1905). *The Protestant Ethic and the Spirit of Capitalism*. New York: Scribner, 1958.

Winnicott, D. (1951). Transitional objects and transitional phenomena. In *Collected Papers: Through Paediatrics to Psycho-Analysis*, pp. 229–247. London: Hogarth, 1958.

_____ (1963). The development of the capacity for concern. In *The Maturational Process and the Facilitating Environment*, pp. 73–82. New York: International Universities Press, 1965.

_____ (1965). *The Maturational Process and the Facilitating Environment*. New York: International Universities Press.

Wright, B. (1960). *Physical Disability: A Psychological Approach*. New York: Harper & Row.

Yalom, I. (1989). *Love's Executioner and Other Tales of Psychotherapy*. New York: Basic Books.

Credits

Index